ALGERIA

M & N Hanhart. lith.

EL KANTARA.

THROUGH ALGERIA

LONDON

DARF PUBLISHERS LIMITED

1984

First Published 1863
Reprinted 1984

ISBN 978 1 850 77037 4

CONTENTS.

CHAPTER I.
A Swallow Flight—Landing at Algiers 1

CHAPTER II.
Place du Gouvernement—Bazaar—Mosque—Arab Court of Justice—Koubba of Sidi Abd-er-Rhaman—Native Streets . 7

CHAPTER III.
Native Population of Algiers 20

CHAPTER IV.
Saint Eugene—A Moorish Interior—Traits of Moorish Life—Point Pescade—Worship of Djins 27

CHAPTER V.
Moorish Wedding—Legal Form of Marriage—Law of Divorce. 35

CHAPTER VI.
The Moresque at Home—Her hopeless Degradation . . 43

CHAPTER VII.
An Aïssaoua Dance—A Negro Dance 57

CHAPTER VIII.
The Maraboo—Maraboo Legends—Algerian Religious Fraternities—The Heretic Mozabite 65

vi   CONTENTS.

CHAPTER IX.

Mustapha Superieur—A New Year's Day—A Moorish Villa—Beautiful Walks—Summer Sunshine—A Wintry Spring—The Cavalcade—Charity in Masquerade—French Superlatives 77

CHAPTER X.

Across the Metidja—Boufarik—Blidah—The Ennekabo Fashion—Beautiful Ravine—A Native Village—The Ramadam—Interview with a Mufti 88

CHAPTER XI.

Gorge of the Chiffa—A Misanthrope—Ravine of Sidi Moussa—Up the Mountain—Lost and Found 98

CHAPTER XII.

The Sirocco—Medeah—A Baulked Plan—A New Start—Across the Col of Mouzaïa—Deserted Mine 111

CHAPTER XIII.

A Morning's Ride—Fastidiousness Punished—Tourists in Difficulty—An Exemplary Corporal—An Algerian Night Scene—Boghari 119

CHAPTER XIV.

A Dreary Valley—An Insulted Caïd—Primitive Accommodation—Arab Hospitality—An Arab Dinner—Mattress versus Carpet—Return to Civilisation 131

CHAPTER XV.

Teniet-el-Had—Hôtel des Cedres—Forest of Cedars—On to Milianah—A Rich Valley—Character of the Lion—Plain of the Chelif 143

CHAPTER XVI.

Milianah—Through the Plain—A Colonist's Prospects—A Desolate Scene—Orleansville—Relizane 152

CHAPTER XVII.

Mostaganem—Storks—A Dreary Journey—Arzew—Oran—Coast Scenery—A Fever-scourged Village—A Mysterious Friend 162

CHAPTER XVIII.

Tlemcen, Past and Present—Beautiful Koubba of Sidi Boumedin—End of Ramadam—A Devotional Dance—Acting the Jackal—A Lady Dancer—Glen of Mafrouck—A Fairy-like Grotto 173

CHAPTER XIX.

Return to Oran—French Proprieties of Sea Life—Journey to Marengo—Tipaza—An English Colonist—A Panther Tale . 190

CHAPTER XX.

Legend of the Tomb of the Christian 201

CHAPTER XXI.

History of Marengo—A Visit—Koleah—A Garrison Garden—Sidi Ferruch—Military Recreations—Matrimonial Experiences—Return to Algiers 205

CHAPTER XXII.

The Feast of Beans—Negro Dancing—An Exemplary Victim—The Feast of the Christian—A Tale with a Moral . . 217

CHAPTER XXIII.

Across the Plain to Dellys—Change of Plan—French Courtesy—A Primitive Mode of Travel—A Beautiful View—Fort Napoleon 224

CHAPTER XXIV.

Great Kabylia—Kabyle and Arab Contrasted . . . 235

CHAPTER XXV.

A Kabyle Village—A Maraboo Host 245

CHAPTER XXVI.

A Trying Ordeal—A Rough Ride—Rough Quarters—On to Akbou—A Delightful Surprise—A Curious Scene—A Civilised Dinner 257

CHAPTER XXVII.

Through Great Kabylia—Beautiful Scenery—A Long Day's Journey—Caïd Ahmed's House—Scenes in Arab Life—A Hospitable Caïd—Entry into Setif 270

CHAPTER XXVIII.

Setif—An Eccentric Gaol—A Dreary Drive—Love in a Cottage 283

CHAPTER XXIX.

A Startling Incident—Tourists in Distress—A Journey under Difficulties—A Midnight Walk—El Kantara—A Saharian Scene 290

CHAPTER XXX.

Biskara—A Negro Village—Palm Grove—Merits of Date Palm—Intense Heat—An Undesirable Ride—Batna—Lambessa—A Wise Judge 302

CHAPTER XXXI.

Constantine—Effective Pictures—Longevity of Ancient Inhabitants—Ladies of Constantine—Cascades—Tarpeian Rock—Garden of Salah Bey—Railroad Enthusiasm . . . 316

CHAPTER XXXII.

Misanthropy Cured—Philippeville—Headland of Stora—Jemmapes—Future Prospects—Another Mule Ride—A Rich Country—A Settler's Wife—An Ornithological Sitting-room 327

CHAPTER XXXIII.

Guelma—Orphan Asylum—Hammam Meskoutine—Curious Scene—Abandoned Fountains—Baths—Arab and Kabyle Legends—Bona—Prospects of Bona—Roman Cisterns—Monument to Saint Augustine—Mount Edoug—Native Hospitality—Embark for Tunis 341

CHAPTER XXXIV.

Algerian Colonisation—Its State and Prospects . . . 354

INTRODUCTION.

A PLEA FOR LADY TOURISTS.

IN every progressing nation, manners and opinions must necessarily, in the course of years, undergo considerable change. But, no matter how reasonable that change may be, society, in the first instance, denounces it vehemently. History presents a record of follies and errors fondly cherished, and reluctantly abandoned. Still, in any country where mental activity prevails, reason is sure at length to overcome the *vis inertiæ* of custom. There, whatever is really rational and right is certain, in the course of years, to be stamped as such by the fiat of society. In lands where the will of the many exercises despotic sway, humanity remains in a state of stagnation —a dull Dead Sea, without waves or tide. There, the mind, weighted and fettered by the power of prescription, continues from age to age inane, powerless, scarce showing a trace of its Divine origin.

Happily for England, however society may endeavour to maintain its prescriptive laws and traditional opinions, it is obliged to yield in time to the force of that individuality which forms a marked feature of the English character, and to which the nation owes its proud position at the present day. The eccentricity of which the English are accused abroad is, in truth, the mainspring of our national progress. However absurd the form which occasionally it may assume, it is yet an element of character eminently productive, on the whole, of good. Without a high degree of originality, which is but another name for eccentricity — a departure from ordinary rule — no man ever accomplished anything great. Watt, Arkwright, Jenner, Stephenson, were essentially eccentric men.

But whilst it may be freely admitted that masculine eccentricity or originality of character is to be admired, very few will allow that any departure from ordinary rule is approvable, or even justifiable, in a woman. We can applaud our grandmothers for overstepping the conventional proprieties of their day, or we can recognise the right of Chinese and Turkish ladies to go about with uncrippled feet and unveiled faces. But, clearly as we can see the follies of our ancestors, or those of contemporary nations, we cling with unreasoning reverence to every restriction on feminine liberty of action imposed by that society amidst which we live. The actual, taken generally not only as the right, but possible, in every sphere of human action, is more especially so, in all that refers to woman. For her, the dogma, 'whatever is, is right,' is held universally as an undeniable axiom; and, acting on this creed, English society at this present day is bringing all its keen weapons of ridicule and sarcasm to bear upon the many rebels to one of its prescriptive laws, which the facilities of modern travel have produced. In bygone days, the rule that no lady should travel without a gentleman by her side, was doubtless rational; but in a period of easy locomotion, and with abundant evidence to prove that ladies can travel by themselves in foreign countries with perfect safety, the maintenance of that rule certainly savours of injustice. For unquestionable as it is that woman's sphere, as wife and mother, lies at home, it is surely unreasonable to doom many hundred English ladies, of independent means and without domestic ties, to crush every natural aspiration to see nature in its grandest forms, art in its finest works, and human life in its most interesting phases;— such being the practical result of a social law which refuses them the right of travel, save on conditions often wholly unattainable. Under these circumstances, and in a land where unmarried women are free from the degrading vassalage in which they are held in France and in other neighbouring countries, it is no wonder that an unnecessary and onerous restriction should be practically set aside, and that the 'unprotected' English lady traveller should have become a familiar sight upon the European continent and in Northern Africa. And if the exploring of foreign lands is not the highest end or the most useful occupation of feminine existence, it is at least more improving, as well as more amusing, than the crochet-work or embroidery with which, at home, so many ladies seek to beguile the tedium of their unoccupied days. Single — for the most part, not from choice but from necessity — the unmarried women of this country are surely entitled to claim the abrogation of a rule, which causelessly forbids their indulgence in not only a harmless, but instructive amusement. Impotent to restrain, it is yet not impotent to wound; and the thought of being exposed to the keen shafts of sarcasm is a rankling thorn in the enjoyment of even the most fearless lady tourist. To convert a now contraband into a legal pleasure, is a boon, which they may reasonably ask, and society as reasonably confer.

But, however essentially just as this claim may be, yet, conscious as I am of belonging to a socially unfavoured class, it needs far more courage than the requirements of travel demand, to present this work on Algeria to the public. The butt of wit and witling, the satirist's staple theme, the 'unprotected' lady looms before the popular gaze as a synonym for that ideal Gorgon, the 'strong-minded woman;' from whose wooden face, hard features, harsh voice, blunt manners, and fiercely-independent bearing, society shrinks in horror. To be confronted with such a fancy portrait of myself, is in truth, no pleasant thought; but as every innovation must have victims, I accept my menaced fate, cheered by the conviction that my immolation will prove of benefit to that class of tourists which, in these pages, I represent. The rearguard of progress passes unmolested over the same ground that the van traversed amidst whizzing bullets. Our great-grandmothers did not exchange their pillion for a side-saddle without being exposed to a fire as brisk as that which now awaits the 'unprotected' lady tourist. The bold, audacious Amazon, dressed in hat and coat, denounced with vehemence in the pages of the 'Spectator,' is now the applauded lady equestrian. The ridiculed bluestocking of the last century is the respected authoress in this. It is no long time ago since the wisest heads imagined that the interests of society required that old women with hooked noses should be burned. Still later, it was an unquestioned doctrine that queues eminently enhanced the dignity of the masculine aspect. Opinions become, in the course of years, quite as ridiculous as clothes whose fashion is obsolete. Every standard of right and wrong undergoes a change, save that which is based on the immutable principles of morality. Doubtless, in the twentieth century, enterprising lady tourists will not feel it needful to preface the published records of their travels with a plea in vindication of the act; for ladies continuing to do what daily experience proves they can safely do, with high enjoyment, will soon be safe from ridicule or reproach, since the unfamiliar, passing into the familiar, invariably becomes a recognised social law.

And undesirous as I am to see my sex infected with a disrelish for home life, and a craving for adventure, I yet feel no fear that these pages will tend to foster such a feeling. The many deeds of derring-do, of which men read continually, exercise no perceptible influence upon the mass of the community. The published records of the Alpine Club do not result in a general masculine rush to find some hitherto unascended snowy peak to climb. The doctor does not forsake his patients from an ardent desire to seat himself on the summit of

Chimboraza. The barrister does not leave his clients to join an exploring expedition to Central Africa. Nor do tradesmen close their shops to wander over the world in search of the picturesque and romantic. And should Robinson-Crusoeish aspirations survive the period of early boyhood, they are speedily extinguished in the mass, by the necessity of earning the means of subsistence. If such is the case with men, still less likely are women to be infected with a craving for adventure. Loving ease and luxury still more than men, not one woman in a thousand can comprehend how hardships and difficulties may be combined with any degree of enjoyment. The fact alone, that the lady of independent means forms but the smallest fraction of society, affords a guarantee that a feminine love of travel can never lead to baneful consequences. As long as the world endures, man, and more especially woman, will seek and find their happiness in the limited sphere of domestic life. To do to-day what has been done yesterday, and to run on in the same groove from year to year, will ever constitute, to all but an insignificant number, one of the essentials of a happy existence. The lady tourist will ever be, to her sex at large, but as a meteoric flash amidst the hosts of fixed stars that stud the sky.

And now, with this exordium, I launch my little bark upon the sea of letters, to float or sink, as may be. And though the hope prove vain, that some amongst the unknown world which I address may bear me willing company along an unfamiliar track, yet not wholly profitless has been my task, since these pages, like a mirror, reflect to me not only many a beautiful scene, and many a quaint picture of human life, but a time, when long days of active exertion in the open air, bracing the energies of a delicate frame, infused through every vein a sense of buoyant health to which I had been long a stranger.

THROUGH ALGERIA.

CHAPTER I.

A SWALLOW FLIGHT — LANDING AT ALGIERS.

A BEAST or bird of prey is certainly no inappropriate symbol of a powerful nation. The French eagle and the British lion well typify many a page in the history of either people. But whilst one phase of English character is duly represented in the royal arms of England, justice requires that the unmeaning, fabulous unicorn should be deposed in favour of some fitting representative of the roving habits of the inhabitants of the British Isles. As the migratory impulse attains its height at the approach of winter, the swallow might reasonably be admitted to a place in our national arms.

But whilst our swallow-like propensity is a universally acknowledged fact, its origin, unlike that of our ornithological model, partakes of a complex character. That the swallow travels in search of food is clearly ascertainable, but the cause of our annual migrations is quite incapable of a similar concise definition, and not unnaturally the foreigner finds it difficult to reconcile our intense pride and love of country with our intense ardour for self-expatriation. Indeed, if we did not admit a lack of sunshine in our native climate, we would be puzzled to give a plausible answer to the question often entailed on us abroad by our openly displayed contempt for manners and usages differing from our own. 'If you think your own country so superior to ours, why do you not stay at home?'

But though love of sunshine acts certainly as a stimulus to foreign travel, its influence is less powerful than that of many other unacknowledged motives which lie at the root of our locomotive tendencies. The same roving spirit and thirst for adventure which made pirates and freebooters of our Scandinavian ancestors prompt doubtless in a high degree the peaceful foreign inroads of their civilised descendants. But inherited restlessness, or a quest of health and sunshine, exerts but an insignificant migratory influence in comparison with that arising from our intense love and reverence for fashion. As to those tourists whose love of travel springs from a desire for information — a wish to study life under varied aspects — their numbers are too insignificant to give them a class existence.

To what head my migratory propensity should be

referred, I do not feel it necessary to declare. Perhaps, to readers of a speculative turn of mind, these pages may afford the means of arriving at a due solution of the question, as to why in the autumn of 1859 I took the swallows as my guide, and followed them to Africa. In general acceptation, a winter in Africa signifies a voyage up the Nile, and an interview with the Sphinxes; but in my case, and in that of a lady who accompanied me, the phrase implied a visit to Algiers, with the supplement of a journey through Algeria.

The air had a keen wintry feel, as we left Paris towards the end of October; and though something of summer warmth greeted us at Marseilles, the fast dropping and bright tinted foliage of the trees indicated unmistakeably the commencement of the reign of winter. But though summer had left Marseilles, it was lingering still at no great distance from its shores, for ere we had been more than twenty-four hours at sea, its hot breath added a pang to an existence embittered by the woes of sea-sickness, a crowded cabin, and the vicinity of two crying children, who, for sixty hours, favoured us almost incessantly with a vocal performance graduating from the low whine of dissatisfaction to the loud shriek of rage.

We had left Marseilles on Tuesday, with the hope of arriving at Algiers at an early hour on Thursday morning, but, notwithstanding there was neither a head wind nor a stormy sea, the steamer lagged so on its way, that the darkness of night had fallen around us before we neared the land. The delay was annoying, for I had heard that the approach to Algiers ranked in beauty with the Bay of Naples and the Golden Horn.

It was a beautiful night when I went on deck; the sea was nearly quite calm, and a light breeze from the land stirred the warm summer-like air. The stars were sparkling brilliantly in the dark depths of a moonless sky, but Orion with all its lustre was a less attractive object at that moment than the light which marked the entrance of the port of Algiers; and as it increased in size and brightness, the deck became crowded with passengers, many of whom, like myself, had just emerged from a two days' seclusion in the lower regions of the sluggish Luxor. Husbands were reunited to wives, and relieved their minds by the interchange of dismal experiences during the last sixty hours of existence. Soldiers and long-robed priests mingled with the crowd of emigrants who occupied the deck. The air was filled with a buzz of many voices, which swelled to an uproar, as at length, when the Luxor stopped, a swarm of half nude Arab porters rushed on deck from the small boats in which we were to land.

From that moment there ensued a scene of bewildering tumult and confusion, for the crowd which pressed eagerly forward to descend the steep ladder by the vessel's side was constantly driven back, to prevent the boats being swamped by an overload. The porters shouted in Arabic, or in a jargon composed of various European tongues, and this, together with the French oaths, commands, and exclamations which rose on high, formed a hurricane of conflicting sound, that had not subsided even after the lapse of half-an-hour, when, wearied waiting, we made our way in the darkness, with much difficulty and perplexity, down a steep ladder into a crowded boat, whose gunwale rose but an inch above the water. Even when we gained the shore our troubles were by no means ended, for we were instantly encircled by a battalion of touters from the different hotels, each of whom thought he could make an easy prey of the two English ladies.

'The ladies will certainly go to the Hotel de la Regence; the best hotel in Algiers,' said one.

The ladies will find themselves best off in the Hotel de Rouen,' called out another.

'No hotel like the Hotel des Ambassadeurs for the ladies,' vociferated a third.

'The ladies will find excellent apartments at moderate prices in the Hotel de Paris,' exclaimed a fourth.

'The ladies will nowhere find an hotel so good and so cheap as the Hotel de France,' shouted out a fifth. But whilst these and other candidates for our patronage were trying to outshout each other in an attempt to impress us with the superior merits of his employer's house, we very abruptly brought the discussion to a close, by ordering our porters to proceed to the Hotel d'Orient.

So far, Africa bore a close resemblance to Europe: had it not been for the unfamiliar sight of our scantily clad Arab porters, we might have fancied ourselves at Boulogne.

CHAPTER II.

PLACE DU GOUVERNEMENT—BAZAAR—MOSQUE—ARAB COURT OF JUSTICE—KOUBBA OF SIDI ABD-ER-RHAMAN—NATIVE STREETS.

NO European unfamiliar with the features of Oriental life can fail to be deeply impressed by a first day in Algiers. The striking contrasts, the various costumes and races, the jostling contact of widely differing forms of life and manners, present altogether a most forcible picture.

But notwithstanding this, my first view of Algiers was somewhat disappointing; for as I looked out from our quarters in the Hotel d'Orient on the large, flagged, tree-shaded *Place du Gouvernement*, I felt aggrieved by the sight of the familiar features of many-storied houses with stuccoed walls, flanked by arcades, overshadowing the doors of cafés and restaurants, that looked as if fresh imported from the Parisian Boulevards. Except for a low domed roof, which rose immediately beyond the *place* on its open seaward side, where it was bounded by a balustrade, I saw no building that was not altogether French in aspect; Moorish Algiers seemed to me dead and buried.

I was far too hasty, however, in this conclusion,

for though the *place* was entirely French in architecture, I had but to watch the crowded thoroughfare, which extended along its inland side, to see an endless series of highly varied and striking pictures of a thoroughly un-French-like character. Here, stalks along the Bedouin Arab, his long thin dark face overhung by a white cloth, bound round the crown by a fillet of twisted cords, and his tall figure picturesquely draped by the ample folds of a large burnous. There, is a Jew; you may know him from his face, which exhibits in a marked degree the characteristic features and expression borne everywhere by his race. A fez, around which a black silk handkerchief is twisted in turban fashion, covers his head. His dark-coloured and braided jacket is encircled at the waist by a crimson silk sash. Grey baggy trousers, terminating just below the knee, are met by a pair of long blue stockings, and large steel buckles ornament his high-heeled shoes. Here, a Jewess, with jaws encircled by a white muslin handkerchief, in a fashion eminently suggestive of toothache, exhibits a rich silk robe too narrow to form a single fold, as it falls down in a straight line from the gold embroidered band around her neck, to her stockingless feet, covered merely at the tip by small heelless shoes, that can only be kept on in walking by a shuffling motion. There, is a Moor whose mild and strikingly handsome face is set off by the folds of a snowy turban, whilst his crimson sash, embroidered jacket, full short lavender trousers, and long snow-white stockings, becomingly array his somewhat portly figure. Only that ghosts do not frequent public thoroughfares in broad daylight, one might suppose yon Moorish woman was an inhabitant of a tomb; for her eyes acquire a preternatural glare from the thick white veil above which they show, whilst the long winding-sheet-like scarf which covers her head, and shrouds her form, imparts to her looks a truly ghost-like character. Here, a negress, her black face peering out from beneath the folds of a long blue striped cotton shawl, displays an ebon arm encircled by two silver bracelets, as she leads by the hand a little child whose head is crowned by a cap, composed of small gold coins. There, a swarthy Spaniard shows a head bound round with a red cotton handkerchief, surmounted by a black felt hat with turned up rim, garnished with tufts of silk. A half-clad Arab porter, with bare legs and arms, follows a braided and epauletted French officer with horned moustaches. Amidst the rattling omnibuses that dash along the street, mingle troops of diminutive donkeys, laden with stones, sand, firewood, or large bundles of palm leaves; and ever and again, the drivers' and the riders' warning shouts are blent with the heavy rumble of a military wagon. As evening falls, a military band, taking its station within the rows of trees that edge the *place*, adds yet another element to the varied sounds with which it re-echoes, from the time that the cannon's voice proclaims the approach of morn, until long after the same voice has declared that the day is done.

The magnificent view visible from the *place* is not the least of its attractions. I have never from the heart of any town seen an equally beautiful prospect as that commanded by the open seaward side of this fine French square, and I think the world can have few more lovely scenes to show than that, presented by the bright blue waters of the Mediterranean, as they roll in and break into wreaths of glittering foam on the white glistening sands of a grand curving bay, bordered nigh hand by precipitous banks of brilliant verdure, and overlooked afar by a lofty range of mountains, crowned by a snow-capped peak.

The *Place du Gouvernement* forms the meeting point of three fine French streets, two of which, bearing the Arabic names of Bab-el-Oued and Bab-Azoun, traverse the entire length of the French quarter. But whilst the conquerors appropriating to themselves the whole seaward portion of the Moorish town, demolished in this quarter with an unsparing hand, they left untouched that part of the pirate's nest which occupied the precipitous sides of the high hill immediately above. Algiers at this present day wears a twofold face—one chiefly European, the other wholly Oriental in every feature.

The jostling of European with African life, in the French quarter of the town, often gives rise to startling incongruities. In the adjacent suburb of the Agha, partriarchal looking Arabs in flowing robes pass before the doors of gay guingettes and restaurants. The frightened camel, laden with dates, recoils from the rattling omnibus with its varied freight — from the epauletted officer down to the wide-mouthed negress; and the one palm tree which overlooks the street, has a block of masonry at its feet, whilst a row of tall French houses tower above its feathery crown.

Yet, French in general aspect as the seaside portion of Algiers has now become, it still shows here and there a handsome old Moorish house. The Governor-General lives in the ancient palace of a Bey, and the building now occupied as a museum is a fine specimen of Moorish architecture. The grand mosque rises also in this quarter, in company with the native court of justice, and these, together with bazaars exclusively tenanted by natives, afford a picture of Algerian life deserving of description.

The bazaars, of which there are some four or five, are built in the form of a covered gallery; and on entering one of them from a new French street, French life recedes altogether from my view, as I pass onward between a line of stalls, in each of which a turbaned shopman sits cross-legged on a bench in a reclining attitude. The rows of shelves around his head are furnished with various articles of native dress and finery. A drapery of gaudy handkerchiefs and miscellaneous brilliant objects hang round the entrance; whilst before him is a narrow glass case filled with numerous trifles of an ornamental character. The Moorish lady's sharp-pointed shoes, glittering with embroidery, lie beside her feathered fan, showing a small mirror in the centre; long pipes with amber mouth-pieces mingle with red leather purses, glistening with tinsel ornament; Arab daggers with shining sheaths lie in the midst of brooches, bracelets, smelling-bottles, essences, perfumes, palm-tree heads, and gilt and enamelled buttons covered with Arabic characters. Each stall seems the counterpart of its neighbour in size and aspect.

It is but a step from the open side of the *place* to a mosque beyond it. This mosque, which is called Djedid (new), is a relic of the old town, and owes its construction to a Genoese architect, who, having had the audacity to build it in the form of a cross, was treated with the bowstring, as the fitting meed for his impiety. By the means of orthodox domes the evil was remedied, but the original figure of the building is still easily traceable.

The interior of this or of any other Algerine mosque consists of a square hall, intersected with pillars. The floor is covered with a mat or carpet; the ceiling shows wooden rafters; and the walls, simply whitewashed, are generally devoid of ornament, with the exception of some ostrich eggs suspended in the niche that indicates the position of Mecca. In each, there is a kind of pulpit, from which the Imaun conducts the Friday's service. It is on that day that I for the first time visit the interior of a Mohammedan place of worship.

In deference to native feeling, I lay aside my boots at the entrance door, amidst the many slippers that are there deposited, and stepping across the threshold, I see long rows of worshippers extending from wall to wall. They are standing as I enter, and each, holding up his hands before his face, prays with a rapid utterance in an under-tone. In the pulpit is the Imaun, who chaunts aloud; and at some signal word of his, down fall the worshippers on their knees, and in another moment each forehead has touched the ground, from which it rises only to repeat the action. Those figures form an impressive sight, as with unwandering eyes and fixed absorbed expression of countenance, they stand, sit, bow themselves, and rise up simultaneously together. The service is not long, and after the Imaun's voice has ceased, the slippers and their proprietors join company once more; an easy process, which the difficulties connected with the resumption of my laced Christian boots make me somewhat envy.

The native court of justice forms an anteroom to the grand mosque, which like the mosque Djedid, is entered from the French rue de la Marine. From the street, a door leads me into a small flagged court, on one side of which is a low narrow room about twelve feet in length, whose open front renders the whole interior visible from the court outside.

Fronting me is the Cadi, a middle-aged man, seated on a low divan, with his left foot resting upon the cushioned seat, while his right hangs downward; his eyes are small, but keen; his beard well trimmed; and over his large white turban he has thrown a bright red scarf, whose long ends, falling down on either side, almost conceal from view his rich embroidered jacket. In his duty of administering justice he is assisted by three men, called adels, clothed in long silk pelisses, and with heads covered by turbans, whose peculiar form give them the look of gigantic balls of cotton. The desks at either side of the room at which they sit are strewn with written papers.

A dispute about some land is the matter undergoing trial; and as each complainant acts as his own lawyer, a beautiful simplicity characterises the whole proceedings. Leaving his shoes without the door, an Arab enters just within the threshold of the court, and after speaking volubly for some minutes the Cadi motions him to silence, on which the defendant Arab advances to tell a tale, soon cut short in a similar manner. With a meditative expression of countenance, the Cadi interchanges a few words with an adel; then uttering his sentence, the whole affair is ended in about ten minutes.

The next complainant is a woman, but her person is invisible to the Cadi, for her shrill voice penetrates to his ear through a small grated aperture in one of the side walls, as she protests that she is defrauded unjustly of her rightful property. The Cadi listens to her complaints with a somewhat contemptuous expression of countenance, and soon summarily dismissing her, the veiled face disappears from view; but I see her again, as, crossing the open court, she clasps her hands together with a gesture of despair, whilst exclaiming in bitter accents, 'All is lost, all is lost, all is lost!'

Nearly opposite the Cadi's court is the still smaller tribunal of the court of appeal, presided over by a Mufti; but as the room in which the high functionary sits, opens off a passage guarded by a porter, who negatives my entrance with a St. Senanus-like gesture, I can see nothing of the interior.

The koubba (tomb) of the maraboo Sidi Abd-er-Rhaman* is also an interesting native sight in the French town. Ascending a steep path opening from the extremity of the new French street, Bab-el-Oued, a few steps suffice to bring me to some low whitewashed walls, crowned by a low dome: entering the building I pass onward through a narrow gallery, to a small hall crowned by an octagonal-shaped dome, underneath which a tomb-shaped wooden cage, hung with

* In country districts, the domed tombs—or *koubbas*, as they are termed in Arabic—serve the place of mosques, which are only found in towns.

silk drapery of various hues, marks the spot where the bones of the saint repose. The banners and lanterns suspended from the ceiling, the walls covered with Arabic inscriptions, and the ostrich eggs hung here and there by way of ornament, make the koubba of Sidi Abd-er-Rhaman well worth seeing as a specimen of native life and customs.

But all the sights which French Algiers can offer to the stranger, are of little interest compared with those that a stroll through the old town affords. It is but a step from a wide French street to a native thoroughfare about four feet wide, scaling the side of a steep hill. The shops on either hand are in European eyes nothing but mere stalls; many of them are not so large as a good-sized wardrobe, and in every case, their open fronts serve the place of doors and windows. Here, is a stall whose entrance is ornamented by pendant bunches of red pepper pods and onions, whilst the proprietor, coiled up upon his bench, has fallen fast asleep. Opposite is a narrow room some five feet long, in which a barber is exercising his skill upon a well-lathered head; and on a bench inside, a handsomely-dressed Moor is evidently waiting to undergo a similar operation. Close by, three shoemakers ply their trade in a recess whose entrance is garnished by pendant strings of shoes, black, red, and green, and showing here and there a resplendent front, glittering with gold and silver twist, and tinsel ornament. A few steps farther up I pass a café, whose walls are lined on either side by a row of cross-legged natives, of whom some smoke, some play at draughts, whilst others sip coffee out of diminutive cups, amidst an almost unbroken silence. In a small recess raised a few steps above the street a solemn greybeard sits, resting on his knees a sheet of paper, on which he is slowly tracing with exquisite neatness some Arabic characters.

An adjoining embroiderer's stall shows four young men, each wearing a fez, from which a flower droops down below the corners of their large dark eyes, whilst their ears are hung with the skeins of gold twist and coloured silk employed in decorating the pieces of cloth or silk on which they exercise their taste and skill. Still mounting upwards, a loud buzz guides me up some steps to the interior of a Moorish school. Glancing over the heads of some thirty boys, all seated cross-legged on the floor of a low dark room, I see a turbaned schoolmaster coiled up in a corner, quietly sleeping, whilst his pupils are vociferating loudly some sentences inscribed on a slate each holds; and louder grows the uproar as the schoolmaster, suddenly awaking, and colouring up at the sight of the unexpected spectator of his slumber, catches up a long wand by his side, and stimulates the flagging energies of his pupils by a wholesale administration of head taps.

The figures I meet at every step are not the least

interesting features of the scene. To the Jewess in her rich embroidered satin robe, succeeds the ghost-like form of the veiled Moorish woman. A negress here, and an Arab there, mingle with the Saharian Mozabite in his striped burnous, the active Biskeri bearing a water pitcher on his shoulder, and the half clad Kabyle, whose cry of *balek* clears the way for his oil-laden donkey. From the Moor in his rich dress of varying colours, to the ragged beggar who asks for alms in the name of the great maraboo Sidi Abd-el-Kader, a native thoroughfare in Algiers is rich in contrasts and picturesque variety.

But if I turn to right or left, the scene entirely changes; for the alleys which branch off at either side are hemmed in by walls, showing here and there a small grated aperture, and a ponderous wooden door studded often with iron bolts, and not unfrequently these jail-like walls meet together above my head, or allow of the sight of but a mere streak of bright blue sky, whilst the dark paths I follow plunge sharply downwards, mount steeply upwards, or wind sidewards in tortuous course. The shrouded figures which I meet at times, add to the air of solitude and mystery that pervades the scene. Now and then, however, as I advance, the dead stillness is relieved by a voice from a terraced roof; and the chance opening of a door gives me an occasional glimpse of a square court arched round, and a pavement on which the bright sunshine traces the dark reflection of a vine or orange tree. Musing upon the life those silent walls enclose, I wander onward.

CHAPTER III.

NATIVE POPULATION OF ALGIERS.

THE term Moor is unrecognised by the many thousand natives of Algiers whom Europeans indicate by that word. According to their own phraseology they are simply Arabs of the town, children of El Djezaïr,* or, in English, Algerines — a term certainly more appropriate to a people whose ancestors may in some cases have been Spanish Moors, but who, for the most part, are descendants of Arabs, Berbers, Turks, Christian slaves, and Spanish or Italian renegades. Yet, withal that varied ancestry, this mongrel race, whom we call Moors, are characterised by similar tastes, manners, habits, dress, and looks.

Generally handsome, and with a fair but colourless complexion, the Moor's large dark eyes and regular features are mostly characterised by an expression mild to effeminacy. Fond of dress and of brilliant colours, he always arrays his somewhat portly person in as costly a manner as his means permit. Indolent

---

* The Arab name for Algiers.

by nature, he never in any grade of life engages but in some sedentary occupation. If belonging to the upper classes, he keeps a stall in a bazaar or native street, where, quite indifferent to the absence of customers, he smokes, drinks coffee, and chats with passing friends. The greatest effort which he makes, is to jog placidly along to his country garden, seated on a broad well-cushioned saddle, borne by a quiet mule. Every act, look, and attitude of the Moor indicates his love of ease.

The occupations of the Moor in a humble rank of life are very limited in number. He embroiders jackets, vests, girdles, purses, shoes and trappings for horses. He makes silk laces, trinkets, and earthenware jars, which he embellishes with coloured streaks in a peculiar manner. The gay trousers worn by the Moorish lady, and the rich jacket of her husband, are both fashioned by his needle. He distils essences of rose and jasmine, and weaves mats and baskets of the dwarf palm.

The Moor has an innate love of beauty. The colours of his dress are well-assorted, and his embroidery designs are graceful. He is passionately fond of flowers — he has them often in a jar beside him as he works, and he frequently inserts them beneath the edge of his fez or turban; the oppressive fragrance of the large white jasmine and the orange flower is his delight. Though loving to lie in shade, he likes to have a gush of sunshine lighting up the scene on which he looks. Polite in speech, his gestures are always graceful; his bearing dignified, and the calm self-possession of his address is never disturbed by the most unexpected incident.

His calm existence, passed underneath a brilliant sun and an azure sky, resembles more a waking sleep than that active state of being which northern nations designate by the term of life. Neither inquietudes for the future, nor frettings over the past, disturb his peace. His strong religious feelings serve as an anodyne for every domestic sorrow, and when some mortal sickness strikes him down, he calmly contemplates his approaching end, secure to enter the ever-blooming gardens of paradise, of which the Koran tells, where, clothed in a robe of rich green silk and lying on a luxurious couch, he will drink delicious wine from the golden cups presented to him by houris with large back eyes, and complexion of the hue of ostrich eggs covered up in sand.

In looks and character the Algerine Jew presents a striking contrast with his Mohammedan fellow-citizen. Impelled, by the destruction of Jerusalem in long byegone ages, to seek a home on the southern shores of the Mediterranean, the ancestors of the Algerine Jew perpetuated in Africa the qualities which have marked the Jewish race in Europe. Patient, cowardly, crafty, and avaricious, the African Jew engages in every pursuit by which money is to be gained; and, alike in Saharian oases as in Algiers, he buys, sells, barters, haggles, and grows rich — the aim and aspiration of his existence.

Cruelly as the Jew for centuries was treated in Christian lands, his position was not so abject there as in Mohammedan Algiers under the dynasty of the Deys. Cursed by the Koran, and denounced by it as a being destined to eternal punishment, the Mussulman thought to show his pious zeal by heaping ignominy on this enemy of God. After the sun had set, he could not leave the quarter of the town in which he herded with his brethren. To strike a Mussulman, even in self-defence, was a crime punishable by death. He was forbidden to mount on horseback, or to walk upon the terraced roof of his own house. He could wear no colour but white or black; and though crippled or infirm, he might not use a stick to aid his tottering steps. He had carefully to avert his glance from every mosque he passed, and children pelted him with stones as he walked along. Despoiled not unfrequently of his hard-won gains, and condemned to death on futile pretexts, he often breathed his last amidst scorching flames, or writhing in agony on iron hooks. Heavy taxes and forced labours were the lightest burdens of a lot which none but an abject servile spirit could have brooked or borne.

In dress, the elder Jews have but little changed from that which they were obliged to wear in former years, but the young Jew not unfrequently arrays himself in a costly and showy fashion. On his head is seen a crimson fez, from underneath which his long black hair hangs down at either side of his clear colourless face; his rich embroidered jacket of purple or emerald-green cloth is girt round the waist by a rose-coloured sash, whilst short lavender trousers, long white silk stockings, high-heeled shoes of varnished leather, and a gold-headed cane, complete the details of his highly-dandified costume.

The Algerine Jew would be handsome if it were not for the usually crafty, sinister expression of his countenance; and a lack of all expression destroys the charm of the Jewess's clear complexion and large dark eyes. A profusion of gold embroidery ill atones for the absence of a single fold in her long robe of satin or brocaded silk, and the white handkerchief she ties round her jaws, forms the very ugliest and most unbecoming head-dress that fashion ever devised. The Jewish girl of nine or ten is often very pretty, and the little cap of gold coins she wears, sets off the youthful charms which generally vanish with maturer years.

The Algerine Jew has engrafted an enormous mass of superstition on the creed of his forefathers; with the negroes he often offers up sacrifices to the djins; with Moors and Arabs he frequently makes vows at the tombs of Mohammedan saints. When ill, he calls in a sorceress, to drive out the evil spirit with which he thinks he is possessed. To avert misfortune, he wears amulets and talismans, and he nails a horseshoe to his house to counteract the evil eye. He is terribly afraid of Satan, and at a Jewish funeral the Rabbi sprinkles gold-dust round the coffin,* which, whilst the avaricious enemy of mankind is engaged in picking up, the soul is able to escape to purgatory, where it must stay for eleven months at least.

The negro population of Algiers amounts to some five hundred, and these—old slaves, or descendants of slaves emancipated by the French—are conspicuous for industry. The women engage in domestic service, or sell oranges and bread, whilst the men employ themselves in various ways; but their speciality is to be whitewashers and sellers of lime.

Lowest in point of number, the Koulouglis wind up the list of the various races forming the native population of the town. Their fathers Turks, their mothers Moresques, the epithet, son of a slave, which their name implies, indicates the lowly position which they held under the dynasty of the Deys; and, repelled as aliens by their mother's race, the Koulouglis willingly rallied round the banner of France on its first appearance on the African shores. Resembling Moors in dress and looks, they only differ from their mother's race in being less strict Mohammedans, and still fonder of dress and show.

A small floating population, composed of emigrants

---

* I saw this ceremony enacted in a Jewish cemetery.

from different portions of Algeria, complete the list of the African inhabitants of Algiers. The Mozabite from the Saharian oasis of Ouad Mzab, migrates to Algiers to open a butcher's stall. Here, also, comes the Kabyle from his mountains, and the Biskeri from his palm-tree grove, to ply the trade of porter. Of kindred race, though wide apart their homes, they show their brotherhood by a vivacity of tones and gestures that strikingly contrast with the staid composure of the Moor and Arab. See that group of swarthy half-clad men, who squat chatting together in monkey attitudes under the arcade in front of the Hotel d'Orient. See how the tallest of the group springs up at our approach, and with a grin that shows a row of brilliantly white teeth, bows half way to the ground as he shouts out, 'Bon jour, Angleterre; comment se va, toi porter bien?'

'Tres bien, merci.'

'Ah, c'est bon; toi rester longtemps. Moi bien aise te voir. Moi aime Angleterre; Angleterre bon beaucoup.'

CHAPTER IV.

SAINT EUGENE — A MOORISH INTERIOR — TRAITS OF MOORISH
LIFE — POINT PESCADE — WORSHIP OF DJINS.

AFTER a short stay at the Hotel d'Orient, in the noisy *place*, we were glad to find ourselves in the quiet suburban district of Saint Eugene, a French village on the sea-coast, about two miles distant from Algiers.

In point of beauty of situation, Saint Eugene is entitled to high praise. Towards the east, the white houses of Algiers, rising tier on tier a-high, form an exquisite foreground to the same grand sea and mountain view visible from the *Place du Gouvernement*. Bold rocks and projecting headlands on the west, and high overhanging banks of verdure on the south, add to the attractions of the scene.

But, with whatever keen consciousness of beauty a tourist may be endowed, the ever-recurring requirements of mortal existence detract much from the pleasure of a residence in Saint Eugene; since, as temporary visitors there are dependant upon restaurants for a supply of food, and as the restaurants, though numerous, range from bad to worse, the necessity of eating becomes a daily grievance of somewhat a serious nature, even to the least fastidious English visitor.

Most of the Moorish villas which plentifully dot the precipitous heights above the village, have now French proprietors, but here and there, one may be found inhabited by a Moorish family, whose jail-like existence is so well indicated by the incidents connected with my first entrance into one of these abodes, that I shall detail the particulars of my visit.

Wandering along the shore one day, we glanced wistfully at a brilliantly white villa close by, approached by a path whose primitive appearance showed it led to a Moorish home. Curious to see a native household, I resolved to try if our desire could not be gratified through the pretext of begging for a glass of water.

Arrived at a massive jail-like door, in a high-walled court, I knocked loudly, on which a shuffling noise and whispering tones inside were shortly followed by the sound of a bolt withdrawn. In another moment a negress was peeping at us cautiously round the edge of the all but closed door. A look of blank amazement was followed soon by a nod of comprehension, as I repeated the word *acqua* several times in an emphatic manner. Instead, however, of being asked inside, the negress brought me out a huge china bowl filled to the brim with water; and, retreating inside, she watched my proceedings by holding the door a couple of inches open. My strategy a failure, I was about to relinquish my vast goblet, when, with a low cry of alarm, the door was suddenly closed and bolted. The panic, incomprehensible at first, was soon explained by the sight of a turbaned Moor close by, advancing towards the house. From his fierce, truculent, piratical aspect, I felt by no means comfortable as he accosted us in an unknown tongue. His acts, however, belied his looks, for at his call the door was quickly opened, and, with a wave of his hand inviting us to enter, we speedily found ourselves in a court, where, besides the negress, we saw a very beautiful young woman, the wife of the grim master of the house.

The contrast between the ill-matched pair was positively startling. With a grisled beard and wrinkled face, which told of nearly seventy years, his stern fierce aspect was enhanced by the effect of a white sightless eye, whilst she, in the bright bloom of girlish beauty, looked scarcely fifteen. Her dress was picturesque. Above a chemisette of gauze she wore a pink silk jacket destitute of sleeves, and her bare arms were encircled by gold bracelets; a striped silk scarf tied round the waist hung down in petticoat fashion over full short trousers terminating at the knee, and in the gay silk handkerchief on her head she had stuck some sprigs of acacia. Her small bare feet and hands were stained with henna; and the beauty of her large dark eyes was somewhat marred by the line of black which edged her eyelids.

The house into which we were conducted was thoroughly oriental in its interior. By a steep stone staircase we gained a long narrow room, with a ceiling of unpainted rafters, a floor of enamelled tiles, and whitewashed walls ornamented solely by a couple of showy brackets. In a recess was a divan, on which we sat, until, finding there was no means of arriving at mutual comprehension, we went away, laden to a most burdensome degree with a parting gift of pomegranates.

Emboldened by success, I soon gained admission into several more of these jail-like-guarded dwellings, and to do so was very easy, for every Moorish gentleman who saw me approach his country-house, asked me unhesitatingly to walk in to see his family. It was thus I made the acquaintance of a young Moorish lady who spoke French, an accomplishment she had learnt from a governess in a European family living in her neighbourhood. She could write French also; an acquirement which made her, as she told me, be looked upon as a marvel by her friends. She shrunk from talking on the subject of the seclusion to which she was condemned by custom, and never uttered a wish for the freedom enjoyed by her European visitors. If I wrote to her she begged I would address under cover to her father, for it was not '*joli*' that a woman's name or existence should become known to strangers; it was not '*joli*' either for her to amuse herself by a song, if a man (even father or brother) was within hearing. As to dancing, I seemed to shock her by the supposition that she could do such an indecorous thing.

This lady had an only brother, heir to what in Moorish eyes would be considered a handsome property; but so little do Moorish and English ideas of social propriety coincide, that the young Moor had erected on his father's grounds by the roadside a wattled shed, in which he made and sold coffee for a sou the cup. Thinking from the primitive appearance of the edifice that it was a place of low resort, I had passed it frequently unentered; but on discovering who the proprietor was, I patronised him by my custom.

Aloes and cacti abound on the hills near Saint Eugene, and domineer over the dwarf palm, amongst which they generally grow. But, common as are these plants, they are not indigenous productions of the soil, for both are originally natives of South America. The sharp-pointed and fibrous leaf of the aloe is traditionally supposed to have furnished Eve with a needle and thread to fashion her garment of fig-leaves; but from my experience of the plant, I am inclined to think that it is much better adapted to perform the tearing than the making process. The cacti produce a fruit bearing the English name of Barbary fig, or of the more appropriate one of prickly pear, since an incautious touch, however slight, never failed to produce sensations which painfully convinced me that the motto 'Nemo me impune lacessit' was rightly applicable to another plant beside the thistle of Scotland.

The good French road which connects Algiers with Saint Eugene terminates at about a mile to the westward of the village, at a small fort on the seacoast, built by the Turks, and now garrisoned by the French. From this, a long reef of rocks project, bearing the name of Point Pescade, and on the extreme verge of its dark beetling cliffs, rise the mouldering ruins of a second fort, whose construction is attributed to the Corsair Barbaroussa. When the wind was high, it was a splendid sight to see the incoming wave shiver against the rocks into great jets of snow-white spray; and whilst listening to the thunderous roar of rushing waters in the great cavern underneath the cliff, I could well imagine how superstition had made of that dark vault the abode of djins.

A far less fitting home for evil spirits, is the djin-haunted spring in a rock by the seaside, immediately below the road between Algiers and Saint Eugene; and here certain pagan rites take place every Wednesday morning in the year. The scene is curious, but disgusting, from the sacrificial nature of the performances. On descending a steep bank by the roadside, amidst an atmosphere perfumed by incense, I saw an old Arab woman crouching near a spring, whilst shrill piercing cries issued from her withered lips. Her weird-looking aspect rendered her a fit minister of those beings whose servant she was supposed to be. Near her was a small pot of incense, with which she fumigated the hands and arms of an Arab, who repaid her services by some sous. Close by, another witch-like woman was engaged in plucking a fowl; whilst nearer the seaside, the same process was being performed by some half-dozen native men and women. Three Jewesses, a little apart, had their faces smeared with streaks of blood. Close to the water a negro knelt upon the sand, and whilst pouring forth invocations in a muttering tone, he held aloft in either hand a struggling fowl, which he waved to an fro above a small vessel of smoking incense. The fowl, thus consecrated, had speedily a sharp knife drawn across their throats, and thrown upon the sand, they struggled towards the water with flapping wings, amidst the shrill demoniac cries of several bystanders; and a young Jewess, rushing forward and dipping her finger in the gushing blood, streaked her brow and cheeks with crimson smears. In a few minutes afterwards, the barbarous scene was re-enacted with slightly varying details; and as I turned away from the revolting sight, a lamb was about to be sacrificed.

This weekly worship of the djins has for its object the cure of disease, which is supposed to be effected through the medium of daubing the face, hands, or feet with the victim's blood. All the various native races of Algiers take part in these proceedings; but though I saw no Christians amongst the group of Arabs, Moors, Jewesses, and negroes assembled around the spring, I heard that it was not rare to see one mingling as a performer in the scene. Truly, however mankind may differ in religion, they agree in superstition.

CHAPTER V.

A MOORISH WEDDING — LEGAL FORM OF MARRIAGE — LAW OF DIVORCE.

IT was after nine o'clock at night, when, in company with a party of English ladies, I toiled up the precipitous streets of Moorish Algiers to the scene of a native wedding. Mounting continually amidst walls which showed not a sign of life, we had nearly reached the summit of the town before we arrived at our destination. Entering by a low door which had been opened instantly at our guide's summons, we ascended by a few high stone steps into a small square flagged court, where two young women, plainly dressed in white, were performing a kind of slow dance to the accompaniment of tambourines energetically thumped by three other women, who were seated on the ground close by, beneath a colonnade surmounted by a gallery.

Whatever the intrinsic merit of the evolutions I witnessed, they had certainly the charm of novelty. Holding aloft a white handkerchief in either hand, the two women advanced, retreated, and changed sides, with a slow measured step, whilst giving a peculiar and most ungraceful undulating movement to their figures, to and fro, ever the same continuously; a more soporific performance I never witnessed, in despite of the well-thumped tambourines. According to Moorish ideas, that noise was music, and those evolutions dancing.

Soon leaving the court, we ascended by a steep staircase to the gallery above, in which the bride's friends and female members of the family were assembled, and not a face or figure that I saw but impressed me with the conviction that its proprietor was fully alive to a sense of her bounden duty to look handsome. If her success did not, in my opinion, correspond with her exertions, that result, perhaps, was owing to a prejudice of mine against eyebrows joined artificially across the nose by a broad streak of black, and eyelids edged with the same colour. Neither did I think that feet or fingers were improved by being stained orange, through the means of henna. The hair of the married women was cut so short as to hang on either side of the face no lower than the chin, whilst the unmarried wore their long tresses plaited into two tails, terminated with bows of ribands. Their dresses, similar in form, varied as to colour, but crimson was evidently most in favour. Over chemisettes of spangled gauze they wore rich silk jackets, stiff with gold embroidery, as was their crimson girdles. A striped gauze scarf hung down in petticoat fashion over wide trousers terminating at the knee; bracelets, necklaces, and rings encircled arms, throats, and fingers. From the gay silk handkerchiefs on their heads to the small pointed gold-embroidered shoes into which their henna-stained feet were thrust, the bridal party showed no lack of zeal in personal adornment. As to beauty, I saw but one handsome face; and even blackened eyes and brows could not destroy the charm of the fine features of the bridegroom's unmarried sister, who, dressed in white, and destitute of ornament, had allowed her magnificent long black hair to stream down about her shoulders.

The wedding festival, which had commenced three days before, was drawing to a conclusion. In most cases the bride, shrouded in a thick veil, is conducted in procession to the bridegroom's house at the termination of the ceremonial; but in this instance, as the bridegroom was going to live with the bride's family, he had come to her dwelling a few minutes before our arrival there, and was now awaiting, in a room apart, the eventful moment when he should look upon the unknown countenance of his bride.

The sight he doubtless longed for, we also desired to see, for the bride was not in the gallery with her friends, and we had to wait some minutes before we were ushered into her presence by one of the wedding guests. At first, however, on entering the room, we saw only a row of frightful old women squatting along the walls; but following our guide to the far end of the narrow room, we soon reached a red curtain hanging from the ceiling to within some three feet of the ground, and by drawing the curtain a little aside, the bride flashed upon our view.

A Chinese god, or a Hindoo idol, were the ideas she instantaneously evoked, as, seated in a cross-legged attitude, motionless as a statue, in the centre of a narrow stage extending from wall to wall, she showed a youthful face glittering with gold paper, stuck in patches on the chin and cheeks, and in broad strips upon the forehead, above eyebrows joined by a black streak across the nose; her head a mass of sparkling jewellery; her bust bare, but for a chemisette of filmy gauze and numerous strings of pearl; her hands, partially blackened and laden with rings, extended flat on either knee, and her eyes fixed in an unwinking stare, formed altogether a sight which made me hide my face behind the curtain to conceal an irresistible tendency to laughter.

Nor did the bride form the sole provocation to merriment in that scene, for by the young lady's side was seated an old woman crowned by a black silk extinguisher-shaped head-dress, some two feet in height; and as it was by her artistic hand that the bride had been arrayed, she rained down radiant glances of exultation on the foreign ladies, which plainly said, 'You never saw in your own land such a beautifully-dressed bride.'

After staring at the motionless figure until we cared

to stare no longer, we sat down on cushions amongst the wedding guests, with whom our interchange of ideas was limited to the utterance of one word, the sole mutual means of verbal communication between us and them. They, examining our trinkets, repeated *buono* with gratifying energy and frequency, whilst we, not to be outdone in politeness, showered our *buonos* profusely on their dress and ornaments. Had the bride's family been in affluent circumstances, coffee and sweetmeats would have filled up the vacuum in the ceremonial between the exhibition of the bride and her presentation to the bridegroom.

In some twenty minutes or more, the welcome tidings came that the last scene of the three days' drama was about to be enacted, and, rising from our lowly seats, we passed out of the room in which the bride was seated, to enter an adjoining one in which the bridegroom, in solitary dignity, lay reclining on the ground, with an elbow resting on a cushion and head leaning on his right hand. As we sat down upon a row of cushions ranged along the wall, he never stirred nor even looked at us. He seemed about twenty years old, and, though far from handsome, his countenance was pleasing.

A sudden din of tambourines soon dispelled the statue-like immobility of the bridegroom, for, springing up at the sound, he hastily seated himself on a divan extending across a shallow recess opposite the door, through which veiled figures immediately began to enter. As the room filled with the white-shrouded ghost-like forms of the wedding guests, louder and louder sounded the tambourines, whilst the din they made, blended with the shrill peculiar cry of joy of the Moorish women. The bridegroom, whose now eager gaze was directed towards the door, had not long to wait for his bride's appearance; and, as her resplendent figure appeared in view, he sprang up to meet her, and, taking her by the hand, he conducted her to the divan, on which she sat down beside him, whilst his beautiful sister, stepping up on the seat, stood erect in the recess, immovable as a statue.

The extinguisher-crowned official who entered with the bride, gave now the last finishing touch to her artistic labours; and whilst the bridegroom looked fixedly towards the door, she divested the bride of a filmy red gauze veil, that had been tied across her face, adjusted a long tress of hair hanging down in front on either side, and, having arranged the many rows of pearls around her neck, and placed her arms in a graceful curve, she advanced the lights so as to throw their full force upon her charms.

If the bridegroom was now entitled to look at his bride's face, he did not avail himself of the privilege, for he was still looking fixedly towards the door when the old woman advanced to pour a few drops of perfumed water into the hollow of his hand; and the bride having drank the contents of this primitive cup, the ceremony was repeated with a change of parts. After this interchange of vows, the bridegroom threw some money into a musician's tambourine, and the old dame wound up the ceremonial by sprinkling the company with perfumed water.

The duration of a marriage festival varies, according to circumstances, from a week to three days; but the family of the bride must be poor indeed, if she be not decked out with jewels, as all her relatives and friends deem it their duty to contribute something to her adornment. A girl is not considered at liberty to refuse any husband whom her parents may select; but a widow may continue single, if such be her wish. The mother chooses for her son, and on her taste depends whether he may have a plain or handsome wife, as he never sees the lady until the conclusion of the marriage festival. On the alliance being definitively arranged between the heads of the two families, the proposed husband goes to the tribunal of the Cadi, in company with a near relative of his intended bride, and there, before two witnesses, he asks the young lady's guardian to grant her to him in marriage on his undertaking to make a nuptial gift of so many douros.*

On the guardian's expressed assent, the Cadi registers the contract; and should a divorce ensue, the lady takes back the nuptial gift with her to her

---

* A *douro* is the Arab name of a five-franc piece.

father's house. From the Cadi's presence, the bridegroom returns to his home to feast with his friends, and to enjoy music and dancing similar to that I have described.

Though the Algerine Moor has frequently several wives during his lifetime, they do not co-exist together; for, through the medium of divorce, which is granted for any cause, one wife is summarily got rid of, before another is installed in the same household. Occasionally, the divorced wife is recalled, but she need not obey the summons against her will. I was told by one of these repudiated ladies, with whom I was well acquainted, that her husband asked her to return to him, but that she refused to do so. Instances are known in which the same wife has been thrice divorced; but, when such occurs, she cannot legally comply with a third recall without being previously married to another man, who, acting on the behalf of the capricious husband, sues for a divorce as soon as the marriage contract has been signed before the Cadi. On the divorce being granted, the Moresque resumes her old position in the house from which she has been thrice ejected.

Thus, a mere tenant at will, liable to dismissal like a hireling should she cease to please, the hapless Moorish wife is dignified by a title which in a Christian sense she has no right to claim.

CHAPTER VI.

THE MORESQUE AT HOME—HER HOPELESS DEGRADATION.

FLAT terraced roofs, small windows, and walled-in courts, form the only invariable features of Moorish country houses, for in form they show a considerable diversity; but one Moorish town house only differs from another in size and decoration, for all are constructed precisely upon the same plan.

Built in the form of a hollow square, the town house turns towards the street a jail-like-looking wall, pierced with a few small grated apertures, and showing a massive door studded with iron bolts. From this door a small dark vestibule leads to a short flight of high stone steps, conducting to a large square court, either flagged with stone or marble, or paved with enamelled tiles. Above a colonnade which flanks this court on every side, rises a gallery, that in all large houses is surmounted by a second. The long, high, narrow rooms which open off these galleries are invariably four in number; for each enjoys exclusive possession of one side of the square, and each is entered by a double door opposite a recess furnished with a divan. A crimson curtain hanging from the wooden ceiling at either end of the apartment converts into a private bedroom a broad shelf extending from wall to wall, and furnished simply with cushions. A few small barred windows opening off the gallery light the rooms. From the highest gallery a steep short staircase conducts to the terraced roof.

The furniture of an ordinary Moorish house consists entirely of carpets, cushions, curtains, and a few gaudily-painted brackets and large chests; but the interiors of the houses of the most aristocratic Mussulman inhabitants of Algiers are half French in look. In the handsome house of Mustapha Pacha — a Turkish Prince — his wife, the daughter of the last Bey of Constantine, received us in a room the walls of which were decorated with prints and handsome mirrors, whilst a costly Parisian clock and several chairs and sofas were also visible. The Prince himself, though dressed in oriental fashion, conversed with us in fluent French; but, as to the Princess, except that she could say *bon jour,* and that she sat on a sofa in a Christian attitude, she was a thorough Moorish woman in dress, mind, and manners. Her eyes were edged with koheul powder, and her only idea of conversation consisted of questions as to whether I were married, and if my father and mother were still living. It was quite a relief when the never-failing coffee appeared, accompanied in this instance with a small glass bowl containing the most delicious preserve I ever tasted.

Coffee is almost invariably served up to visitors, and is presented in a tiny porcelain cup inserted in a still smaller cup. No offering of any kind can be refused without gross rudeness. I have often left Moorish houses laden with great branches of rosemary and gigantic bouquets of daffodils and narcissus, which I ungratefully flung aside on leaving the presence of the donors.

The rich gala costume of Moorish ladies has been described in the account of the wedding at which I was present. On ordinary occasions, her in-door costume is of the simplest character. A black silk handkerchief crossed behind and tied in front, constitutes her head-dress. From beneath a narrow scarf, flung round her shoulders in the winter season, emerge a pair of full short coloured cotton trousers, terminating immediately below the knee. Bare legs or stockings seemed equally fashionable, and as for shoes, they are shuffled on and off continually. The freedom that the feet generally enjoy, confer on them a highly admirable industrial vocation; for I have seen a Moorish lady stitching away at a piece of work which she dexterously held between her toes.

The outdoor costume is very different. The veil, that all-important article of a Moorish lady's dress, is composed of a square of muslin doubled in two, which, passed tightly across the face just below the eyes, is tied behind. A long wide cotton scarf thrown over the head descends in front to touch the brows, and, brought together on either side beneath the chin by a dexterous twist, it is held inside by two invisible hands; whilst below the ends that hang down in front is seen a thin woollen drapery descending to the knees over immensely-full cotton trousers, drawn in round the ankle by a string. A pair of stockings sometimes, but always a pair of small black shoes, complete the dress. The effect of the costume, as I have said before, irresistibly suggests the idea of a ghost. With a cambric handkerchief and a small sheet or table-cloth, used as substitutes for muslin veil and scarf, any lady of an experimental turn of mind can easily convert her face into almost a fac-simile of that, with which the Moresque confronts the world; and if, when thus arrayed, she stands before a glass, her perceptive faculties must be keen indeed if she can recognise herself.

But notwithstanding what seemed to me an impenetrable disguise, Moorish women do recognise each other in the street; and a veiled figure by whom one day I was affectionately tapped upon the shoulder in Algiers, seemed extremely surprised that I stared at her glaring eyes in complete bewilderment, as to who their proprietor might be.

Nature has endowed the Moorish race with no small amount of beauty. But in this respect the men are pre-eminently distinguished; for, whilst all their features are generally regular, the charms of the Moresque are often limited to the possession of large black eyes and long curling lashes. Grey eyes are rare, and fair hair is so disliked, that the girl to whose lot it falls, hides her misfortune through the medium of a dye that changes the offending hue to a reddish bronze, which gives place to black when she is married. Before this important epoch of her life, her hair hangs down in two long tails behind her head; but matronly dignity involves the amputation of the tails to the level of the chin.

Koheul and henna are quite indispensable to the completion of a Moorish lady's toilet. With koheul, a black powder, she edges her eyelids, and often joins her eyebrows across her nose, and with the dye she extracts from the leaves of the henna plant she stains her nails bright orange. Her hands, wrists, feet, and ankles are also frequently embellished in a similar manner. In an artistic point of view, nature seems in every land to be considered an arrant bungler.

In addition to the merits of koheul as a beautifying agent, the Arabs allege that it strengthens the eyes, and acts as a preservative against ophthalmia. Tracing its origin to the burning bush on Sinai, they allege, with somewhat of an anachronism, that it was employed by Sarah and Hagar to increase their charms in the eyes of the patriarch Abraham. And as to find favour in a husband's sight is declared by

Mussulman divines to be the means by which a woman can obtain favour in the sight of God, the toilet arts of a Moorish woman assume the attributes and functions of religious duties.

The road to Paradise being thus opened to Moorish women through the medium of black-edged eyes, it is no wonder that those of a philanthropical turn of mind should urge their European visitors to adopt a similar practice. If the Mohammedan masculine heart can be won and kept by such a process, why should not the Christian heart* yield to the same influence? This assumption, far from illogical, gave rise to the following adjuration, addressed one day by a Moresque to a French lady in whose company I was:—

'Do let me blacken your eyelids and brows; it will make your husband love you so much better.'

The lady thus addressed, was at first unwilling to submit herself to the love-inspiring operation, but after renewed urgent entreaties, she finally consented. On this, there was produced a diminutive vial, into which a short knitting-needle-shaped piece of wood was inserted, and drawn forth covered with a fine black powder, that left a very decided line of black

* It would seem as if a belief in the heart-enthralling power of black-edged eyelids does extend to Christian communities, as this practice is now prevalent amongst the fashionable ladies of France and England; and, from the bungling way in which I have seen the process performed, I should recommend the ladies who resort to this oriental system of beautification, to visit Algeria for instruction.

upon the edges of the closed lids, between which the implement was lightly drawn a couple of times. This done, the artist gave some very effective touches to the eyebrows; and as I looked on the metamorphosed blonde, I felt assured that her appearance was undoubtedly calculated to produce a very deep impression on her husband, if he were not the most stolid of mortals.

Highly satisfied with her performance, the artist earnestly besought me to allow her to exercise her skill upon my face; but, whilst consenting to her wish, I limited her operations to my eyebrows, which, under her skilful hand, were so altered and amended as to give me a very decided martial aspect. In spite, however, of the approbation our appearance evoked, we had so little faith in the talismanic force of blackened eyes and brows, that the instant we left the house, we reciprocated the friendly service by endeavouring to efface every mark of the beautifying process we had undergone.

I was present in the same house at a congratulatory visit paid to a young mother soon after the birth of her child. The heroine of the scene lay on a silk cushion on the broad shelf which generally extends across the end of every Moorish room, and whilst a striped amber and white silk scarf served for a counterpane, her head was overhung by hangings of crimson silk, embroidered with gold. Here and there, the same rich material decorated other portions of the room, which now, in its gala dress, suited well with the brilliant aspect of the company, who were seated on silk cushions ranged along the walls.

The ladies all belonged to the first Moorish families of Algiers, and were dressed with a splendour befitting the position they occupied. Koheul had been most liberally used, and many a massive gold or silver ring encircled bare ankles stained with henna. Small rich silk jackets and girdles, stiff with gold embroidery, were worn by all. As the Moorish lady now dressed, so dressed her twenty times great-grandmother; a somewhat startling fact to one who had come from a land where old-fashioned is a word of reproach, and 'the last novelty' a phrase irresistibly attractive in feminine ears.

Each new arrival, having bestowed a profusion of kisses on her friends, sat down on a cushion in tailor fashion; and after sipping a cup of coffee, and exchanging a few conventional observations with her neighbours, she apparently concentrated her whole faculties of mind upon the European ladies, who were plied with a series of questions.

Was I married?—a standard question, and put by every native I came across. Were my father and mother living? Had I brothers and sisters? Since I was not married, how had I money to travel? What was my age? Why did I wear a black dress? — it was not a pretty colour.

In the midst of question and answer, the attention

of the company was diverted from us by the entrance of three plainly-dressed young women, with a very bold disagreeable expression of countenance. As they passed onward through the circle, each lady held out her hand to be saluted; and room being made for them beside the most distinguished-looking of the party, they sat down, and commenced to talk with volubility.

'Who are these women?' I asked.

'Musicians,' was the reply; and knowing the infamy that name implies in Mohammedan lands, I thought the proprieties of Moorish life were somewhat singular in permitting noble ladies to have such associates. As to the ladies themselves, it was only natural that amidst the *ennui* of a secluded, unoccupied life, they should welcome such companions, and listen eagerly to their words.

Not less strange, either, was another feature of Moorish life which was brought strikingly before my notice by a visit which we paid to two sisters, the daughters of a Moorish gentleman. Both were married, the eldest some eight years ago, but not finding favour in her husband's eyes, he had returned her to her father. The younger, who was only sixteen, had not been married more than a few months when we made her acquaintance.

Received as usual at the entrance door, we were conducted upstairs by the younger sister to a room which she announced to be her husband's apartment, and which, as it was furnished in French style, she naturally supposed would be agreeable to us. Seated on a divan, she conversed with us in French, whilst her elder sister squatted on the floor beside us in true Moorish fashion.

We had not been more than a few minutes in the room when, with an exclamation that indicated alarm, the elder sister bent forward her head in an attitude of eager listening; then, starting up almost immediately to her feet, she said a few words in Arabic to her sister, and rushed precipitately from the room. The young wife also showed symptoms of discomposure, and she asked us in a nervous tone to come and see her room. Before, however, we had passed through the central court, off which the apartments opened, the sound of approaching footsteps caught my attention, and, looking round, I saw a very handsomely-dressed young Moor coming up the stairs. 'It is my husband,' said our hostess, in answer to my look of enquiry, and, turning again alternately red and white, she leaned against a pillar close by in a state of very evident nervousness.

The young man, advancing towards us, addressed us with great politeness in fluent French, with which language he seemed perfectly acquainted. But little formidable as were his looks and manners, his wife quite coloured with nervous shyness as he said a few words to her in reference to her visitors; and her answers were given in a tone and with a look that breathed of a slave's humility.

The appearance of the young man explained the mysterious cause of the sudden panic of both the sisters; for whilst the elder sister had rushed off to conceal her unveiled face from her brother-in-law, the young wife feared that her husband would be angry at the liberty she had taken in receiving her guests in his room. I afterwards heard that, except in the case of youths, or of brothers marrying sisters, propriety requires that the faces of the wives should be veiled in the presence of their brothers-in-law. From the instance given, it will be seen that this strange code is not relaxed even in the case of sisters living under the same roof.

From her birth to her grave, the Moorish woman has no recognised existence in the world, beyond the circle of her home, and of her female friends. She lives and dies an ever-shrouded mystery. Her husband's dearest friend has never heard him mention her; and though the friend might chance to learn through his female relatives that she was dangerously ill, he could not say, 'How is your wife?' or 'I hope your wife is better,' without being guilty of a gross breach of decorum, which would not improbably be rebuked by the indignant answer, 'It is no business of yours to hope or care about my wife, or to concern yourself in any way about her existence.' Except under the comprehensive terms, How are your family? how is your house? how are your people? all enquiries relative to the health of the female inmates of any Moorish house are an insult to its proprietor.

The strictness of the code of etiquette in reference to this subject was strikingly exemplified to me one day by the mode in which a gentleman, proprietor of a native café, invited me to visit his wife, who lived in a neighbouring villa. Had he been alone, he would have said at once, 'My wife will be glad to see you, pray visit her;' but being in his café amidst a dozen of its frequenters, he merely said, '*They* will be very glad to see you in my house, should you pass that way.'

As might be expected from her secluded life, the mature Moresque is in tastes and faculties but a grown-up child. The reason which she is debarred from exercising, remains totally undeveloped, and her blighted intelligence might well give rise to the idea that she was an irresponsible being, destitute of a soul.* Acting under the influence of the belief that the evil was curable through the medium of education, a philanthropic French lady, named Madame De Luce, established in 1845, in Algiers, at her own expense, a school for girls. In this school, which is now entirely supported by Government grants, instruction is given in the arts of speaking, reading

---

* The Koran does hold out the hope of a paradise to women, but is silent as to the nature of its enjoyments, whilst entering into minute details as to the blessings reserved for the pious Mussulman.

and writing French, as well as in plain work and embroidery. But so little do parents value the Government offer of gratuitous tuition for their daughters, that it requires the premium of three sous a day to procure a scholar. At this present time Madame De Luce has not a pupil belonging to any but the very poorest class of the community; and out of some two hundred girls I saw assembled in the school, not more than one was the daughter of a former pupil. That such was the case is only natural, for under the Mohammedan social code, literary knowledge is to a woman absolutely useless, to which consideration may be added the still stronger one derived from the position assigned to her by the Koran. Nor can it be denied that in many cases the knowledge imparted in the school of Madame De Luce has led to evil, for the young French-speaking Moresque generally prefers a Christian lover to a Mohammedan husband. But apart from this result, the knowledge of French cannot possibly counteract the pernicious effects of the home influences to which the Moresque is subjected from her childhood.

Short of Christianity, no teaching can elevate the character and position of Mohammedan women in any land; for, as long as she accepts the Koran as a rule of faith, she will unhesitatingly acquiesce in the mutilated life to which by it she is condemned; and if, in despite of this mighty influence, her mental faculties could be developed by education, she would probably purchase wisdom at a heavy price, galled by the bonds she is too weak to break, but whose weight she had learned to feel. Degraded by her religion into a toy or slave, a toy and slave she will continue, as long as the name of Mohammed is reverenced by her race. But prostrate as she lies, she yet takes ample vengeance for the injuries of which she is the victim; for, fatally sapping the native vigour of the Arab as well as of the Turkish race, she has doomed them both to stagnation and decay.

CHAPTER VII.

AN AÏSSAOUA DANCE—A NEGRO DANCE.

THE worship of the Mohammedan religious fraternity of the Aïssaoua* presents a companion barbaric picture to that offered by the weekly invocation of the djins, near Saint Eugene.

The Aïssaoua have no mosque belonging to their order in Algiers, and they assemble for worship in a dwelling house in a native street, called by the French, the rue Klebér. On entering this house, under the guidance of a member of the fraternity, I found myself in a flagged court, at whose further end a number of natives were seated on the ground, beneath, and before one side of a colonnade which flanked the inner walls. Amongst this company a group of eight were made conspicuous by tambourine-shaped instruments, which they struck, whilst an old man performed some slow and not ungraceful evolutions, facing a miniature table, on which was a chafing dish, and a large bunch of flowers. A silk banner drooping from each corner, a gallery crowded

---

* This word should be pronounced as if written Aïssawa, *ou* in Arabic sounding like *w*.

with white veiled figures, and the partially dismembered carcases of two sheep, lying on the flags, completed the details of the scene. A seat was immediately given me beneath the colonnade; but disliking the sight of the butcher-like operations which were pursued in my vicinity, I joined the veiled occupants of the gallery.

For some considerable time, the proceedings below were of a very monotonous character, consisting principally of most dolorous-sounding chants; but after the last portion of the dismembered sheep had been carried off, and the court well washed, the musicians began to beat their instruments with an energy that made me fear the permanent destruction of my sense of hearing.

But though the deafening din exercised on me a kind of stupifying influence, it seemed to produce an intoxicating effect on the assembled congregation; for before long, up sprang a young man from beneath the colonnade, and, bounding into the court, he flung his head and body about in a frantic manner, jumping up and down with scarcely a change of place; his fez falling off, and his top knot of long black hair tossing wildly about his face, combined, with his contortions and frantic yells, to give him a truly fiendish aspect. And still more was this the case, when the Mokaddem —the priest of these strange rites—slipped over his head a long white burnous, that enfolded him like a shroud.

A DEMONIAC DANCE.

Five minutes had not elapsed, when, with a bound and yell such as I had previously seen and heard, another man joined in the demoniac dance. Another, and still another, was soon added to the group; and when the whole four were jumping together side by side, each tossing his head with frantic violence and uttering howls like savage beasts, I could scarcely bear to look upon that spectacle of degraded humanity.

In the midst of this revolting scene, the Mokaddem, advancing into the court, raised up his hand, and when at that signal the din was hushed, the dancers staggered as if they had been shot. One fell back with a deep groan into the Mokaddem's arms; another dropped to grovel on the ground; and the two others went reeling to and fro, uttering savage roars, which mingled with the shrill cries of delight of my veiled companions in the gallery.

The young man in the Mokaddem's arms seemed utterly exhausted. He tried to stand erect, but, with piteous moans, he fell back into the same position, and he continued apparently in a half lifeless state until, on inhaling the fumes of incense from a small vessel that was brought to him, he revived, and no sooner did the tambourine-like drums begin to sound once more, than he sprang forward to join a dance as frantic as the previous one.

Amongst this second set of dancers I particularly remarked one young man as transcending all his companions, by frantic contortions and violent gestures; and when the din was once more suddenly hushed, he dropped on the ground, moaning fearfully: but, revived by the fumes of incense, he soon got up, and taking a large round stone from the Mokaddem's hand, he began to knock it against his breast with great apparent violence, and finally giving a loud howl, he flung his arms about the neck of the Mokaddem, who had been clapping him on the shoulder during the process.

Another similar dance succeeded, lasting, like the others, some twenty minutes. On its conclusion, the fumes of incense were again required to revive the staggering, howling dancers; and the same young man who had knocked his chest, favoured the company with a second performance of a somewhat similar character, for, being presented with a short iron spike, he held it against his breast, and hammered it with the same stone he had used previously. In a few minutes, the process was brought to a conclusion by the stone shivering into fragments; and rising up from the ground on which he had been sitting, he reeled to and fro across the court, uttering deep moans. But when an apparently bloodless spike was drawn forth by the Mokaddem, into whose arms he shortly sank, I regarded this circumstance as an evidence, not of miraculous interposition, but of the presence of a breast-plate of wood.

Another mad dance succeeded, and at its end a new horror was enacted, by a new performer, who, seizing

the iron spike, deliberately inserted it into his right
eye, so as to force out the ball beyond the socket;
and though I turned away from the revolting sight,
I knew by the loud delighted cries of the women by
my side that the exhibition lasted for at least three
minutes; when I next looked round, the eye-ball was
in its place, and the late performer was rubbing it
with his fingers.

Again the din of drums was followed by another
frantic dance, the prelude of a new startling exhibition. This time, a man approached a brazier, and
taking up the burning embers, he rubbed them
between his hands. Another, subsequently, champed
fragments of glass. A succeeding performer passed
a red-hot poker several times across his forehead.
After him, a member of the fraternity displayed his
piety by standing barefooted on the edge of a sabre,
whilst a man sat on his either shoulder, and when,
sick of horrors, I left the gallery, an Aïssaoua was
wandering howling around the court with his lips
bristling with needles.

Making my way with difficulty through the mass
of women who thronged the narrow staircase, I
gained the court, where my guide Abdul the Aïssaoua
soon cleared a path for me.

'Was it not a beautiful sight?' he asked, in French.

'No, Abdul, in my opinion it was a very ugly
sight; to force out the eye is an especially horrible
looking thing.'

'How so?' he rejoined; 'it does not hurt or do any harm, if done in a right state mind.' My eye always felt quite right again after I had rubbed it with my fingers.

'And if you did not dance beforehand, you could not force out your eye without doing it injury. Is that the case?'

'Yes, certainly,' returned Abdul, with a look and tone of undoubting faith. 'It is the power of Allah whom he invokes, that keeps an Aïssaoua from being harmed.'

Many as were the horrors which I saw, the Aïssaoua repertory of startling sights was not nearly exhausted when I left their presence; and doubtless, had I remained, I would have seen them put vipers and scorpions into their mouths, chew the prickly leaves of the cactus, and wreath head, neck, and arms with venomous serpents; besides committing many other revolting extravagancies. How far the juggler's art mingled with the fanatic's exaltation I cannot say, but I feel assured that both combined to produce the sights I witnessed.

The origin of these extraordinary rites of worship is attributed to an alleged incident in the life of the maraboo Sidi Aïssa, the founder of the order; for on one occasion, it is said, his disciples, who had followed him into the wilderness to hear his words, having nothing to eat, he commanded them to satisfy their hunger by swallowing the scorpions, serpents, sands, stones, and thistles, which abounded on the spot, and which, by the grace of Allah, was converted into nourishing food. According to the Aïssaoua belief, a miracle of a similar nature is performed on every occasion that the members of that order meet together in public worship.

The negro dances, which take place in a house in the native street termed Sidi Abdallah, present features not much less revolting than those just described; but whilst the Aïssaoua invokes the inspiration of Allah, the negro summons Satan to his aid, and his demon worship is fitly mated with his demoniac dance. But, like as are the negro and Aïssaoua dances in frantic violence of character, there is this great difference between the two: that whilst negresses take an active part in the demon worship, no woman is permitted to join in the Aïssaoua performances.

Many negresses array themselves in a very elaborate manner for these occasions. The most brilliant-coloured striped silk scarfs often adorn their persons, and the graces of their ebon necks and arms are invariably set off by necklaces and bracelets. The finest dressed ladies were always the quietest dancers, I remarked; probably, they feared to discompose their finery by any very energetic devotional exercises: and if such was the fact, a love of dress was in their case a highly commendable passion. After each frantic dance came to a conclusion, the dancers were evidently supposed to be endowed with some occult power, for the spectators eagerly pressed forward to enjoy the privilege of having their heads twisted from side to side, and their arms pulled out, by the late performers. After every operation of this kind the operator received some sous. As in the Aïssaoua worship, the noise called music was quite deafening in amount.

'*Oh! Mon Dieu, mon Dieu, que c'est epouvantable, que c'est affreux?*' exclaimed a French lady with clasped hands, as she told me of the negro dance, from which she had been taken out in violent hysterics. Another French lady, who accompanied me to see the Aïssaoua dance, rushed out horror-stricken in ten minutes' time; whilst an English lady followed her example, under the impression that Satan was present within the walls. To the lovers of horrors, Algiers supplies an ample feast.

CHAPTER VIII.

THE MARABOO—MARABOO LEGENDS—ALGERIAN RELIGIOUS FRATERNITIES—THE HERETIC MOZABITE.

THE koubba* of Sidi Abd-er-Rhaman Talebi, mentioned in a former chapter, is only one of many tombs of saints visible in and around Algiers, and all constructed in similar fashion. In a rural district they serve for mosques, and are frequented more or less according to the popular reverence for the maraboo whose bones they cover. The term of maraboo is by no means limited, however, to such as have earned it by reputed miracles or peculiar sanctity of life; for as every male descendant of a maraboo is privileged to assume this name, the appellation, as far as existing maraboos are concerned, is merely a title of nobility, since no Algerian saint has been enrolled in the Mohammedan calendar during the present century. All existing maraboos have been born maraboos, and, for the most part, owe entirely to their birth the influence they enjoy. It is

* The French most inaccurately apply the term *Marabout* to the saint's tomb. The word koubba signifies in Arabic, a dome, which forms the characteristic feature of all these structures. Maraboo (in Arabic M'rabeth) signifies, attached to God.

TA - E

an exceptional instance when reputed wisdom or sanctity of life heightens the reverential feelings with which they are regarded, as was the case in the instance of the maraboo Mahi-ed-Din, the father of Abd-el-Kader.

Peculiarly distinguished thus by birth, the famous chief owed more to it than his own genius his election, at an early period of the French war, to the post of commander of the Arab forces, and to this source also may be assigned the origin of the popular superstition which regarded him as a special heaven-appointed agent to drive the infidels from the land. On two occasions it was believed the mission was miraculously revealed. The first took place in 1828, when, after a pilgrimage to Mecca, Mahi-ed-Din and his then young son repaired to Bagdad, to prostrate themselves beside the tomb of the great maraboo Sidi Abd-el-Kader, who appeared in person there to his two worshippers, under the figure of a negro, holding three oranges in his hands.

'These oranges are for the Sultan of the west,' said the disguised saint, proffering the fruit to young Abd-el-Kader as he spoke.

'We have no Sultan,' replied old Mahi-ed-Din.

'You will have one speedily,' returned the negro, and giving the oranges to Abd-el-Kader, he vanished from sight, to re-appear in 1832 once more on earth, when, on the eve of the day fixed by the Arab chiefs for the election of a supreme head, he intimated in person to an Algerian maraboo that Hadji Abd-el-Kader must be the nation's choice.

This Sidi Abd-el-Kader may be considered as the king of maraboos, for whilst other Mohammedan saints only enjoy a local fame, his name is known and venerated throughout entire Islam, and though Bagdad enjoys the distinction of possessing his sacred bones, yet koubbas rise to his honour in every portion of that vast region where the name of Mohammed is adored. Pilgrims flock in multitudes to his tomb. The sick, unfortunate, and afflicted never fail to implore his aid. No enterprise can succeed without his favour, and even robbers seek to propitiate his goodwill by vowing to decorate his shrine, should they succeed in accomplishing a projected theft. His intercessory power is even considered to be greater than that enjoyed by the messenger of Allah. The Italian beggar not less invariably solicits charity 'for the love of God and the blessed Virgin,' than does the Mohammedan mendicant invoke an alms in the name of ' Allah and Sidi Abd-el-Kader.'

The intercessory power of the great saint was the reward conferred for a peculiar sanctity of life, which procured him the distinguished honour of being appointed by Allah to bear alone the burden of three-fourths of the 380,000 ills which annually descend in the month of Safar on the earth—a load ordinarily divided amongst twenty pious men in different parts of Islam, thus leaving to weak sinful man only the endurance of a small portion of a burden which in its undiminished amount would crush him to the dust. But pious as was Abd-el-Kader, his sanctity did not render him insensible to the heavy load of ills appointed him to bear; and though he died in fearful torment before the lapse of forty days, his sufferings have been indemnified by the glorious intercessory privileges he now enjoys, and which, with unbounded benevolence, he exercises in favour of not only the faithful, but even of heretical Jews and Christians who on any emergency earnestly invoke his heavenly aid.

The order of which Sidi Abd-el-Kader was the founder, constitutes one of seven religious fraternities existing in Algeria at this present day. With this exception, the founders of these various orders were all African saints, two of whom are specially deserving of notice from the marvels connected with their histories.

Sidi Abd-er-Rhaman was a native of Algiers, and founded there a religious order, whose rule consisted in repeating 3,000 times a-day, 'There is no god but God, and Mohammed is the messenger of God.' The fraternity increased rapidly in numbers, but to extend it further, the maraboo left Algiers to seek disciples amidst the mountains of Great Kabylia, where he died, and was buried with all the honours due to a person of great sanctity. But no sooner did the Algerine members of the order hear of the death of their great head, than they formed a plot to wrest his precious mortal relics from the possession of the Kabyles; and from an ambush near the tomb they rushed forth one night to seize the coveted prize, and bore it off in triumph to bury it near Algiers. A rumour reaching the Kabyles of their loss, they hastened in dismay to the violated sanctuary, but to their delight they found the remains of their venerated saint apparently untouched, for lo! the body of the maraboo had been miraculously multiplied into two. From this circumstance the designation of *bou kouberin* (man of the two tombs) has been added to Sidi Abd-er-Rhaman's name. The largest native cemetery at Algiers extends before the Algerine koubba of the revered saint.

Still more marvellous is the history of Sidi Aïssa, the founder of the order of the Aïssaoua. More than 300 years ago there lived in Meknès, a city of Morocco, a pious man of lowly birth, who daily returned from his fervent devotions in the mosque to a home filled with the hunger-stricken faces of his numerous family. But poverty had no terror for the pious Aïssa. On the brink of starvation, he still, with an untroubled countenance, exclaimed, 'Blessed be Allah; his ways are right.'

Thus years passed on; until one day, on his return from the mosque, his wife, with a joyful countenance, thanked him for the supply of food that he had sent; and as he looked in bewildered surprise at a large heap of provisions of various kinds piled up against the wall, he heard how an unknown man had brought them to his door and had given them to his wife with the words, 'Sidi* Aïssa sends you that.' 'Blessed be Allah,' said the pious Aïssa, 'it is surely heaven sent food;' and from that day forth, the angelic messenger never failed to make his appearance each morning at the door with gifts that soon made Aïssa so rich that Moulei Ismael, the Sultan of Meknès, growing jealous of his wealth, banished him from the town to a waste piece of ground some miles off. There, Aïssa lived, surrounded by an ever-increasing circle of disciples, whose numbers at length provoked the ever-jealous Sultan to order Aïssa to quit his dominions at once.

'Nay,' said the holy man, 'I will not move again; but if you do not choose to have me in your kingdom, I will buy it of you at any price you fix.'

'The Sultan, thinking that he now would have fair grounds to get rid of him, named an enormous sum as the price of the contemplated purchase; and, appointing a day for the execution of the sale, he went, attended by his officers of state, to the dwelling of Aïssa, who led them to a large olive tree, around which he invited them to sit.

'Aïssa,' said the Sultan, 'here is the act of sale. Give me this moment the stipulated price, or I shall drive you from my kingdom as an impostor.'

* A title of nobility.

'So be it,' said the Saint, as, raising up his stick, he struck the tree, on which there fell down from it a shower of golden coins, amounting in value to thrice the required sum.

'Late Sultan of Meknès,' exclaimed the triumphant maraboo to his discomfited enemy, 'I, Sultan now, order you, Moulei Ismael, to leave my dominions.'

'Pardon, pardon,' exclaimed the contrite Moulei, as he and all his retinue prostrated themselves before the holy man, whose sanctity had been so abundantly proved by that miraculous shower. Satisfied with his triumph, Aïssa gave back his kingdom to the repentant prince, on the condition that, every year, for the period of seven days in a certain month, all the inhabitants of Meknès who do not belong to the order of the Aïssaoua, should be compelled to remain indoors.

The convention is stated to have been faithfully observed from that time up to this present day; but the annual proclamation made by the authorities of Meknès in conformity with the maraboo's demands, inflicts no grievance on any of the inhabitants of the town, since all are followers of the order of Sidi Aïssa.

No particular miracle seems to have illustrated the lives of the heads of the remaining number of the seven religious orders in Algeria. Each is believed, however, to have received in sleep an intimation from Mohammed of the mode of worship to be followed by the brotherhood he was ordered to form. Each raternity has an existing head, called *Khalifa*, who designates his successor before he dies, and the *Khalifa* appoints delegates, named *Mokaddems*, who preside in his name over every assembly of the fraternity. Like the freemasons, these orders have each a particular password; and the entrance into one of these religious bodies is indicated by the phrase 'to take the rose.' 'What rose do you wear?' is a question not unfrequently put by one Algerian Mohammedan to another, who, if not a member of any order, answers, 'I wear no rose; I am simply a servant of Allah.'

Though very rare, a koubba rises here and there throughout Algeria over the remains of a female saint. The white-domed tomb of Lella* Gouraïa at Bougie perpetuates the remembrance of a woman of noted knowledge and piety. But her fame is eclipsed by that of Lella Messaouda, whose koubba rises amidst the sands of the Sahara. Such a marvel of wisdom as well as of sanctity was she held, that strangers came from afar to submit their differences to Messaouda's arbitration; and of her it was declared by the popular voice, 'What she judges is judged, what she writes is written; after Messaouda the sage has spoken, there is no longer doubt.' A remarkable tribute to a woman amongst a woman-despising people.

The temptations of St. Anthony find a counterpart

* Lady.

in those of the maraboo Sidi Omar, whom Satan accused before Allah of being a hypocrite.

'Villain,' replied Allah, 'slander not my most faithful servant.'

'Only let me tempt him,' rejoined Satan, 'and you will find my words come true.'

'Tempt him, then, if you will,' returned Allah. 'To-morrow, from earliest dawn to sunrise, I surrender him to your temptations, on the condition that, if you fail to make good your words, you shall be his slave for life.'

'Agreed,' said Satan, and joyfully went off.

With the earliest dawn the maraboo was at his well to draw water for the prescribed ablutions before prayer,* but on drawing up the unusually heavy bucket he found it filled to the brim with silver. Casting like rubbish the glittering metal on the ground, and uttering an exclamation of disdain, he lowered down again the bucket to raise it up a few minutes afterwards, filled up this time with gold.

'Oh, blessed Allah!' exclaimed the holy man, 'I wish for no glittering worldly dross. I desire nought but water, that I may purify myself according to thy law.'

After flinging the gold upon the silver, Sidi Omar again lowered the bucket, and once more it returned to his hands laden with riches—this time in the form of precious stones, which casting upon the heap, he

---

* A prayer at dawn is obligatory on every Mussulman.

fervently exclaimed, 'Oh, gracious Allah! it is then decreed that, like a pilgrim on a journey through the desert, I must perform my ablutions with sand.' But no sooner had these words been uttered, than the gold, silver, and precious stones melted into a fountain of pure sparkling water, which has never ceased to flow from that time to this day.

'God is great,' exclaimed the maraboo in a holy ecstasy at the sight; and, having performed his ablutions and said his prayers, he returned to his house, where he saw before the door two beautiful young girls, and a negro holding the bridle of a magnificently caparisoned horse.

'I am thy servant,' said the negro, as he prostrated himself before the saint, 'and these beautiful girls, and that matchless horse, are also thine, gifts from the Sultan of Fass, who has heard of thy great virtues and poverty.'

'Take back the gifts to him that sent them,' said Sidi Omar, 'and tell the Sultan, with my thanks, that I desire no horse or slaves. With the labour of my hands I have wherewithal to satisfy my wants.'

With the last words spoken, the sun arose, and on the instant, horse, girls, and negro disappeared, whilst the air resounded with the baffled demon's cry of rage and disappointment. History is unhappily silent on the subject of the tasks allotted him by the saint.

The Chefaï, the Hambli, the Hanafi, and the

Malki, constitute the four orthodox sects into which the followers of Mohammed are divided. All other sects beyond this pale are considered heretical by Mussulman divines. The Algerian Malki and the Turkish Hanafi respect each other as good Mohammedans, but both hold in aversion the heretical Ouhabi, who occupy the Saharian oasis of Oued Mzab. In spite of the extravagant worship of the Aïssaoua, his orthodoxy is unquestioned, but the mode in which the Ouhabi Mozabite performs his devotions is an abomination in the sight of the orthodox faithful. In Christian eyes it may seem a trifling matter that the Ouhabi, contrary to the usual Mohammedan practice, divests himself of his inner garment before he prays; that he then allows his hands to hang down by his side, instead of raising them up in the ordinary way before his face; that he unties the cord wound round his haik-draped head, and exhibits some independent notions as to the spot in which he leaves his shoes ere entering the mosque. But to orthodox Mussulmen such practices are so odious, that the Mozabite's acknowledged purity of life and probity of character cannot save him from being an object of aversion and contempt to his Mohammedan brethren.

A love of donkey flesh is another of the grievous sins imputed by the orthodox Algerian Malki to the heretical Mozabite, and the Malki firmly believes that, as a punishment for indulging in this abominable taste, the Ouhabi's ears in death lengthen out suddenly to the dimensions of those of the animal on which he has feasted during life.

And enlightened as we deem ourselves, have we no political, social, and religious Malkis in England? Haters, from trifling differences in opinion and practice — detractors of merit, inventors of calumnies?

CHAPTER IX.

MUSTAPHA SUPERIEUR—A NEW YEAR'S DAY—A MOORISH VILLA —BEAUTIFUL WALKS—SUMMER SUNSHINE—A WINTRY SPRING —THE CAVALCADE—CHARITY IN MASQUERADE—FRENCH SUPERLATIVES.

AFTER a month's residence at Saint Eugene, we spent the succeeding month in a Moorish house near El Biar, a French village situated on the heights above Algiers. But, magnificent as was the view, the site was so exposed that we were very glad to migrate again to another Moorish dwelling situated a short way down the heights of Mustapha Superieur, a surburban district lying eastward of Algiers.

As Algiers is now resorted to by English invalids, some information connected with the best place of residence there may be of use; and, speaking from experience, I have no hesitation in giving a decided preference in every respect to Mustapha Superieur. In Algiers the stranger or invalid has little choice but to be domiciled in an hotel in the *Place du Gouvernement*, or immured in an indifferent lodging in some wynd-like mongrel French and Arab street. In the first, there is a fine view and abundance of fresh air, but incessant noise; in the other, there is quiet, but a close atmosphere and abundance of foul odours. Saint Eugene is pleasant quarters for a person who has health and strength to climb the steep hills inland, but an invalid has scarcely any walk but a public road overhung continually by clouds of dust produced by ever-plying omnibuses. El Biar is exposed and cold, but Mustapha Superieur enjoys for the most part a warm southern aspect, whilst protected by steep banks from the often high, and sometimes keen north and west winds. In addition to these advantages, it commands views of exceeding beauty, and a variety of charming walks through winding paths and lanes bordered by luxuriant foliage.

But let no invalids be tempted by the very attractive exterior of Moorish houses to select them for their place of residence; for, notwithstanding the fine climate, they will find their interiors chilly, as they are constructed entirely with a view to summer enjoyment. Their windows mostly face the north, dead walls the south, whilst if any stove or fireplace exist within, it is altogether a modern innovation. The Moorish house we occupied at Mustapha had very recently been vacated, at a considerable pecuniary loss, by an English family with an invalid, who had taken apartments there for the whole winter season; and even with two additional stoves, our rooms could not altogether be called comfortable, in the English acceptation of the word. The difficulty of finding really good accommodation, is the great drawback at present to a winter residence at Algiers, but each year this difficulty diminishes; for though the French residents at Mustapha may not love us, they yet love our money, and the desire of obtaining some two, three, four or five hundred francs a month is yearly inducing many to try to adapt their rooms to English tastes. House rent is ordinarily somewhat dear, living cheap, but meat of a very indifferent quality. In a good, well-situated, but somewhat expensive English boarding house at Mustapha, the invalid or tourist will find very comfortable accommodation.

With cliffs on high, ravines below, and precipitous banks clothed with luxuriant verdure, amidst which a multitude of villas sparkle with star-like brightness, Mustapha Superieur would be beautiful, even without the splendid view it commands of a noble curving bay, and the fine mountain range bounding the long narrow plain of the Metidja. As I watched the sun rise, on New Year's Day, from our dwelling on these heights, I thought I had never witnessed a more glorious prospect. Sent to my window before six o'clock by the cannon's voice which proclaimed the approach of dawn, I watched the first rays of filmy light creeping upward from the horizon, and which, gradually warming into a ruddy glow over north and east, brought out in strong relief the waving outline of the looming masses of the distant mountains. And, whilst the varying tints above were mirrored in the glassy sea below, the red hues changed into a golden radiance, amidst which the glorious disc of a cloudless sun arose. Then glittered the snow-capped Djurjura, and the glassy sea of the grand curving bay, dotted here and there with the bird-like sails of small fishing craft, flashed in the bright light of morning; whilst near at hand the heights and slopes of Mustapha, and the steep banks beyond, were gemmed with the diamond sparkle of innumerable white villas, each in a setting of luxuriant verdure. No English summer day was ever born amidst such a wealth of azure sky and gushing light, as was that 1st of January at Algiers.

A brief description of our dwelling at Mustapha will afford a general idea of the characteristic features of a Moorish villa. The entrance was through a garden, containing many of the productions of a warm clime. The banana, with its slender stem and long drooping narrow leaves, rose in the vicinity of large orange and lemon trees, whose golden fruit showed brightly amidst the dark green foliage. Dead leaves lay thick upon the pavement of neglected baths, past which the path led onward up a steep wall of rock, festooned with wreaths of large-leaved ivy, and crowned by high white walls irregularly pierced with French and Moorish windows. Passing through a large walled-in court, from which the house was entered, a small door and a steep flight of high stone steps led to the suite of rooms we occupied, and which we rented from a French gentleman who, with his family, lived in the basement story.

The house having been modified to suit European tastes, presented a very mongrel aspect; and the walls of our sitting room were so averse to all innovation, that, absolutely refusing to accommodate themselves to a square German fireplace, it projected into the room in a manner very distressing to a mathematical mind. In my French furnished bedroom, a small grated Moorish casement was placed so high that I had to stand upon a chair to look out through it; but, thanks to a modern innovation in the front wall, I was able to survey the outside world without being obliged to have recourse to such a laborious process. Under the dome where the prophet had been adored in prayer, our easy chairs were placed, and with a wedge formed of the sheets of a London newspaper, I very impiously filled up the hole in the walls by which, in former times, the water used in ablution by the faithful had been let off. Queer recesses, eccentric apertures, and quaint passages, characterised the house; and my stature would so ill accommodate itself to some of the low Moorish doors, that I thought, at times, it would be extremely convenient if, like St. Denis, I could have managed to carry my head in my hand.

The neighbourhood of this villa was rich in varied

and beautiful walks. From the summit of the Sahel, of which the heights of Mustapha form a part, there extends inland an elevated tract of land, intersected by numerous ravines. Amongst these, the valley of the Hydra is peculiarly beautiful, from the fine arches of an ancient but still perfect aqueduct which spans the steep and richly wooded gorge. A handsome light blue iris grows here abundantly, close to a ruined Moorish house, used as a native café, where I sometimes paused to take a cup of coffee, which would have cost me but one sou if I had not enacted the munificent by adding to it another.

But prominently picturesque as is the valley of the Hydra, it forms only one of a thousand beautiful walks abounding in the neighbourhood of Mustapha Superieur. In whatever direction I might wander, beauty was ever present in varied forms; and, until the month of February, every charm of scenery was enhanced by brilliant sunlight and warm skies. Up to that time there had been no winter but in name; for, though the wind was often very high, it was not cold, and the rain had been so trifling in amount that alarmists prophesied there would be a famine cry that year amongst the colonists of Algeria. Ordinarily, November and December shower down a copious supply of fertilising water on the parched soil; but, not having done as they were wont to do, it was a much-agitated question if January or February would perform the old year's duties, and as in the course of time it was found that January very decidedly declined that office, it was strongly suspected that February would follow the example of its predecessor. Faces grew very long, and heads nodded very portentously, when January expired amidst still unclouded skies and magnificent sunshine.

The prospects of the colonists did look bad, I thought, as I saw almond trees and beans in flower, hedges starred with bright yellow jessamine, the thorn showing clusters of opening buds, and butterflies fluttering across my path with a summer-like frequency. From a philanthropical point of view I wished for rain, but as, from a tourist's point of view, I was averse to it, I cannot say that my stock of philanthropy was sufficient in amount, to reconcile me altogether to the cold heavy sleety showers with which February almost entered on its existence. If February rained, it ought reasonably to have done so warmly, as befitted its position in an Algerian year.

But as the days passed on, February rendered itself still more obnoxious to my censure, for on the morning of the 15th I arose from my bed to see a snow-covered ground. For many a year, such a sight as that had not been visble at Algiers. Our native servant, a young woman of Spanish origin, eighteen years old, clapped her hands in wonder at the marvellous scene, and after repeatedly exclaiming, '*Oh! qu'il fait beau*,' she wound up her reflections on the subject by uttering no less energetically '*Oh! qu'il fait froid.*' As to myself, the familiar but now unexpected sight inspired me with sensations akin to those that a dupe may feel, on discovering he has been grossly taken in; and the keen breath of this white-faced visitant, from which I had fled from my native land, was here still more odious in my eyes, from the absence of the mitigating influence of great fires of blazing coal. Very shortly, too, the grievance assumed a still graver character, for the melting snow insinuating itself through various small chinks in a flat roof unused to such visitations, innumerable cascades commenced to fall from the ceilings; and though cascades are undoubtedly agreeable sights amidst rocks and trees, they cannot but be considered an objectionable feature of scenery in one's bedchamber, or sitting room.

Algerian vegetation was as little fitted as were Algerian houses to resist the snow, for after the thaw, which speedily set in, our bananas looked quite spectral, and the orange and lemon trees showed many a broken bough. Calamities of a similar kind abounded throughout the neighbourhood of the town.

Keen piercing winds, and cold, sleety, drenching rains succeeded the snow. Roads, lanes, and paths converted into beds of mud and mire, forbade all pedestrian strolls. Thus confined indoors, I made considerable progress in Arabic, which I had commenced in the previous month, to learn by ear in a child-like manner; for the sight of the many hieroglyphical letters of the Arabic alphabet had made me fling aside an Arabic grammar with a shudder. Under the system I adopted I had two teachers — one a young French lady, who had picked up some slight knowledge of the language from a negress servant; the other, an Arab lad, some twelve years of age, who, understanding French, consented, for a certain consideration, to teach me through that medium his own language. His system I thought admirable, for intuitively arriving at my well-reasoned conclusion that rules of grammar in a foreign tongue were unjustifiable restrictions on English liberty of speech, he most liberally allowed me to make my nouns masculine, feminine, singular, or plural, as I found most convenient.

Winter, tardy in coming, showed no haste to leave. The same desponding spirits who had previously prophesied a famine drought, began to predict an interminable deluge as March approached the term of middle age, amidst cold drenching rains that fell day after day incessantly. '*Les pauvres*' were pitied exceedingly, for the weather was too bad to permit the annual *cavalcade*, an invention allied in nature with those English balls and fairs in which pleasure masks itself in the garb of charity. The possibility of relieving *les pauvres* in any other way seemed an idea beyond the mental grasp of French high life in Algiers.

After many postponements the *cavalcade* took place on the 15th of March, and the sun, for the first time for weeks, benevolently showed an unclouded face as a long procession of huge decorated cars, richly arrayed cavaliers, and carnival-dressed figures, defiled along the streets of French Algiers, whilst charity on high, with sparkling eyes and beaming smiles, rained down its silver or copper coins on philanthropy, pleasantly impersonated to mortal eyes under the form of dashing young officers. It was a brave show for a holiday — a success as such; a mockery as a charity, since the expenses of an expensive fête deducted from the receipts would leave *les pauvres* almost nothing. The jay who decked himself in borrowed plumes, was a type of this *cavalcade*. Ever the same old story since the world began: poor Sense rebuked, snubbed, put into the corner, her ears well boxed; whilst Folly, petted, kissed, and patted on the head, is encouraged to jingle her bells right merrily.

Strangely enough, the pageant excited no interest amongst the native inhabitants of the town. With rare exceptions, the spectators of the show were Europeans. Whilst in French Algiers, crowds filled the streets and shouts the air, not a stall seemed closed in the native town, nor a café empty, and beggars in their native haunts whined forth their cry for charity in the name of the great maraboo Sidi Abd-el-Kader.

Towards the end of March the weather became so bright and warm, that we determined to start at once on our projected travels through Algeria. Our first destination was Blidah, a town on which French tourists and authors lavish such superlatives of praise that their literal construction would have induced me to believe I was about to visit a terrestrial paradise. '*Une corbeille des fleurs,*' '*une ville embaumée*' in the midst of '*environs enchanteurs, magnifique, ravissant,*' are words highly stimulating to an English imagination; but a familiar acquaintance with French forms of speech had taught me to accept a French superlative of any kind at never more than one-half its apparent value. A *desolé* as little indicates a deep amount of woe, as an *enchanté* does a state of overflowing happiness. To judge by words, the whole French nation knows no medium between the highest bliss and the deepest misery.

CHAPTER X.

ACROSS THE METIDJA — BOUFARIK — BLIDAH — THE ENNEKABO FASHION — BEAUTIFUL RAVINE — A NATIVE VILLAGE — THE RAMADAM — INTERVIEW WITH A MUFTI.

A VISIT to Blidah usually follows a winter in Algiers. The Parisian tourist, seldom venturing inland beyond this point, quickly returns to his loved boulevards to entertain his friends with an account of his Algerian travels — an enterprise which does not task his energies of mind and body in a high degree, as a comfortable diligence conveys him from Algiers to Blidah, over an excellent road, in four hours' time, and the railroad now in progress will soon reduce the journey to a much shorter period.*

Taking our seats in a diligence that passed along the Mustapha road, we wound up the heights amidst a brilliant sunshine, that shed a radiant glory upon every beautiful feature of the magnificent Bay of Algiers. The deep azure masses of the Little Atlas mountains towered grandly in the distance; brightly

---

* The railroad is now open.

flashed the settlers' houses in the plain: and, whilst Moorish villas sparkled amidst the rich verdure that clothed the slopes and the precipitous sides of the Sahel range, Algiers 'the white'* rose tier on tier, like a great chalk cliff, from the edge of a boundless expanse of bright blue sea. '*Vedi Napoli e poi mori*,' says the Italian proverb; but, to my mind, Naples has scarcely a scene to show which surpasses that, viewed from the heights of Mustapha, on a fine sunlit day.

On gaining the summit of the Sahel, we plunged into one of the numerous ravines by which the range is intersected. Some twenty minutes brought us to Birmandrais, a picturesque French village, situated in a hollow overlooked by wooded peaks, at the entrance of a beautiful ravine called the '*Femme Sauvage*,' which no visitor to Algiers should fail to explore. Passing onward, through a highly undulating tract, bright with sprouting corn and dotted with settlers' houses and white Moorish villas, a few miles brought us to the military station and small French settlement of Birkadem. From that, cultivation gradually decreased, till, before long, it almost seemed finally to cease, as, gaining by a gradual descent the eastern limits of the Sahel, we entered on the long narrow plain of the Metidja.

For some miles on, the desolation on either side of

* 'El bahadja,' an Arab epithet.

the fine road over which we travelled, was only very occasionally relieved by the sight of a small humble cottage and plot of corn, dotting a waste of brushwood principally composed of the dwarf palm and lentisk, and showing many a patch of marshy land and pool of stagnant water, reeking with the same pestilential exhalations which lay like a low white cloud over the distant portion of the Metidja. But on approaching the centre of the plain, swamps and brushwood disappeared, to give place to large well-cultivated cornfields, extending around substantial dwelling houses rising amidst groves and orchards. As we entered the clean, trim, prosperous looking village of Boufarik, by a road overhung with trees, the immediate scenery conjured up a vision of England.

And yet, not a single French settlement in all Algeria bears such a death-fraught name as Boufarik. Nowhere throughout the land, as here, has civilization gained a victory at such an enormous cost. Wasting ague or malignant fevers cut off both old and young. Under the hot autumnal sun the exhalations from a swampy soil became a virulent poison, which the strongest could not withstand. 'They died off like flies' is the significant spoken epitaph of the several successive generations of colonists that tenant the graveyard of the now large, flourishing, and healthy village. To the genius of misrule, which planted a military station and agricultural settlement in the midst of a thicket hemmed around with marshes, the melancholy distinction of Boufarik is to be assigned.

After leaving Boufarik, brushwood reappeared, but in much diminished quantities, and almost vanished to the distance, as, approaching the mountains, we passed the small French settlement of Beni Mered. From that to Blidah is a distance of but four miles, and, as we neared the town, white villas gleamed brightly out of the dark verdure of evergreens which skirted the base of the mountain. Orange gardens have a poetic sound, but the very narrow belt of these through which we passed before entering Blidah, showed me that I had acted prudently in considering the '*corbeille de fleurs*' and '*la ville embaumée*' in the light of poetic fictions. Through straight, wide streets, bordered by tall houses, we gained a fine hotel, as French in character as was the tree-shaded *place* on which it looked.

Probably these poetic epithets were in former times much more appropriate to Blidah than they are now, for many an orange garden was remorsely cut down to make way for the French ramparts. Moorish Blidah can scarce be said to exist at all, for, destroyed by an earthquake in 1825, it was never rebuilt. The labyrinth of low ruinous walls amidst which the natives live, are fraught with an ominous meaning, both as regards the past and future. Seldom does a year go by without an earthquake shock in some portion of Algeria.

All the picturesque costumes of Algiers are visible at Blidah. The Moresque, however, shows herself here in a somewhat different guise; for, instead of favouring the public with the view of her two eyes, she keeps one entirely eclipsed, and the other nearly so, as the immense white scarf which envelopes her from head to foot, is drawn over her face in such a way, that she can only peep out through an aperture about half an inch in width. An Arab told me that the Blidah fashion was called *ennekabo*; the Algerine, *yeadjero*.

'How do these ennekabos manage to breathe in hot weather?' I asked an Arab.

'They turn towards a wall when oppressed, and, uncovering their mouths, take a few mouthfuls of air,' was a reply not particularly suggestive of enjoyment in connection with the ennekabo fashion.

The koubba of the maraboo Sidi Yakob, spared by the earthquake that ruined the town, rises amidst a grove of large olive trees said to have been planted by his hand. The koubba is much frequented by the sick, who bribe the holy Sidi to intercede for them by the promise of a donation to the poor, should they recover. Nor does the Mussulman alone expect to gain the blessing of long life by the aid of alms, for he feels assured that it is only through their means he can walk without hurt, or falling across the sabre-edged bridge which leads to paradise. He ever remembers, too, that the angel standing at the gate of heaven incessantly cries out, 'Who gives alms to-day will be satiated to-morrow.'

At two miles distance from the town, in the grand ravine of the Oued-el-Kebir, is the equally venerated koubba of Sidi Mohammed Kebir. No poet could desire a more lovely resting-place in death than that the saint enjoys, close to a stream that winds through a magnificent mountain gorge, at whose entrance Blidah stands. At the time I visited the spot, the mountain tops above my head were crowned with snow, and the dark rocky masses which they showed on high, gave an added brilliancy to the luxuriant verdure of the richly-wooded banks of the deep narrow gorge below. In the loveliest part of a lovely scene, the koubba of Sidi Mohammed rises in the middle of a cemetery extending round his holy remains and those of his two sons. A low pillar, crowned with a mushroom-shaped capital, rises at the head of either grave,—but that of the father is peculiarly distinguished by a kind of wooden cage, draped with coloured handkerchiefs.

The common graves were for the most part indicated by little mounds of earth, encircled by a few irregular oblong-shaped stones; but in the vicinity of the maraboo's tomb the graves were covered with flags, or enclosed by a low ledge of slates, with a headstone showing the figure of a crescent carved on its top. To rest in death beside the maraboo was evidently a privilege that wealth could purchase.

A few yards from the cemetery is a native village, which I entered through a large doorway in a mud-wall rampart, and on gaining a small court enclosed by dwellings, at whose doors several women and children were visible, I became speedily the centre of a crowd, and the object of wondering exclamations. Old crones came forth from the recesses of dark windowless huts to see the *Roumia* (Christian), as they termed me; and on my telling them my country, the word *Inglesa* passed from lip to lip in tones that showed I was looked upon as a truly remarkable personage.

Amongst the circle which formed around me, I saw some very well-looking young women, decked out with ornaments of a somewhat costly character. One wore a necklace of gold coins, and, whilst all showed a profusion of bracelets, each ear was distended by the weight of not less than three massive gold ear-rings. A handsome woman, wearing a bright red scarf, acted as the principal speaker on the occasion. 'Where was my husband?' she asked. My answer was re-echoed by the circle in tones of wonder. It was evidently a relief to them to find that I had a father and once a mother; and consequent on the discovery that, after all, there was a link of connection between me and them, they grew more familiar— shouted with laughter as they attempted to pronounce my name, and did me subsequently the honour of minutely examining my dress. The pockets in my jacket produced a very deep sensation; but when the handsome woman in the red scarf exhibited, in a very unequivocal manner, her admiration of my embroidered collar, by proposing that I should present it to her, I thought it was judicious to bid goodbye to the assembly.

The evening of this day I went, in company with friends, to visit the two principal mosques of Blidah, which were filled with worshippers, assembled there to celebrate the opening of the holy month of Ramadam. In themselves, the buildings were insignificant, but their interiors were rendered strikingly picturesque by the long rows of white-robed figures extending across the matted floor. Numbers of small oil lamps hung from the ceiling, and shed a mellow light upon the scene. An Imaun from the pulpit led the prayers, and I have never seen in any Christian church an air of such intense devotion as that evidenced by these followers of Mohammed.

Adjoining one of these mosques was a small room, whose wide-opened door, as we passed by, allowed us a view of several richly-dressed natives, seated cross-legged on a bench, at either side of a very solemn, dignified looking Moor, wearing a large white turban. 'That is the Mufti,' said a Blidah gentleman of our party, in an undertone; and he had scarcely spoken, when the Mufti waved his hand to us as an invitation to enter. I held back, for, being expected to represent my nation in a conversational capacity, I was quite awe-struck at the idea of talking my stumbling Arabic in such a distinguished presence. But, stimulated by several very urgent 'come ins' from a voice close by, I advanced to discharge, as best I could, the very formidable task that was assigned me.

'Peace be upon you,' I said to the Mufti, with a low bow, on which the learned man responded by such a grand-sounding '*Salamou alaikoum*' as put my timidly-uttered salutation to shame.

'You come from far to see our country?' said the Mufti.

'Yes, from England,' I answered.

'All the way from England,' said the Mufti, in a tone of animation. 'The English are good, very good; the Arabs love them. Your husband brought you here.'

'I have no husband.'

'No husband!' echoed the Mufti. 'And did you cross the seas from England, all the way from England, without a husband to take care of you?'

'Even so.'

Thinking it prudent to take advantage of the momentary paralysation of the Mufti's power of speech caused by my announcement, I brought at once my representative functions to a conclusion, by a compliment to Algerian scenery and skies; and giving the sage and his friends, on behalf of myself and party, a solemn benediction, we retreated amidst a general chorus of '*emchi besslema*' (go in peace).

Returning to the hotel through the Arab quarter of the town, we saw the native cafés filled to their utmost capacities. Some of the company smoked, others drank coffee out of tiny cups—enjoyments, no doubt, highly enhanced by the rigid requirements of the Ramadam, which had that day begun. For unworthy of the name of Mussulman is he, who eats and drinks during this holy month, from the instant 'that the light of dawn affords the means of distinguishing a white from a black thread.'* Even a pipe is considered a sinful indulgence. Though a scorching sun be overhead, and the furnace blast of the desert may fill the air, a sip of water to cool the parched tongue is a crime punishable by fine, imprisonment, or the bastinado, according to the pleasure of the Cadi before whom the delinquent is brought.

* From the Koran.

CHAPTER XI.

GORGE OF THE CHIFFA — A MISANTHROPE — RAVINE OF SIDI MOUNSSA — UP THE MOUNTAIN — LOST AND FOUND.

AN excellent French road running from Blidah to Medeah, through the gorge of the Chiffa, affords to the most unenterprising and delicate of tourists the means of seeing without toil or trouble the great sight of the vicinity. What the Coliseum is to Rome, that is the gorge to Blidah; and in fulfilment of our duty as pilgrims in quest of the picturesque, we lost no time in obtaining a carriage, which, after a short drive of some three miles through the plain, brought us to the entrance of the deep defile to which the river Chiffa gives its name.

The beauty of the gorge, commencing at its very entrance, increased with our advance, as, passing along a road that had been cut out of the face of perpendicular cliffs, we wound through a narrow pass overhung by dark mountain masses, clothed towards the base with luxuriant vegetation, where, amidst the dark green foliage of evergreen oak, cork, and carub trees, the yellow broom and laurustinus showed their bright blossoms.

Arriving before long at a small restaurant, close to a brook called Ruisseau des Singes, we halted there for a few minutes in order to try to get a sight of the monkeys which are said to frequent the spot; but I was obliged to content myself with a view of the portraits of two specimens of the race that decorated the front of the restaurant, and which, if correct representations of the habits of the long-tailed denizens of the Chiffa, show them to have attained to a high degree of civilisation, as, seated socially together, one smoked a pipe whilst the other drank a glass of wine.

Leaving the Ruisseau des Singes, we advanced amidst scenes of ever-increasing grandeur, till the gorge, contracting more and more, showed at its farther side great sheets of almost perpendicular rock, streaked with numerous glittering streams; and while they confronted us in downward leaps from a height of some 300 feet, innumerable small rills shooting forth from the steep bank above our heads dashed down upon the road, or, trickling from overhanging blades of grass, fell close beside us in a fringe-like shower. The dark mountain masses towering overhead, the luxuriant blossoms of broom and laurustinus which dotted the luxuriant foliage of the banks around, and the sparkling water which filled the air with its many voices, formed altogether a scene of peculiar beauty.

After leaving the vicinity of the cascades, the gorge diminished so much in grandeur that, after proceeding a mile or more, we readily assented to our driver's wish to halt and feed his horses, in preparation for our return; and to fill up the interval we scrambled up an eminence close by, to visit the locality of some recently abandoned mines. As we approached a solitary house built upon the summit of a low hill, the furious barking of a watch-dog brought to the door a woman, who, advancing, addressed us in French. On exchanging with her a few words, I found to my surprise that she and the dog were the sole tenants of the dwelling.

'Do you not feel lonely?' I asked.

'Better to abide alone in peace, than with many in strife,' was the bitter reply. 'It is a bad world we live in—the evil tongue falls foul of the best—hatred, malice, and envy pursue us from our birth to the grave.'

'But the world is not all evil.'

'Perhaps not your world, but my world is evil to the heart's core. I was glad when my companion left me six months ago—I did not miss her, not a bit; my dog is better company by far.'

Notwithstanding her misanthropic words, she urged us to enter the house and drink a cup of coffee, an invitation we declined; and, bidding the recluse good-bye, we followed a path leading through a thicket of sweet-scented white heath, whose fragrance mingled with that of the wild lavender which strewed the ground. At the bottom of a small glen, a dilapidated-looking shed marked the entrance of the deserted mines. On every side the view was very fine, and as I looked down on deep ravines, overhung by snow-crowned mountains, I thought how the winter winds, as they swept howling through narrow defiles, would speak in sympathetic tones to the ear of the lonely misanthrope. Does she give them words, I wonder? Does she make them shriek out denunciations of human malice and perfidy, and wail and groan over the sins and sufferings of mortal existence? And then, does she feel a gleam of joy when the wild voices of the night wind, speak to her in tones that seem to echo her gloomy thoughts and morbid fancies?

Sitting beside the driver on our return, I was enlightened by him on the subject of the culinary merits of the various wild beasts of Algeria. 'A slice of lion,' he said, 'was extremely good, and the General, his former master, was always presented with the most delicate joint of any lion that might be killed in his neighbourhood. The wild boar was excellent. The panther tasted like chicken. The jackal was not bad, but a man must be very hungry to relish a bit of a hyena.' Knowing that the hyena was addicted to feasting on the tenants of graveyards, I gave full credit to the last assertion.

On the succeeding day, if I had been experimentally inclined, I could have easily ascertained if panther and chicken were allied in taste; for on being conducted to see a panther which had just been killed in a forest a few miles distant from the town, a Blidah gentleman (to whom I mentioned our driver's simile) most politely offered to forward a joint of panther to the hotel for our especial benefit. Having refused the offer, the chicken and panther relationship still remains a question to be elucidated by enquiring minds.

The ravine of Sidi Moussa must be visited on foot or horseback, but a somewhat toilsome ascent of a steep native path is well repaid by the beautiful view seen from the koubba of the holy man who has given a name to the locality. The maraboo who has the custody of the sacred precincts, did us the honour of conferring on us a munificent donation of oranges.

But by far the most exciting of our excursions around Blidah, was an ascent of the snow-crowned mountain which rose immediately behind the town. To ascend a mountain is always an enterprise invested with a certain degree of dignity, and as we heard that the cedar forest which grew amidst the snowy heights could be reached in a few hours on horseback without difficulty, we determined to devote our last day at Blidah to this achievement. Having made the necessary arrangements for carrying out this purpose, we were grieved to find that the sun did not accommodate itself to our convenience, since, as we mounted our horses for the mountain trip, he showed a strong inclination to remain hid behind a veil of clouds. Hoping, however, to soon see his face, we started.

On leaving the town, a few minutes' ride amongst fruit and orange gardens sufficed to bring us to the commencement of the ascent. The tortuous native path we followed, resembled the half-dried bed of a mountain torrent, and the menacing branches projecting on either side, necessitated a skilful navigation. Emerging at length from this wooded region, we entered upon a tract of bare mountain land, dotted with some thorny shrubs and tufts of wild lavender. In measure as we advanced, the scenery increased in gloomy grandeur, and the continued absence of the sun tended to enhance the stern, solemn aspect of the snow-crowned peak above our heads, as well as of the dark chasms which opened out before our view as we proceeded.

As we ascended, the temperature decreased in warmth; but even on entering amidst a thicket of evergreen oak, where patches of snow lay on the ground, the air was by no means cold, though chilly enough to make an additional shawl or cloak agreeable. The ascent was easy—easier than that of any mountain I had ever previously ascended. Our only difficulty was the ever-increasing amount of snow, which, however, troubled us little until we had passed an ice-house, whose guardian, who lived close by, could scarcely fail to find his eyrie-like dwelling a somewhat uncomfortable residence in the winter time, when icy blasts swirled up the deep ravines, or, rushing across the snowy heights, howled amidst the branches of the cedar forest, on whose verge his home was placed.

A cedar forest has such a magnificent sound that I was inclined to quarrel with the somewhat insignificant-sized trees amidst which we now entered, but this censorious state of mind was speedily checked by my being obliged to concentrate my whole faculties on my horse, which began to flounder onward very uneasily amidst ever-deepening drifts of melting snow. Before very long, some rather startling equestrian evolutions had the effect of arresting the progress of a lady and gentleman who accompanied us. We, however, determined to persevere on horseback as long as safely practicable; on foot, when obliged to dismount. By careful management of the docile Arab horses we rode, we had arrived within a short distance of the summit of the mountain, before we found it necessary to alight. Giving the horses into the care of our Arab guide, with the injunction to await our return, we proceeded onward on foot; and in a short time, though after a somewhat inelegant floundering style of progress, we stood on the summit of a bare peak that rose above every other mountain mass in our vicinity.

Much as the still overclouded sky and misty air detracted from the beauty of the prospect, it, even

A FINE VIEW.

under these unfavourable circumstances, was very fine. Towards the west, the long narrow plain stretched out from its high inland boundaries to the sea; whilst towards the east and south, ridge after ridge of lofty mountains rose upward in long parallel lines, until their wave-like crests became undistinguishable in the distance. Immediately below, were dark grim precipices, looking all the more grim and dark in contrast with the snow-crowned peak on which we stood. The dusky foliage of the cedars which climbed to the summit of the neighbouring heights, added also, in no small degree, to the sombre beauty of the scene. Longing inexpressibly for a gleam of sunlight to lift the veil which hung over the distance, we remarked with joy that the sky above our heads showed a patch of blue, whilst the bright spot which marked the sun's position in the heavens looked larger and brighter than it had yet been that day. Assuring ourselves that the sun was about to show his face, we agreed to wait a little before we began to descend.

Whilst waiting for the coming sun, we wandered onward for some ten minutes over the mountain-top, in search of a glacier of which our guide had spoken, but finding nothing that answered in our ideas to this term,* we retraced our steps after adding some

---

* A confusion between the words glacier and glacière (icehouse) on the part of our Arab guide gave rise to our vain search for what has no existence amidst the Atlas mountains.

stones to a small cairn that was raised upon the highest pinnacle of the mountain. Having thus commemorated our achievement, we looked impatiently at the still clouded sky, where, to our regret, the patch of blue had very visibly dwindled in dimensions, as had also the spot of luminous haze from which we had augured so favourably. Soon thoroughly convinced that we must accept a clouded sky as an enduring fact in that day's history, we trudged off through the snow to regain our horses. Feeling that we had been somewhat spendthrifts of our limited time, we walked fast; but, make what haste we might, we knew full well that night could not fail to overtake us before we reached Blidah.

With this conviction, we were before long most unpleasantly startled by finding that the path by which we had ascended, seemed to have utterly vanished. The snow lay untrodden before our view, and not a sign of guide or horses was visible. The disagreeable truth, that we had lost our way, became soon too clear. On this discovery, we turned back at once, and scrambling through snowdrifts to the mountain-top, we walked along the ridge, looking for the ravine by which we had ascended, regretting bitterly that search for the glacier, by which our geographical ideas had been evidently much confounded. After a short survey of our position, we agreed in the propriety of seeking the lost trail in a certain direction, and, entering the forest again, we

AN UNPLEASANT PROSPECT.

descended along the side of a steep bank, hoping soon to strike upon our missing track. But our hopes proved vain—no track, guide, or horses could we discover. The prospect of passing the night amidst the snowy summits of the Atlas mountains became somewhat painfully distinct and near.

In this emergency we consulted on the most judicious course to be pursued. The question was perplexing, and whilst still undecided, the sight of a bare eminence not far off, suggesting a means by which it might be possible to obtain some information as to our position, after some more scrambling and floundering amidst the snow, we gained the brink of a cliff that commanded a full view of the surrounding regions.

No lost tourists ever looked on a more discouraging scene. Before us were frowning precipices, whilst at either side were deep ravines clothed sparsely with dusky cedars, amidst which we vainly tried to scan one sign of life. The ice-keeper's cottage was nowhere to be seen, and we could not recognise one feature of the prospect except the long plain, which looked in the gathering gloom to lie at an immense distance below our feet. Our doom seemed sealed, and it appeared more than probable that, for the future, we should be qualified to sing 'My lodging is on the cold ground,' with a touching pathos derived from practical experience of its discomfort.

Unpleasing as was the prospect of a night amongst the cedars, its thought inspired no fear, for several reasons. Despite the snow-strewed ground, the air was far from cold, and a dry spot in a sheltered nook was easily procurable. No wild beast was likely to be found amidst these lifeless solitudes, and by daybreak, Blidah would certainly send out legions to our rescue.

But though resigned to our menaced fate, we did not the less exert ourselves to escape its infliction; and whilst relinquishing all idea of regaining the missing path before nightfall, we commenced to holloa in a most energetic manner, in hopes that our voices might reach our guide and bring him to our rescue. Not a breath of wind stirred the branches of the cedars; not a bird's note rose on high; and the air was so deadly still, that the shout after shout we gave, went ringing across the deep ravines with a strength that might seem to argue the sudden acquirement of stentorian powers. In the deep silence which prevailed after each successive shout, we listened anxiously for an answer, and at length we heard a faint vague sound, which gradually assumed ere long a definite existence as the voice of a human being. With the certainty of help at hand, our suspense was ended, and advancing in the direction of the welcome sounds, we floundered down the side of a ravine through deep treacherous snowdrifts with the most heroic indifference to the difficulties which beset our progress, during which, on looking up towards the opposite bank, we saw a tall white-clad Arab descending rapidly to meet us. No words were needful to tell the errand on which he came, for under his arm he bore two well-known shawls, unequivocal tokens of his mission.

Under the Arab's guidance we commenced to scale the opposite side of the ravine to that, down which we had just descended. The snow had melted here, but the gravelly bank afforded such an insecure and yielding footing that we had often to seize on projecting twigs and branches to avoid a fall. Striding on before us with an enviable indifference to the difficulties of the ascent, our dark-visaged guide seemed to look somewhat impatiently at our comparatively slow progress. At length, after one of the most arduous scrambles I ever had, we emerged upon the missing path at a point where some half dozen Arabs were seated together, evidently waiting our approach. Greeting us in the most friendly manner, they begged we would sit down and talk with them a little while, but declining the polite invitation on the score of the lateness of the hour, we passed quickly on to rejoin our guide and horses, awaiting us close by.

We found young Mohammed, our guide, far from being recovered from the state of agitation into which he had been plunged by our disappearance. His eyes were red with weeping—an evidence of grief which would have been truly touching had not his remarks led to the conclusion that he feared he would lose his head if he did not bring us safely back to Blidah. He had a deal to tell about all the exertions he had made to find us. How he had searched and shouted, and how, when our voices reached him, he had sent to our assistance a man well acquainted with the mountains. It will be long before poor Mohammed forgets the Inglese who put his head in danger of being cut off, by losing themselves amidst the heights of the Atlas mountains.

As we mounted our horses, the sun was very near the horizon, but though clouds still concealed his face from view, he changed their dull gray hue into gorgeous tints of gold and crimson. The plain was steeped in a soft purplish light, and the mountain ridges in the distance stood out in strong relief against the glowing sky. But all too soon the splendid pageant vanished from our sight, and the deep shades of a moonless night found us afoot, stumbling along a rugged, steep descent, down which in darkness it was not safe to ride. It was a happy moment when at length we safely arrived at the door of the fine Hotel de la Régence.

CHAPTER XII.

THE SIROCCO — MEDEAH — A BAULKED PLAN — A NEW START — ACROSS THE COL OF MOUZAÏA — DESERTED MINE.

THE sirocco was blowing violently as we left Blidah for Medeah, and the stove-like temperature which prevailed was accompanied with a leaden sky and a thick misty atmosphere; but before we were half-way through the gorge of the Chiffa, the influence of the desert wind was no longer perceptible, and I breathed the fresh air of the mountains with a sensation of intense relief. If this, I thought, be the sirocco at the end of March, God help the settlers in the plain in the hot months of July and August, when the scorching desert-blast is a frequent visitor.

After passing the limits of our former drive, we soon left the valley of the Chiffa, and wound up the side of a bare mountain, amidst scenery of a somewhat dreary character. As we neared Medeah, a few vineyards and fruit trees became visible, but being scarcely yet in leaf, they failed to neutralise the bleak aspect of the unwooded hills around.

Medeah itself has a cold cheerless look, from the absence of the luxuriant evergreen foliage which gives in winter a summer-like charm to the neighbourhood of Algiers and Blidah. Not an olive, orange, or lemon tree was visible on the bare height on which the town is built, at an elevation of nearly 4,000 feet above the sea. Medeah has, in fact, a climate and vegetation much more partaking of a European than of an African character. The winter there invariably brings snow and frost, and the sun (even in the dog-days) never becomes an oppressive tyrant. Notwithstanding, however, its salubrious position, the number of colonists' houses in the neighbourhood of the town is as yet inconsiderable.

Previous to the French conquest, Medeah was the Arab capital of the province of Titteri, but is now for the most part a new French town, much inferior in size to Blidah. Whilst a well-built military wall, pierced with gates, has superseded the old crazy ramparts, its native streets have given place to tall French houses, built in formal lines. Here, and there, a few Arab dwellings have escaped the general doom; but their numbers are too insignificant to detract in any appreciable degree from the French character of the town. At this present day, Medeah derives its sole picturesque attraction to a tourist from the close vicinity of a fine ancient aqueduct, whose double tier of arches are in a state of excellent preservation.

A BAULKED PLAN.

As to the population, it presents a mere miniature likeness of that of Blidah. The Jew with crafty face, the Jewess with bandaged jaws, the Arab of the plain with cord-girt head, the Moor in fez, or turban, and the ghost-like *ennekabo*, make up, with French officers and soldiers, the living furniture of the streets.

As we intended to proceed inland from Medeah by native roads not practicable for carriages, we had procured at Algiers an official letter for the head of the Bureau Arabe at Medeah, who, we were told, would, on our requisition, furnish us with mules and guides for the prosecution of our contemplated journey. Receiving us with the utmost politeness, the *chef* of the Bureau at once expressed his willingness to forward our views; and, assuring us in answer to our enquiries that we would incur no risk in carrying out our project, he promised us mules and trusty guides for the ensuing morning.

Ready to start betimes, we waited impatiently for the tardy mules, but when they came at length, they exhibited such a lamentable quantity of raw sores that we would not mount them. Informed on good authority that no uninjured Arab mules* would be procurable in the neighbourhood, we resolved to try and carry out our scheme in some other manner, and

---

* The natives treat their mules and donkeys with terrible barbarity; it is rare to see one of these animals without a bleeding sore.

finding that Medeah would not furnish us with the requisites for our projected journey, we started off by diligence to Blidah, where, we were fortunate enough to be able to hire riding horses to convey us to Milianah, by the circuitous route of Boghari and Teniet-el-Had, a district yet untraversed by roads.

It was a beautiful March morning when, mounting our horses at the hotel, we once more left Blidah for Medeah. Our attendant, who rode the baggage-horse, having been a soldier, declared his ability to guide us by the old Arab road to Medeah across the Col of Mouzaïa, the pass by which the French had advanced to the attack of Medeah in the year 1830. Our proposed route involved the speedy abandonment of the fine French road, and after passing the entrance of the gorge of the Chiffa we entered upon a winding native mountain path, the lowest portion of which was in some places so obliterated by disuse that Philippe had to refresh his memory by application to the Arab herdsmen of the vicinity.

As we ascended the pass, the vegetation around us varied in a very marked manner. In the neighbourhood of the plain, we passed through brushwood composed of the wild jujube thorn and dwarf palm, whilst patches of bright green corn were here and there visible, close to some small native dwelling. On ascending higher, the palm and jujube brushwood gave place to a low thicket of lentisk and wild olive. Still higher, we wound upward amidst a scanty vegetation composed of coarse grass and a few prickly plants, until, approaching the summit of the pass, there rose above our heads the dusky foliage of a forest of cork and evergreen oak.

A brilliant sunlight enhanced the beauty of the views, commanded by the heights we traversed. Immediately beneath was a narrow ravine, through which a small stream marked its sinuous course by a curving line of fruit trees, corn plots, and bright verdure, and the plain, sparkling here and there with clusters of white houses, lay in quiet beauty at the foot of dark masses of lofty mountains. High in the air rose up the peak of Zakkar above Milianah, and the great bulk of Chenoua above Cherchel frowned gloomily in the distance. The small Lake Alloula,* the plague spot of the plain, gleamed bright as silver below the pyramidal Mauritanian monument called Tomb of the Christian, crowning the low Sahel range directly opposite. To the left, long parallel ridges of the Little Atlas mountains extended westward in undulating lines, whilst to the right, and high overhead, the crags and cliffs which overlooked the pass were fitly crowned by the sombre foliage of the dusky forest. The cloudless sky, the bright sunshine, and the air whose stillness was only broken by the cuckoo's voice, all

* A hotbed of malaria. The convicts employed by Government to drain this death-dealing lake, died off so fast that the works were discontinued.

combined to add in no small degree to the beauty of the scene.

As our horses scrambled up the rude, steep mountain path, it was difficult to realise the fact that we were following in the track traversed nearly some thirty years before by a French army, who gained here a victory which bears a foremost place amongst the French military achievements in Algeria. The passage of the Col de Mouzaïa,* in the face of an opposing army, is a feat to which the French ever refer with pride. Strongly posted on the heights, stood the Bey of Titteri and his men, whilst the French, scrambling upwards as best they could, cut to pieces or put to flight the opposing troops who barred their passage to Medeah. 'It was a glorious victory,' said Philippe, after pointing out to me where the Bey was posted, and where the French first came in deadly grapple with his army. As with the words there rose up vividly before my view a picture of the terrible reality—the blood-stained ground strewed with writhing figures and mutilated corpses, the air filled with every sound of agony, from the deep hollow moan to the dying gasp—I thought what an absolute mockery it was to apply the term 'glorious' to any human shamble field.

On the highest point of the Col there extends across the pass a wall of rock, broken by a narrow gap, bearing the name of Porte de Fer. On passing

* Sometimes called Col de Teniet.

through this *iron gate* we commenced to descend towards Medeah, through a forest of cork trees, by a precipitous track covered with rubble stone, that tried the sure-footedness of our excellent horses somewhat unduly. On emerging from the forest, we passed along the sides of great banks of red clay all furrowed with streams, and towards Medeah, the unwooded country looked as if it had been suddenly changed from a liquid to a solid state, when its surface was heaved up in billows by a storm. After a considerable descent we passed by a desolate closed-up house, whose title of 'Hotel des Mines' indicated pretty plainly that the present shareholders in the copper mines of Mouzaïa were by no means likely to realise large fortunes — a fact that was still more unequivocally evidenced when, after passing through a small patriarchal olive wood, we dismounted at the entrance of a large square of what seemed at first to be quite uninhabited buildings.

Whatever the future of Mouzaïa Les Mines may be, it has a corpse-like aspect now. The engines raised to crush the ore rust uselessly away. The water brought at great expense from far has got no work to do. Not a single tenant had the miners' many rooms. Offices, workshops, stables, magazines, baths, café, and bakery were all closed. As I crossed through the square of the deserted village, I thought I had never seen a more striking picture of bankruptcy and desolation.

A Jew and a couple of lounging Arabs were the only signs of life that met our view within the enclosure, and the Jew, poor young man, looked only half alive, for his thin face was deathly pale from the effects of the malaria fever. He had been ill for several months, he said, a circumstance that by no means impressed me with the idea that Mouzaïa Les Mines would be a particularly salubrious place of residence. He showed us specimens of copper; and, speaking of nickel and silver being constantly found in combination with that ore, he declared that with an outlay of only 200,000 francs an English company could work the mines with enormous profit.

From Mouzaïa Les Mines to Medeah, the ride was very uninteresting, and after a tedious ascent up bare hills, we arrived at the town, just as the last rays of the setting sun were gilding the arches of the fine aqueduct.

CHAPTER XIII.

A MORNING'S RIDE—FASTIDIOUSNESS PUNISHED—TOURISTS IN DIFFICULTY — AN EXEMPLARY CORPORAL — AN ALGERIAN NIGHT SCENE — BOGHARI.

ON starting the succeeding morning from Medeah, our riding-party was reinforced by the addition of an English lady and two native youths, her attendants. Seated with a jaunty air of perfect ease on the back of our baggage horse, Philippe's keen, shrewd, and energetic countenance formed a striking contrast with the pleasing but languid and effeminate faces of the two Arabs. A conquering and a conquered race was severally stamped on either brow.

Medeah is connected with Boghari by an imperfect French road, which in summer is practicable for carriages; but though the deep ruts and holes which the winter rains had caused were gaping round us as we rode onward, the road, wretched as it was, might be pronounced a magnificent specimen of engineering skill in comparison with the ancient Arab highway over which we had passed the preceding day. The low hills, scantily clothed with rusty grass, which lay around our course on leaving Medeah, offered no attraction in the way of scenery, and the features of the country continued unchanged, when towards noon we arrived at the caravanseraï of Ben Chicao,* where we halted.

But though the propriety of a halt was a step on which there could be no doubt, the length to which the halt should extend was a question for consideration. Boghari, we were assured, was unattainable that night, and between it and the caravanseraï we should nowhere find a comfortable night's quarters. When we looked, however, at the scanty furniture of the cell-like whitewashed rooms of Ben Chicao, we finally agreed that it were better to risk our fate elsewhere, than to waste in inaction the best portion of a beautiful day. The wisdom of this course became apparently still more clear, when, on speaking to a young Egyptian officer in the caravanseraï, we were told by him that at a station called Quatorzieme we should find beds and food. With this goal in prospect, we remounted our horses and set off.

On resuming our progress the scenery much improved. Leaving the bare bleak hills behind, we proceeded along the brow of wooded heights over-

---

* An Algerian caravanseraï consists of a one-storied range of buildings enclosed by a high wall, and furnishes the traveller with a clean bed, a good roof overhead, and a sufficiency of homely fare to still the pangs of hunger. Erected by Government in troubled times, the walls are for the most part pierced with loopholes.

THE SPAHIS FARM.

looking narrow winding valleys, dotted here and there with a bright corn plot—the only visible indication of inhabitants, for not a dwelling of any kind was visible. Mountains steeped in an exquisitely soft purplish haze, rose upward in the distance, as we advanced amidst a solitude, the stillness of which was only broken very rarely by the faint bark of an Arab dog, rising from some invisible gourbi, in the vale below. Until, after a ride of many miles, we approached a military agricultural settlement called the Spahis farm,* we saw not a trace of European life or civilisation.

Whilst passing through the farm, where two or three cottages rose up amidst an inconsiderable extent of bright green corn, a man advanced from an humble dwelling near the roadside and offered us accommodation for the night, but with a somewhat disdainful glance at the exterior of the house, we declared our intention to proceed onward to Quatorzieme. But after we had advanced a few miles beyond the farm, I began to be haunted with certain misgivings as to the wisdom of our resolve to proceed onwards, for the road grew worse and worse—its roughness aggravating the fatigue arising from a lengthened ride. It was a pleasant sight to all when the two white houses of Quatorzieme came into view.

But a near approach to the station filled us with

---

* The farm is laboured under Government superintendence, by a troop of Spahis; a name given to the native cavalry soldiers.

consternation, for the two white houses we had eagerly descried from afar, proved on our advance, to be utterly untenanted; and nothing but a miserable cottage in the vicinity showed signs of life. Fatigued as we were, we hearkened willingly to Philippe, who said that, if we were not too tired to proceed, we would certainly fare better in a small roadside inn, which he remembered was to be found a short distance further on. Buoyed up by the hope of speedily obtaining rest combined with decent quarters for the night, we continued on our way.

On leaving Quatorzieme, the road somewhat improved, and finding the slow pace of my companions more fatiguing than a quicker movement, I urged on my horse in advance. With the sun rapidly nearing the horizon, I looked out eagerly for the house where we were to pass the night, but kilometre after kilometre stone was passed, without my seeing aught of what I sought. My only solace was the scenery, which increased in beauty as the shades of evening began to fall. Mountains which rose in the distance loftier and loftier in the darkening air, served as a grand background for lovely wooded glens, overlooked by the heights along whose crests I rode. But the solitude continued unbroken by any sign of life, until a turn in the road brought full into view the white conical tents of a troop of soldiers. With the certainty of receiving definite information, I rode up quickly to a Zouave who had just ceased working on the road, and asked him if there was any house in the neighbourhood where ladies could get accommodation for the night. 'The nearest house is that of a *cantonnier** who lives some five kilometres beyond this spot; your only chance of finding a bed or food is there,' was the disheartening answer.

A three-mile further ride, with a chance at the end of it of finding a bed and dinner, was not a particularly cheering prospect, but as there was no other alternative I proceeded onward amidst the glow of a magnificent sunset sky, which brought out into strong relief the dark masses of the distant mountains. But the golden and crimson radiance had died quite away, before I saw in the distance a dwelling several degrees humbler in appearance than the house at the Spahis' farm, from which we had turned away disdainfully. But 'experience teaches,' says the proverb, and thus enlightened I approached the house in a deeply humble frame of mind, fervently hoping that three soldiers I saw lounging near the door had not forestalled us in the occupation of the desired quarters.

'Can you accommodate three ladies for the night?' I anxiously, eagerly enquired of a woman standing at the threshold of the door I approached.

My question was met with a mute look of

---

* A man employed on roads.

amazement and a fixed stare, which argued considerable mental doubt as to whether or not I was to be considered an inhabitant of the earth ; but my question, repeated in a pathetically suppliant human tone, seemed to solve the problem, for on its repetition I received the answer that an officer of engineers, who had just arrived, occupied her only spare room. As she spoke, a young French officer appeared at the door.

'No matter — no matter,' I said; 'a shakedown in the kitchen will do quite well.'

'The kitchen has been engaged by the soldiers,' was the crushing answer.

'But have you not another room?' I exclaimed, despairingly.

'Only a lumber closet, where I sleep. Though my husband is away in hospital, it is too small to accommodate your party.'

'Not at all; we shall make it do.'

A torrent of *impossibles* burst from the Frenchwoman's lips, in the midst of which, the officer broke silence in words that sounded in my ears like the sweetest music — 'I will give up my room to the ladies. I can sleep in the kitchen with the men.'

'What an excellent young man — what a treasure to his mother — a credit to his country,' I thought.

Alas, for human frailty and fallibility of judgment: for on the arrival of my companions the excellent young gentleman vanished from view, and the mistress of the house informed me that Monsieur le Lieutenant had changed his mind and would keep his room. Decidedly, his mother was not the fortunate being I had thought her.

However, bed or no bed at our disposal, we resolved to stay. Some sort of dinner was promised us, in waiting for which we discussed the attractions of the open air *versus* those of the lumber closet; but whilst we were still ruminating sorrowfully over the dark colours of our fate, a burly corporal, entering the kitchen where we sat, asked the mistress of the house where the ladies were to sleep, and, on hearing her answer, burst forth with an indignant 'bah,' followed by a declaration that the ladies need neither sleep in the lumber closet or in the open air, as the kitchen was altogether at their service; for what did it matter one whit to him and his *camerades* if they should pass the night outside — a thing they had often done, and would do many a time again. Had I been a queen I should on the spot have dubbed the corporal a knight; not wearing a crown — for which mercy I am truly thankful — my admiration of his chivalrous conduct sought vent in thanks.

The important bedroom-question settled, that of dinner absorbed our minds. We were promised that when Monsieur le Lieutenant had dined, we should have something to eat, and as the stewpans were still frizzling on the fire for the gentleman's dinner, the prospect held out to us was somewhat painfully distant. As for Philippe and the Arabs, they regaled themselves outside by munching dry bread.

A weary while elapsed before Monsieur le Lieutenant had concluded his repast, which he dallied over in the most merciless manner; and as he walked forth with a cigar in his mouth, we walked into the room and the table he had vacated, to partake of a dinner to which hunger gave a much needed relish.

During our dinner, the kitchen was cleared and swept, and converted into a bedroom, through the effective assistance of the corporal and his *camerades*; and to our surprise we were greeted with the sight of a duly furnished iron bedstead, and an unexceptionable shakedown bed upon the floor. Before, however, profiting by these luxuries, we took a look outside at the sleeping arrangements of our attendants. The Arabs, rolled up in their burnouses, lay side by side upon the open ground, but Philippe, with a horserug to serve as mattress, and a burnous as quilt, had encircled his sleeping place with a number of empty wooden boxes he had somewhere found. Our horses had for a stable a side wall of the house, furnished with iron rings, to which they were tied. The night was fine and almost warm. The jackals cried around, and as a bright moon shed a silvery light upon every unfamiliar picture of the scene, I realised for the first time the fact that I was in barbarous Africa.

The voices of cocks and hens mingling together in a glee of cackling and crowing, aroused me from a sound sleep to the consciousness that another day had dawned, and, after a hasty toilet, accomplished under considerable difficulties, we partook of some bread and coffee before starting onward.

The scenery of our morning's ride, though fine, was inferior in beauty to that through which we had passed the previous evening. Though still overlooking ravines and glens, the heights along whose brows we journeyed were of inconsiderable elevation; and though fir and juniper grew plentifully around, they scarcely attained beyond shrub-like dimensions. Like, as on the previous day, we traversed a country where apparently nature exercised an uncontested dominion. From time, to time, we met an Arab going towards Medeah, or a mounted Spahis seated on a crimson high-peaked saddle, and draped in his ample and exquisitely picturesque crimson cloak.

After some hours' ride, and a steep descent through a fir wood, we emerged upon the extremity of a narrow treeless plain, where, close to the edge of a shallow stream we forded, I saw for the first time an encampment of Arabs. Those tents, no less than the arid burnt-up look of the hills at either side, afforded an unequivocal indication that we had reached the frontiers of a region, where nature grudges to man the first necessaries of existence. Behind us lay the rich corn lands of the Tell,* before

* Algeria is divided by nature into two distinct zones, to which have been severally applied the names of Tell and Sahara. The

us were the scanty pastures, palm-tree oases and the lifeless sands of the Sahara. The rusty vegetation of the narrow plain we traversed was in keeping with the bleak bare hills on either hand, and on one of which was plainly visible the white houses of Boghar, a French military station, lying directly opposite the small European settlement of Boghari, to which we were proceeding. Our destination remained, however, invisible, until a sharp turn of the road showed us close at hand two or three one-storied European dwellings, rising at the base of a precipitous and arid height, on whose brow a small Arab town was perched. Dismounting at a rustic inn, a humility, the growth of our late experiences, made us look with a sensation of satisfaction on the accommodation we were offered. That each should have a bedroom to herself was an unexpected luxury, and we were not inclined to quarrel with the deep twilight obscurity which, even at noonday, shed a becoming dimness and indistinctness on the walls and scanty furniture of our apartments. Our first lesson in the art of roughing it, had not been thrown away.

Some nomade tribes, which, with at least a hundred camels, defiled in a slow procession before the inn on our arrival there, afforded a sight of

Tell borders the sea coast, and extends from that, inland, to a line at which corn ceases to grow, or forms a very exceptional product. From that line the Sahara begins, and stretches southward in an archipelago of pastures and palm oases, until it merges into the lifeless sandy ocean of the Great Desert.

striking novelty. First came a dark-skinned woman with unveiled face, her brow surmounted by a kind of turban structure; and following her were other women presenting a similar aspect, and who, as they walked beside the troop of camels, mingled with tall, thin, dark-visaged men, with cord-girt heads, and figures draped from head to foot by the ample folds of the Arab cloak. On the last camel of the troop was placed a litter, above whose open top, a woman's head and throat emerged, glittering with ornaments. The rear was closed up by a flock of sheep. The migration northwards of these Saharian Arabs in quest of fresh pasture lands, showed that the parching Saharian summer had already commenced.

In the afternoon we clambered up the steep cliff behind Boghari, to explore the small Arab town which crowns the heights. In the appearance and steepness of the streets, the Ksar, as it is called, presented a microscopic likeness of native Algiers. In the stall-like shops I saw many of the proprietors sound asleep—a truly excellent way of passing one of the long, hungry, weary days of the Ramadam.

A troop of dancing girls came forth from dark cafés to see and wonder at the Christian ladies. The poor degraded creatures were literally weighed down with ornaments in the form of huge earrings, thick chains, and massive bracelets and anklets. All had resorted to the aid of koheul for their beautification, and one had enhanced her charms by a broad streak of light brown paint across her forehead, which was joined in the centre by another effective streak commencing at the tip of her nose.

On descending from the Ksar we crossed the narrow plain to mount to the military station of Boghar, for the purpose of procuring from the Bureau Arabe an official letter in our behalf to the Arab Caïd, in whose dwelling we purposed to find shelter on the following night. Bleak, bare, and perched upon a height exposed to every wind, Boghar was as dreary a looking place of residence as I ever beheld. But the view that it commanded was not devoid of interest, for looking over a range of hillocks which to the south bounded the little plain, I saw a Saharian desert-like expanse extending on one side to the horizon, and on another backed in the far distance by a long mountain range, bathed in a lovely azure hue. These mountains, called by the French 'Les Montagnes Bleues,' bear more properly the name of the Djebel Amour, and are one of the loftiest of the many chains of the Great Atlas.

The officer at the head of the Bureau Arabe granted our request most courteously, and his wife was so loth to part with the '*femmes guerrieres*, as she termed us, that we did not reach Boghari until the jackals had begun to cry out around us with startling distinctness; but, harmless as they are, there was a something in the sound of that wild-beast cry which made us well pleased to reach the inn.

CHAPTER XIV.

A DREARY VALLEY—AN INSULTED CAÏD—PRIMITIVE ACCOMMO-
DATION—ARAB HOSPITALITY—AN ARAB DINNER—MATTRESS
VERSUS CARPET—RETURN TO CIVILISATION.

ON mounting my horse the ensuing morning, I was much concerned to find that his shoulder had been galled by a badly stuffed side-saddle, and by his languid pace I saw that the poor animal was in pain. Our day's journey was commenced by an ascent to Boghar, to obtain a guide; as Philippe, somewhat humiliated by his previous mistake in reference to the promised inn, spoke doubtingly of his ability to conduct us there. By the order of the polite *Commandant*, to whom we were referred from the Bureau Arabe, a mounted Spahis of the name of Abd-el-Kader, was speedily added to our party. Thus provided, we redescended the hill to enter a narrow treeless valley leading towards the west.

The narrow, shallow valley into which we turned, was bounded on either side by low, arid hills, on one hand, almost destitute of vegetation, and on the other only very scantily dotted towards the summit by stunted firs and small bushes of juniper. Here and there, as we passed along, we came upon a small patch of barley, but in many places the arid valley would have been utterly bare save for the presence of a small tufted plant, and a sweet smelling herb, which the Arabs called respectively *ketaf* and *sheah*.

Amidst the monotonously dreary scene, it was a relief to arrive in the neighbourhood of an Arab encampment, with its surroundings of sheep and cattle, and wishing for a draught of milk, I advanced with Abd-el-Kader, amidst a furious charge of dogs, towards the circle of tents, which were composed of united stripes of dirty, dark, brown woollen cloth, that in most instances presented a very tattered and dilapidated appearance. As Abd-el-Kader went round the tents to enquire for milk, I halted before one, whose scanty covering permitted me to see the dark and elaborately tattooed face of a youngish woman in an apartment some four feet square, furnished simply with an earthen pot, a sieve, and a small piece of carpet.

In a few minutes, Abd-el-Kader returned to tell me that no milk was procurable, on which I was about to proceed onward, when an Arab, standing before a distant tent, signing to us to advance, presented me on my approach with a small tin of milk, which to my disappointment proved somewhat sour. From the poverty-stricken aspect of the tent

I did not hesitate to offer its proprietor a few sous as an acknowledgement of his courtesy, but my offering was refused with the words *ma kan hadja,*[*] uttered in an indignant tone. Shortly afterwards, some sentences exchanged between our native attendants, which I chanced to overhear, aroused me to the consciousness that I had unwittingly committed the grave offence of offering a Caïd a money payment for his hospitality. The tidings somewhat shocked me, not truly, from remorse of conscience for the deed I had done, but for the vision it suggested of our quarters for the approaching night. I was, however, in some degree relieved, by the assurance of Abd-el-Kader, that the Caïd Ahme el Hadj, whose guests we were to be, was an infinitely richer and greater personage than the insulted chief.

Amidst a chorus of barking dogs, who yelped and snapped viciously at our horses' heels, we left the encampment, and continued along a valley that showed ever the same dreary features. From time to time we passed an Arab encampment, as wretched looking as that, at which we had halted. Some sparkling morsels of mica which in one place strewed the ground, and a few daisies, dandelions, and marigolds, which here and there sprung up, were a grateful relief to the eye, amidst the stunted rusty

[*] Literally, 'It is nothing;' a phrase used in Arabic in the sense of the French 'Il n'y a pas de quoi.'

vegetation of the parched soil. A plot of barley now and then, however, showed that the ground was not actually so barren as its present aspect indicated. Desolation without grandeur, and dreariness devoid of solemnity, formed the unvarying characteristics of the scenery of our morning's ride. With nought to interest the eye, combined with a powerful sun, and the slow pace of the injured horse I rode, I was heartily glad when, about four o'clock in the afternoon, Abd-el-Kader pointed out the tents of the Arab tribe whose Caïd's hospitality we were about to seek. Had not our guide, however, informed me that the Caïd lived in a stone-built house a little way beyond the wretched tents I saw, the announcement of the near approach of the end of our day's ride would scarcely have been of a pleasurable nature.

After passing the tents, ten minutes brought us to the Caïd's residence, a low one-storied building forming three sides of a square, and enclosed on the fourth by a wall, in the centre of which was a small door where we dismounted, amongst some half dozen retainers of the chief. Asking for the Caïd we were told to enter, and on advancing into the court we were met by a tall, dark, dignified-looking, middle-aged man, draped in the voluminous folds of a brown burnous. On presenting our letter, he opened, read it, and courteously bowing, said in very good French, 'With or without letter, you are welcome. I regret extremely that my family is not here to make you comfortable; they are still at Blidah, where I was living till lately.'

Turning away, he spoke to his attendants, who disappeared, to reappear quickly, laden with mats and carpets which they spread for us on the earthen floor of an empty room extending along one side of the enclosure. The lesson of humility which we had been lately taught was not now unneeded, for two small unglazed apertures did duty for windows, assisted by a doorway, which, being without a door, possessed very valuable light-giving qualities. Overhead, the thatch was visible amidst the rough branches which formed the ceiling. For furniture we had a few mats and carpets. Diogenes himself could not have discovered any luxurious superfluity in our accommodation.

To refresh myself, I went to wash my face and hands in a small stream close by, and the Caïd's dog was so startled by my unfamiliar appearance that he ran away. But reflection seemed, unfortunately, to have revived his courage, for on my return he flew at me with a ferocious bark, and was satiating his animosity on my dress, when an Arab rushed to my rescue, and with a stout stick sent off my assailant howling.

Taught caution by this incident, I summoned to my side an effective bodyguard of natives, to attend me on the visit I wished to make to the tents in our vicinity, and on my arrival there a legion of dogs rushed forth to meet me with such ferocious demonstrations of hostility, that had not my retinue assailed them vigorously with sticks and stones, I should certainly have experienced a far more severe calamity than that from which I had recently suffered.

Conducted to a tent, of which one of my escort was the proprietor, a goodly company came flocking to the entrance to see the wonderful *Inglesa*. Overlooking a low partition of carpeting that divided the tent in two, I saw several women, one, young and rather well looking, the others, elderly, and extremely ugly. All were tattooed on face, arms, and hands, and wore a quantity of roughly-fashioned brooches, necklaces, and bracelets.

I was asked, as usual, a variety of questions about my family, and, when this topic was ended, my hat was discussed with considerable animation. After that, I was requested by the master of the tent to state, if I did not think one of the elder ladies in company to be extremely ugly.

'The old are never so handsome as the young,' I replied, evasively.

'Oh, she is ugly, and good for nothing; it is time for her to die,' was the contemptuous rejoinder.

Some infants, brought to me by their proud fathers to be admired, roared so loudly at my sight, that they happily were obliged to be withdrawn, before I had an opportunity of expressing my opinion on their charms.

My host, having disappeared for a few minutes, returned with some half-dozen raw eggs, which he offered for my acceptance. Knowing the course that civility enjoined, I accepted the tribute, and, with many misgivings as to the probable result, I filled my pockets with the frail commodity.

Seated on a carpet in the centre of a circle of Arabs, I did not scruple to try and entertain them, in spite of their grave demeanour, in a manner suitable to children; and, judging from the immense sensation my watch produced, I have no doubt that the marvellous little wheel which said tic, tic, and went round so merrily of its own accord, was a thing to be remembered and spoken of for many a day.

As daylight began to fade, I rose to leave, on which the master of the tent invited me in the most earnest manner to remain; he said he would kill a sheep forthwith; that, besides, he had fowl and eggs in plenty, and would give me a good carpet to sleep on. Pleading my previous engagement to the Caïd, I declined, with thanks, the alluring invitation.

By well-aimed blows from sticks and stones, the dogs were once again prevented from assaulting me; and thus, being baulked in their intentions, they vented the exasperation my appearance caused, by fighting with each other. One cunning dog profited by the tumult to pounce upon a fowl, but, seen by watchful eyes, he was speedily made to drop his prize, and he skulked off, yelping and howling, from the effect of a violent blow.

On my arrival at the Caïd's house, I found four horses picketed near the door in Arab fashion: each had his forelegs immovably fixed, by means of a cord close encircling the pastern, and fastened to pegs driven into the ground at certain distances from each other. They had no covering of any kind; and in the depth of winter their position, I heard, was precisely similar.

The bright morning's sunshine had been succeeded by dark clouds, which completely obscured the sun; and, as one of our young Arabs, looking up wistfully towards the sky, expressed his belief that the obligatory long day's fast had ended, the Caïd, who stood close by, turning on him a look befitting one who had earned the title of El Hadj, by a pilgrimage to Mecca, sternly reproved him for his impatience. Had the Caïd known that the youth had taken a furtive sip of water from the stream close by, a sin of which I knew him guilty, the offender would, undoubtedly, have been sentenced to undergo a bastinado.

Like the young Arab, I also longed for dinner, but the darkness of night had set in before we were gladdened by any sign of the expected repast. A bougie, in a low tin candlestick, was its precursor; and, when I saw the candle flaring and guttering away from the draught which entered through the doorway and unglazed windows, I thought very decidedly that civilisation had considerable advantages. Next arrived a small round pewter tray, which was placed before us on the carpet, and served as a foundation for a large pewter dish, containing apparently some savoury fricasee, and garnished round the edge with thin white cakes. Immediately afterwards, a second dish, of a very dignified aspect, was added to the entertainment, for it was raised on a pedestal at least a foot and a half in height, and, from the appearance of its contents, we pronounced it at once to be the great national Arab dish called couscousou,* of which I had once partaken in Algiers. Small, shallow wooden spoons were the only implements of eating given us.

'Do at Rome as Rome does,' says the proverb, but though I am anything but an admirer of the doctrine embodied in that phrase, I conformed from necessity to its teachings in this instance, by eating my dinner in the mode practised by my forefathers, before the human mind had attained to the grand

* The manufacture of couscousou employs a large portion of the time of Arab women. Wheat ground, not into flour, but into small grains, is the basis of the composition, but these grains are not fit for use till after they have been moistened and worked through the hand, so as to combine into pellets, which are then passed through a sieve to ensure their being of nearly uniform dimensions. This done, the heap of pellets is put in a cloth and laid on the top of a steaming pot of boiling mutton or chicken. Some savoury herbs are added, and when sufficiently cooked, the whole mess is mingled together in a large dish for eating.

conception of inventing forks. The excellent condiment of hunger, made us, I rather fancy, pronounce the white-cake-edged dish to be very good, but as for the couscousou, which came second in the repast, the verdict passed upon it was by no means favourable.

Shortly after our dinner, we agreed that it would be proper to visit the Caïd, who, had we been gentlemen, would certainly have dined with us; and sadly perplexed the poor chief must have been to decide what were the proprieties to be observed in regard to such an unprecedented set of guests. On entering the presence of the Caïd, he was reclining on a cushion in a room, almost a fac-simile of the one we occupied. He received us very courteously, begged of us to sit down on a cushion beside him, and again lamented that, through the absence of his family, he could not make us as comfortable as he could wish. From this we diverged into general topics of conversation. He spoke with deep interest of the war between Spain and Morocco; and we were able to give some later intelligence on the subject than he knew. He alluded, with thorough contempt, to the rude tribes over whom the Government had lately placed him as chief; and he drew comparisons between French and Arabic customs. In manners and conversation, the Caïd Ahmed el Hadj was quite the gentleman.

It would be a mere figure of speech to say that we

went to bed that night, since a double ply of carpet on the earthen floor served each for mattress, a travelling rug for blanket, a shawl for quilt, and a leather travelling-bag for pillow. But though I suppose that, by dint of practice, I might be quite reconciled to such sleeping arrangements, I avow, that, by the time the dawn appeared, I had arrived at the conviction that soft mattresses and down pillows ranked amongst the most admirable creations of man's inventive genius.

The Caïd had not yet emerged from his room when we started on our journey, and doubtless it was owing to the Ramadam that we were offered no coffee previous to our departure. Had it not been for our private store of food, I should have been unwillingly compelled on this occasion to enact the part of a true believer. Having distributed some francs amongst the Caïd's retainers who had waited on us, we rode off.

The country through which we passed, though barren and desolate, was not altogether so dreary in aspect as that which we had traversed the preceding day. Arab encampments, with cattle, and plots of barley, were more numerous, and the arid ground, in some places, was beautified by the presence of a little plant, with small green leaves, amidst whose long woolly hairs the dew glittered bright as diamonds.

On approaching Teniet-el-Had, the scenery began to improve. Rusty grass gradually merged into a bright green hue, and, as we advanced, the hills around our course showed summits thickly studded with juniper. Still nearer Teniet, the crests of lofty mountains rose upwards in the distance. As we approached the town by a steep ascent, the dense black clouds which had gathered overhead, made us quicken our pace, and we had scarcely time to dismount, about four o'clock, at a small tavern bearing the dignified title of the Hotel des Cedres, when hailstones of enormous size dashed thickly and furiously on the pavement.

CHAPTER XV.

TENIET-EL-HAD — HOTEL DES CEDRES — FOREST OF CEDARS — ON TO MILIANAH — A RICH VALLEY — CHARACTER OF THE LION — PLAIN OF THE CHELIF.

A FEW large military buildings, and a few rows of, for the most part, one-storied dwellings, form the present features of Teniet-el-Had. Built on the side of a hill, bare almost to its summit, and facing another bare hill whose crown of cedars is scarcely visible from the town—Teniet, in its situation and stage of growth, strongly reminded me of an unfledged bird.

The cold, rainy, stormy day which succeeded the evening of our arrival at Teniet, we devoted to rest; but our enjoyment of that luxury was much diminished by the character of the quarters in which we were. Bare rooms and poor fare I could have borne without a murmur; but my philosophy was not proof against the dirt, disorder, and vile odours of the tavern bearing the title of the Hotel des Cedres.

Our landlady, a young, handsome Frenchwoman, was a thorough sloven, and seemed to devote her whole mind and time to the task of trying to satisfy the ravenous appetites of a flock of children ranging from six years to six months old. Both eating and sleeping rooms were hung round with articles of her attire, mingled with masculine garments belonging to her husband. The walls and ceilings were draped with spiders' webs, and my bed would have afforded a rich field of study for any entomologist. A good fire of cedar wood was the only set-off to our manifold grievances, and within a limited circle it overcame the vile odours of the miserable place.

On the following day we mounted our horses to visit the forest of cedars in the neighbourhood, and in less than half an hour, a steep and winding path amidst the hills brought us to the commencement of a wood composed of evergreen oak, which shortly, as we advanced, began to give place to somewhat stunted-looking cedars. Still continuing upwards, the cedars increased in size, till we came to truly noble trees, that towered above huge gray crags, along whose base we passed, and the effect of their grand beauty was enhanced by contrast with dead cedars, whose skeleton forms rose up barkless, leafless, white, and gaunt, from trunks blackened and charred by fire—whilst the corpse-like wrecks that strewed the ground under a roof of wide-spreading branches and luxuriant foliage, combined to render the scene one of the most striking I had ever witnessed.

As we neared the summit of the height, the cedars diminished in size and number, but their place was well supplied by venerable oaks, whose gnarled boughs were covered with moss and lichens. From the peak, which was bare, save for a few distorted stunted trees, I had a grand and varied panoramic view of the surrounding country; here, mountain ridges and luxuriant vegetation; there, flatness, bleakness, and sterility. The contrast between the Tell and Sahara could nowhere be more strikingly seen than from the summit of the cedar forest of Teniet.

The desert, visible from the heights of Boghar, formed, with the long distant line of the *Montagnes Bleues*, the chief feature of the southern portion of the picture; and that flat, treeless expanse, stretching out to the far-off horizon, was characterised by an air of dreary, but of that solemn grandeur, with which an image of infinity is ever associated. Towards the east lay the arid hills, amidst which we had so lately journeyed, and whose rusty hue enhanced in an eminent degree the effect of the richly wooded peaks that, towards north and west, showed their lofty crests in ridges running parallel to each other, whilst at the back of a narrow plain, into which we looked there towered aloft the dark masses of Zakkar, one of the highest peaks of the Little Atlas mountains. In the foreground were heights and valleys clothed with evergreen trees, and dotted here and there with plots of corn, whose rich emerald tint had its brightness heightened by the brilliant sunshine. The death-like stillness of the air was unbroken by a sound; but a few yards below me a large prostrate uprooted cedar, with its boughs still green, spoke of a time not long gone by, when the now profoundly peaceful and silent air resounded with the loud roar of a furious tempest. Regretfully I descended the hill, to return to Teniet.

At daybreak the ensuing morning, we mounted our horses to start for Milianah. Our parting with the landlord of the Hotel des Cedres, was somewhat stormy, as we not unnaturally demurred to pay a bill drawn out on a scale suitable alone to a first-class French hotel.* But our well-grounded pleas for reduction were vainly urged, and they moreover brought upon us the rebuke of being unduly fastidious in finding fault with accommodation which had given thorough satisfaction to a French General who had lately honoured the Hotel des Cedres with his presence. Yielding to the logical force of the landlord's reasonings, we paid the disputed bill and rode off.

Shortly after we left Teniet, the sun rose amid the golden radiance of an almost cloudless sky. Our course lay along the side of a small stream that ran through a glen, of which the hills on either side, were wooded to the summit. The thuya, a species of cedar, mingled its dark foliage with that of

---

* With the exception of the Hotel des Cedres, I never found any reason to be dissatisfied with the French Algerian hotels.

the evergreen oak, and of the abounding lentisk, whose small glossy green leaves were thickly studded with clusters of tiny flowers of a coral-like look and colour. At times the trees closed overhead, at other times the bright green sward over which we passed lay open to the sunlight. Here, and there, the glen contracted into a narrow pass, faced on either side by rocks, between which we passed by entering the bed of the little stream whose course we followed. The feathery leaves of the giant fennel were everywhere abundant, the yellow jessamine and coronella tapestried the banks with their bright colours, and occasionally a burnt tree, rising up charred and gaunt, heightened the effect of the luxuriant and rich-hued vegetation.

Crossing and recrossing the stream innumerable times, we advanced onwards, amidst a solitude unbroken by any sign of life, save that afforded by the sight of a troop of soldiers engaged on the construction of a road between Teniet and Milianah. Not a hut or plot of corn gave evidence of even one Arab inhabitant of this beautiful and evidently fertile region. From a tourist's point of view the absence of all traces of civilisation was a decided benefit, for the settler's axe would have infallibly robbed the scenery of its most beautiful features.

Yet notwithstanding the absence of all traces of civilisation, its influence had made itself felt, even in the luxuriant wilderness through which we journeyed, for we passed right across a tract which, only a few years ago, was a favourite haunt of lions. But formidable as this word sounds in English ears, I found from both French and Arab testimony that an interview with an Algerian lion was not an incident from the thoughts of which a tourist need recoil with terror; yet I own, that, although I was frequently assured ' *si vous ne dites rien a lui, il ne dira rien a vous,*' I fear that my equanimity would have been somewhat disturbed by finding myself unexpectedly confronted by his imperial presence.

The Arabs say that if unassailed, no lion will in the day-time attack a man, but that his pacific disposition ends at nightfall, for in the hours of darkness he is a dangerous enemy. Even then, however, they assert, that, if he be confronted unblenchingly, he retreats from the presence of his intended victim. But though some of the many Arab statements on the subject savour strongly of romance, the ascendancy of courage over the lion is an incontestible fact.*

From my own experiences I am not able to corroborate the truth of French and Arab testimony on this subject, for as we passed through his haunts of former years I saw nothing of the wild beast species,

---

* The lion in death, as in life, is highly respected by the natives. His skin is considered a suitable offering to a maraboo or chief; and, used as a couch, it is a talisman against demons, misfortunes and certain ailments. The skin of the forehead, worn on the head, confers boldness and energy on the wearer; and a lion's claw set in silver is an ornament highly prized by Arab women.

not even a jackal. After a ride of many hours through scenery whose luxuriant beauty of feature continued unaltered, mid-day brought us to a large caravanseraï, where we halted; and whilst the horses ate their barley, we partook of an entertainment consisting of bread, fried eggs, and sardines. Had we remained for dinner, a death warrant would have been certainly executed on a couple of the several fowl which, in happy ignorance of their eventual destiny, were placidly pursuing researches for stray grains of corn within the enclosure.

On leaving the caravanseraï the scenery changed considerably; for whilst the hills on either side diminished very considerably in height, they receded from each other so as to destroy the glen-like character of the valley that lay between them. Small yellow butterflies, with orange-tipped wings, fluttered over great beds of glowing marigolds. Bright green lizards darted continually across our track, to hide themselves amidst the grass growing up amidst the slender branches of the wild jujube, which, though spring was in the air, wore still a white corpse-like look. As we proceeded, the hills, still diminishing with our advance, died away at length into a brushwood covered plain, at whose further side we saw the white houses of Milianah perched half way up the side of a dark mountain. Some miles of brushwood passed, our approach to an inhabited country was indicated by small clearings showing plots of grain, and a little further on, we emerged into an open plain sparsely dotted with the square whitewashed dwelling of the settler. We had entered on the plain of the Chelif — a long narrow level valley traversed from east to west by the river from which it derives its name.

But though the Chelif ranks as the largest river in Algeria, and, though rising in the Sahara, it had been winding many a mile before we reached its bridgeless banks, it was yet so contemptible, in point of size, that its waters scarcely reached our horses' knees as we forded it.

About a mile from the river, we commenced to ascend the mountain, high up whose side Milianah is situated. The spiral windings of the road we followed led us amidst luxuriant gardens, filled with fruit trees, which displayed an exuberant mass of blossom. And, whilst a richly wooded ravine below increased in beauty as we ascended, the perpendicular cliffs above, on whose summit the town is built, showed even grander as we approached them. The dark peak of Zakkar, towering over all, completed the chief features of a scene of no ordinary beauty.

On entering inside the walls of Milianah I saw a waste and almost desolate space, with here and there a couple or a trio of European dwellings, ranged in a line together. As we advanced, the houses became more plentiful, till at length they formed a street, through which we passed into a large square, ornamented with platanus trees. From that, it was but a few steps to a large hotel, whose bright aspect was indescribably agreeable after our recent tavern experiences at Teniet-el-Had.

CHAPTER XVI.

MILIANAH—THROUGH THE PLAIN—A COLONIST'S PROSPECTS—
A DESOLATE SCENE—ORLEANSVILLE—RELIZANE.

MILIANAH is situated at a height of nearly 3,000 feet above the sea, on the southern slopes of a lofty ridge of the Little Atlas mountains. From the summit of the precipitous cliffs on which it stands, it commands a grand and extensive prospect. Immediately below, is a winding ravine, opening upon a narrow plain, backed in the distance by the wooded hills of Teniet; and above, it is overlooked by the bare craggy peak of Zakkar.

It was, probably, much more the military than the picturesque advantages of such an elevated site that induced the Romans to select it for the foundation of a city, which, under the name of Malliana, attained to a high degree of prosperity; and traces of this era may be seen in the coins, columns, statues, and fragments of sculpture, abounding in the ground. But though Milianah existed as an Arab town for many centuries, and did not become a French possession before the year 1840, a space of twenty years has sufficed to give it, in its architectural aspect, an almost thoroughly European look. As the officer lounges beneath the platanus trees of the Grande Place, to listen to the music of the military band and exchange the gossip of the day with his friends, he might easily forget he was so far from his well loved Paris if it were not for the occasional sight of a turbaned Moor or white-cloaked Arab. A few uninteresting fragments of the Arab town alone remain.

As Milianah had no attraction to offer beyond that of the fine view it commands, we resolved to lose no time in carrying out our purpose of proceeding to Oran by land. Having got into a region where conveyances could be used, we dismissed our horses, and secured places in a diligence plying at certain intervals between Milianah and Orleansville, the first stage on our journey through the plain of the Chelif.

The day had scarcely dawned when we started; but by the time we entered on the plain the sun had appeared above the horizon. In the vicinity of Milianah the colonist's white house was visible here and there; but in a very short time the only dwellings to be seen were occasional groups of miserable Arab huts, fenced round by piles of cut branches of the prickly jujube.* With the exception of this

* Arab villages are thus fortified to guard against the midnight depredation of jackals, and more especially hyenas, which, though liking their food in an advanced stage of the state called 'high,' will

shrub the plain was destitute of brushwood, and offering as it did a clear expanse, requiring apparently no preliminary expense or toil to fit it for cultivation, I wondered to see the narrow limits to which, as yet, the European colonisation of this fertile region was confined. A Government surveyor, a fellow passenger in the coupé, speedily enlightened me on the subject.

'It is the fever,' he said, 'that scares colonists from settling here; they die off like flies in the hot season. All take the fever. It generally kills off at once the new comers, and those who survive that time may expect to keep their bed for many days each year. Last summer I passed four days in the plain, and I kept my bed for four months afterwards.

'Cannot the climate be improved?' I asked.

'Yes, undoubtedly; but it takes time. With the cultivation of the land the fever disappears; but here, as in the Metidja, the turning up of the soil brings

---

not yet despise, when hungry, a fresh killed fowl. By man himself the Algerian hyena is so little feared, that an Arab armed only with a stick does not hesitate to attack it in its den. The common Arab phrase 'as cowardly as a hyena,' plainly shows that the Algerian or Barbary hyena does not the least bear out the statement of Buffon, that ' for its size, the hyena is the most terrible of all quadrupeds, an assailant of man, and a match for the panther in fight.' I was sorry not to have seen a hyena, which one day in winter came prowling in search of food beneath the walls of our country residence at Algiers, but our maid servant told me that it ran away from her, even more speedily than she ran away from it. The natives sometimes chase the hyena for the sake of eating its flesh, but they believe they would become mad if they swallowed a morsel of any portion of its head.

sickness, even if there be no marshy land in the neighbourhood.'

'The first colonists, then, in any spot, find death almost at their threshold on arrival?'

'Yes—few survive.'

'And their successors have a better chance of life?'

'Yes, considerably better; and the third generation of colonists have a fair prospect of doing well.'

God help the Algerian colonist, I thought, as I heard the surveyor corroborate in every melancholy particular the statements of the European settlers in the Metidja. Before the riches of Algerian plains can be developed by European hands, of how many heart-breaking tragedies will they be the theatre? Follow out in thought the history of the stalwart emigrant who, flushed by delusive hopes, leaves, with wife and children, his native land, to seek a home in Africa. See the arm, in whose strength he trusted to gain his fortune, fall nerveless by his side; and the cheeks, all white and hollow, which, only a few months before, wore the bright glow of health. See, too, his stricken wife and his wailing children, languishing to that death which unites them before long in one common grave. What tragedy so sad as that which has been enacted *once* at least, in every red-tile-roofed dwelling that rises amidst Algerian plains! The bright hopes that have there, been quenched in the thick darkness of despair, the vain regrets and longings that have there, preyed like a canker within the breast, the bonds of affection that have there, been severed, and the breaking hearts that have there, been stilled by the cold hand of death—would fill one of the saddest volumes of human history ever penned.

About nineteen miles from Milianah, we arrived at the small French settlement of Duperré, whose melancholy aspect plainly showed that it had not yet emerged from the malaria-fever stage of its existence. After passing beyond the immediate vicinity of the village, we entered once more on an uncultivated waste, which looked indescribably desolate and dreary from the barren hills by which the narrow curving plain was bounded on either side. The road was miserable, in truth it was nothing more than a track worn by wheels; and when ruts became more than ordinarily deep, the driver improvised for himself an original road, either to right or left, as seemed most desirable. Had it not been for the abounding wild flowers, our long day's journey would have been utterly devoid of interest; but the marigolds, sweet pea, mignionette, and many bright-hued unfamiliar flowers which in some places quite carpeted the ground, tended to dissipate in some degree the monotonous dreariness of the surrounding scenery. Towards the middle of the day, we passed on our right hand a low chain of mountains, whose name of Dahra has gained a mournful notoriety, from the terrible tragedy that was consummated there by the orders of General Pelissier.*

It was evening when we arrived at Orleansville, a small bright town, as thoroughly French in aspect as it is in name. The natives call the place El Esnam, and this term, signifying the cross, it owes to the many remains of Christian sculpture found in the locality. An inscription, bearing the date of the year 476, points to that era as one in which the unknown predecessor of Orleansville was a flourishing town.

As in the case of other French Algerian settlements, the illustration of '*les mouches*' was freely used in describing the great mortality of Orleansville in its early years. But its salubrity had so much improved since then, that, although the malaria fever is still prevalent in the hot season, it has lost its malignant character. The many flourishing trees which give to the town an exceedingly bright and pleasant look, tended, doubtless, in no small degree, to improve the climate.

Orleansville is as yet the centre of only a very small agricultural colony; and though their bright green fields of corn proved the fertility of the soil, the land lay almost uncultivated around several Arab

* The barbarous destruction of nearly six hundred Kabyles, by a great fire kindled at the entrance of a cavern to which an entire tribe had fled for refuge, is an incident in the history of Algeria which will ever remain a foul blot upon the arms of France.

villages in the vicinity, and these villages were about the most wretched native structures I had yet seen. The contrast was very striking between them and the well-built French town in whose vicinity they rose; and I could not but feel, here, as elsewhere, that a people who showed themselves so unworthy of the rich land they occupied, did not deserve to be compassionated for their lost independence. The French in Algeria, as the English in Australia, both serve the interests of the human race.

As Orleansville, towards the west, is unconnected by a diligence line with any French town, we were obliged to seek a private conveyance for proceeding onward, and the only one procurable was a britska that presented the most forcible illustration of the word 'shabby' it was possible to conceive. It was shabby in every way; the greasy corduroy lining of the inside fitly matching the paintless outside, which was thickly streaked with varying hues of mud; but for all its manifold demerits in civilised eyes, we could not avail ourselves of its services save at a price which showed that the proprietor's estimate of its value was very different from ours.

It was not long, however, after we had started onward on our journey before our opinion of the britska underwent a change, for the tremendous jolts that it bore uninjured, and its admirably-maintained equilibrium under the most trying circumstances, could not fail to make us feel that its good qualities atoned for its demerits in looks. Except for the constant excitement arising from the imminent danger of being upset, our long day's journey would have been most monotonously tame, for the plain of the Chelif, through which our course still lay, showed ever the same unvarying features of an expanse of coarse, scanty, yellowish vegetation, bounded on either side by a low chain of barren, treeless hills. An Arab village, even in the distance, was a rare sight.

It was late in the afternoon when, reaching the termination of the plain of the Chelif, we passed through a series of low hills, and by a diminutive salt lake, to the small plain of Relizane, in which was the French settlement of the same name, where we were to pass the night. After our long dreary drive through an expanse of rusty vegetation, the bright verdure of the fields around the village was a grateful sight; and on alighting at a small inn we were glad enough to be assured of beds, even though the public dining room was the only quarters for the night that could be assigned to us.

Relizane was in its infancy, a term associated here, as in the plains of the Chelif and the Metidja, with the death-dealing autumnal pest of malignant malaria fever. In the preceding August, nearly the whole population of the village lay stricken down upon a bed of sickness, from which many were borne to the graveyard. A mere village now, Relizane will probably expand into a town, and have a prosperous future, should French colonisation wrestle successfully with the still rampant scourge of fever.

Relizane is a long day's journey distant from Mostaganem, for which we started on the ensuing morning in the wake of a public conveyance proceeding to that town. The unexpected sight of this evidence of civilisation gave us the pleasant assurance that our tribulations on the score of an upset would be considerably less this day than it had been the preceding one; and, though seen from a European point of view, the road to Mostaganem would assuredly deserve to be pronounced miserable, yet by the light of our late experiences we looked on it with considerable satisfaction. The scenery along our course, though uninteresting, was not nearly so bleak and desolate as that which characterised the features presented by our two days' journey through the plain of the Chelif. Here, was an Arab village buried in a plantation of Barbary figs; there, a conical hill crowned by the white koubba of a maraboo. In some places the ground was a garden of brilliant coloured flowers, and as we advanced, we saw now and then the beautiful spring foliage of a small grove of figs, in the vicinity of a European colonist's whitewashed house. As we approached Mostaganem, we gained a rich narrow valley dotted with gardens, orchards, and white Moorish villas. From that, a short ascent brought us to the walls of a large town, and, entering through a military gate, our shabby but highly meritorious britska soon conveyed us to the door of the many-storied Hotel de France.

CHAPTER XVII.

MOSTAGANEM—STORKS—A DREARY JOURNEY—ARZEW—ORAN—
COAST SCENERY—A FEVER-SCOURGED VILLAGE—A MYSTERIOUS
FRIEND.

GEOGRAPHICALLY speaking, Mostaganem is a seaport town, but the epithet is more nominal than real, for, except in the calmest weather, vessels fear to approach the exposed rock-bound coast of that portion of the Gulf of Arzew on whose shores the town is built.

Under the dynasty of the Deys, Mostaganem was a place of considerable importance, and, though now more than half French in aspect, some four thousand Arabs, cluster together in a quarter thoroughly native in point of architecture. Built on the steep banks of a narrow ravine, the town is divided in two by the small river Safra, which runs through the gorge, and which also for the most part forms a boundary line between the dwellings of the Arab and the European population. On the heights around rise buildings of a size and character which show that Mostaganem is one of the chief French military stations in Algeria.

The appearance of the principal *place* in the town itself, announces the existence of a large military force within the walls. As I look down from my room in the Hotel de France, I see soldiers swarming underneath the long arcades of the fine square, and amongst the rows of trees by which it is ornamented. The numerous cafés and restaurants which open off the arcades are filled with officers, to whom the business of satisfying the *besoin de s'amuser* forms the chief end of life. And here this great end is happily attained, if it be true, as is stated by a French authority, that 'Mostaganem est la ville de l'Algerie ou l'on s'amuse le plus.'

The varied costumes of the natives of Algeria mingle picturesquely with the uniforms of French officers and soldiers. Draped from head to foot by the voluminous folds of their long cloaks, a group of Bedouin Arabs stand in close vicinity to a general officer decked out in all the bravery of plumed hat and flashing epaulettes. The Spahis, in his deep crimson burnous, and the Turco* with braided jacket and turbaned head, combine, with the characteristic costumes of Jews and Moors, to form a varied and striking picture.

The storks, which abound in Mostaganem, compose

* The Turco is a native soldier dressed nearly as the Zouave, with merely a difference of colour.

highly important class of the community, from the reverence of which they are the objects. In all ages indeed, storks have been the most fortunate of birds in securing human respect and protection; and though Egypt alone paid them the homage of worship, the Dutchman of the present day would no more molest his long-legged favourite than would the Arab drive away the stork, which comes, he knows, as a harbinger of good luck, to build her nest upon his roof. He knows also — what you do not know — that these birds have human souls imprisoned in their forms, and when the stork, throwing back its neck and raising its head aloft, makes with its bill a peculiar sound, he is well assured that that sound conveys a prayer to Allah, denied expression in any other mode by the righteous judgment which condemns the Thaleb* who has broken in aught the holy Ramadam fast, to expiate his guilt by a term of imprisonment in the body of a bird. Under these peculiar circumstances, it is evidently quite natural that the stork should be, as is the case, a melancholy bird, addicted to solitude and meditation. From this point of view, the Arab theory on the subject must unquestionably be considered highly satisfactory.

After passing one day at Mostaganem, we started the ensuing morning before daybreak for Oran, in a diligence that offered us only the uncomfortably

---

* Thaleb, learned man.

elevated seats of an uncovered *banquette*, which we accepted, in preference to losing our time by waiting till we could secure places in the *coupé* or *interieur*. In fine weather our position would have been rather enviable than the reverse, but in the drizzling rain amidst which we started before the dawn, we felt by no means inclined to consider the *banquette* as a place at all conducive to human happiness. Burying ourselves in shawls and waterproofs we longed for dawn, and when daylight came, it showed us a country as sombre and dismal as was the leaden sky above our heads. Far or near, not a tree was visible, and far or near I saw nothing around, save a waste of low brushwood intermingled with bushes of gorse. Multiply dreariness by bleakness, and the product by desolation, and the result may convey an idea of the general features which characterised our whole long day's journey.

Nearly midway to Oran we halted for half an hour at the small seaport town of Arzew, which, notwithstanding it possesses one of the best natural harbours to be found along the whole Algerian coast, yet presented a picture of stagnation and decay. Scarcely a sign of life was visible in its streets, and many houses were utterly destitute of inhabitants. Pre-eminently lying under the curse of malaria, Arzew contains now the scanty surviving relics of a European population ravaged by cholera and fever. The saline nature of the soil, from which, for miles around, not a drop of pure fresh water is obtainable, has tended doubtless in no small degree to make French Arzew at this present day a monument of failure.

In the neighbourhood of Arzew, the brushwood-covered ground was dotted here and there with a settler's house and farm, and we passed through a small village, of which the few inhabitants whom I saw gave me the idea that brackish water was very far from being an inspiriting beverage. After leaving that, the brushwood closed in around our course again, and the opiate influence of the scenery was only counteracted now as previously, by the violent lurching movements of the lumbering diligence in which we were, since for the most part our road owed to man, only the labour expended in cutting down the brushwood along its course — wheels had done the rest. A simple system, but one I should say not altogether commendable in the eyes of nervous-minded travellers, particularly if perchance they occupy seats in the *banquette* of a high French diligence.

On nearing Oran, the sight of the magnificent headland which rose immediately above the town effectually relieved the monotony of the prospect. Still, not a tree was visible, and the settlers' houses which began to show amidst the dreary brushwood waste were few and far between. Until we actually reached the very confines of the town, the whole scene presented a dull dingy hue, which was suddenly transformed into the most brilliant verdure as, attaining the summit of a hitherto unseen ravine, we gained the town by a steep descent amidst luxuriant fruit gardens. After the discomforts of our dreary journey, it was supremely pleasant to find ourselves within the walls of one of the largest and best-looking hotels that I had yet entered in Algeria.

Having expected to find Oran with Spanish features, I was much dissatisfied at the sight of its almost thoroughly French face. Here and there, indeed, I saw a fragment of a house or archway that was evidently of Spanish origin, but such relics were too inconsiderable in number to counteract the effect of the tall square white modern houses which lined the streets. The almost utter extinction of Spanish Oran is due to a fearful earthquake, which, in the year 1790, reduced the town to a mass of ruins. The formidable Spanish forts, that were, with the ramparts, almost the only survivors of this catastrophe, repaired and improved by the means of modern science, have, with a change of masters, lost the names which indicated their origin. Santa Cruz has become Sainte Croix, whilst San Gregorio and his numerous fellow saints which guard the town from every quarter, have undergone a similar transformation.

The very scanty amount of the native element in Oran, both as regards architecture and population, tended also to make me view it with disfavour. One handsome minaret rising above a mosque was the only striking architectural memento that I saw of the native inhabitants of the land. Here, were no dark mysterious alleys lined with prison-like walls, nor Jewesses in their quaint rich dress, nor the veiled Moresque's ghost-like form. The picturesque and varied features of Algiers were absent from Oran.

Yet, though deficient in interest, as a town, Oran most undeniably possesses the charm of a magnificently grand situation. Built in the centre of the shores of a deep curving gulf, Oran rises tier above tier on high, along the precipitous side of the dark masses of Mount Mergiagio, which towers above the town. The fort, Sainte Croix, which crowns its lofty summit, and the no less formidable fort of St. Gregoire some way below, add to the frowning grandeur of its aspect. Towards the east, the waves beat against the base of a long range of lofty perpendicular cliffs, terminating in the distance in a cape rising to a height of two thousand feet above the sea; and toward the west, the view is immediately closed in by the beetling rocks of a fort-crowned point, beyond which, at some two miles' distance, is seen the mole-like extremity of the noble heights which form the bay of Mers-el-Kebir. Those who love nature in its grand stern aspects, will find in the iron-bound coast of Oran a picture whose solemn beauty stamps itself indelibly on the mind.

Exposed to the full fury of the dangerous north wind, the term of seaport town, as applied to Oran, would be, as in the case of Mostaganem, a mere geographical expression, were it not for the vicinity of the noble bay of Mers-el-Kebir, which, closed in towards the north by a pier-like projecting range of lofty rocks, offers to vessels a secure retreat amidst the fiercest winter storms of the Mediterranean. A magnificent road, five miles in length, hewed for the most part out of the face of beetling cliffs, connects the town of Oran with its port. But fine as is the harbour, the scanty shipping it contains most plainly shows, that, at this present day, Oran is a mere French military stronghold, and nothing more.

Towards the south-west of Oran, European colonisation has made considerable progress. At four miles' distance from the town, is the flourishing-looking village of Senia, and between it and Oran the road passes through a trimly cultivated district, dotted with large well-built European houses. But a dry sandy soil and want of water, prove formidable obstacles to the colonist. No tree will grow unless tended and watered in its early years like a tender garden flower, and grain crops give a scant return. But vines do well; and to them, and to his carefully-tended mulberry trees, which yield a good silken harvest, the colonist looks for repayment of his toil.

Having determined to extend our westward

excursion through Algeria to Tlemcen, a town situated near the borders of Morocco, some seventy miles south of Oran, we secured seats in a diligence plying between the towns, and we once more made another ante-daybreak start — this time away from the sea shore, towards the interior of Algeria.

The scene revealed by the light of morning might vie in dreariness with any I had yet seen in Algeria. Around us lay an utterly desolate plain, covered with low brushwood; and to the left, bounded in the distance by the waters of a long, narrow saline lake. At about eighteen miles from Oran we reached the European settlement of Bou Tlelis, where we were detained for a considerable time by the accident of a wheel taking fire. Through this delay, I obtained from the inhabitants of Bou Tlelis such information as warrants me in saying that a residence at Bou Tlelis may, at this present time, be considered in the light of a respectable mode of committing suicide.

For miles on miles the same dreary brushwood accompanied our advance, and, save an occasional small roadside tavern, I saw no signs of life, not even an Arab gourbi or a flock of sheep. Our road was for the most part constructed in the primitive style I have previously described, and our driver, apparently emulous of engineering distinction, improvised a new line wherever the brushwood did not interpose an effectual barrier to the developement of his constructive talents.

Owing to our delay at Bou Tlelis, we did not arrive at Tlemcen until long after dark. When daylight left us, we were journeying amidst an undulating grass-covered tract of country, a pleasant sight after the expanse of desolate brushwood through which we had passed. But far pleasanter even than that sight was the one which greeted us when, after a long day's journey, we alighted at the door of the good-sized and comfortable-looking Hotel de France, where, on our entrance, we were greeted by the landlady with the most unexpected assurance that our rooms were quite in readiness for our immediate use.

'Our rooms! we engaged no rooms!' was our somewhat startled rejoinder.

'But Monsieur Georges did, for you.'

'We know nothing of any Monsieur Georges; it is some mistake.'

'No, it was no mistake,' the landlady affirmed; for it was quite incredible that two parties of English ladies should arrive at Tlemcen the same day. Being unable to contend against the force of this reasoning, I began to fancy that M. Georges must be a beneficent geni watching over the comfort of unprotected lady tourists, when the remembrance of a certain letter given us by the Vice-consul of Oran led rapidly to the discovery that M. Georges was the prefix to a long-syllabled Italian name inscribed upon the document we bore. From what source

M. Georges had received notice of our intended arrival, it required no sphinx to guess.

After all, I was not far wrong in classing the enigmatical Monsieur Georges in the ranks of beneficent genii, for, on the ensuing morning, when he came to visit us, he put himself, wife, daughters, house, carriage, and riding horses at our command during the time that we might remain at Tlemcen.

CHAPTER XVIII.

TLEMCEN, PAST AND PRESENT — BEAUTIFUL KOUBBA OF SIDI BOUMEDIN — END OF RAMADAM — A DEVOTIONAL DANCE — ACTING THE JACKAL — A LADY DANCER — GLEN OF MAFROUCK — A FAIRY-LIKE GROTTO.

TLEMCEN is decidedly an ill-used town, for, in spite of having played a distinguished part in some not long byegone centuries, its name is buried in oblivion. Such at least is my belief, as well as hope, for I do not wish to avow a humiliating degree of ignorance in declaring that previous to my visit to Algeria, Tlemcen was to me an unknown word. For the benefit of similarly benighted minds, I shall sketch the past history of the town in a style suited to the requirements of an age, already groaning under the weight of an appalling burden of historic lore.

Like other Algerian towns, Tlemcen had a Roman ancestor which, under the name of Pomaria, flourished some 1,700 years ago, but attained to no distinction, save that it enjoyed from the abundance of its apples, to which particular attribute it owed its name. In the fifth century Pomaria, under a change of masters, merged into Djidda, which subsequently formed the capital of a Berber kingdom that was overthrown in the eleventh century by the great Moorish chief Youssef ben Tachfyn, whose victorious arms founded a vast dominion that comprised the south of Spain and an uninterrupted line of territory extending from Morocco to Algiers.

As Pomaria had given place to Djidda, so Djidda now in its turn underwent a similar extinction in favour of Tlemcen, which speedily became in riches and importance, one of the first cities of northern Africa. But Tlemcen did not attain to its culminating point of glory until the thirteenth century, when, on the dismemberment of the great empire of which it formed a portion, it became the capital of a powerful kingdom governed by the Beni Zian — a Berber race. Under the successive sovereigns of this dynasty, who employed their wealth in beautifying the town, mosques rose up which vied in splendour with the richly-decorated halls of the Alhambra. Renowned professors taught in schools, whose walls were ornamented with mosaics. Spacious caravanseraïs afforded accommodation to the foreign merchants who thronged the markets to buy the produce of the interior, as well as the rich carpets, fine woollen stuffs, and the exquisitely wrought harness that came forth from the workshops of the town. Pure sparkling water, brought by subterranean channels from the hills, bubbled up in numerous fountains, and supplied large public baths. In the centre of the town arose the lofty walls of the

Mechouar, the vast and splendid citadel palace of the kings. Innumerable white villas gleamed amidst the luxuriant gardens, and the forest of fruit and olive trees which encircled the city walls. The magnificence and riches of Tlemcen were a source of wonder and admiration to the adventurous traveller of those days.

But the greatness of Tlemcen was of no long duration, for, exposed to the almost incessant attacks of the rulers of neighbouring states who coveted the rich prize, its prosperity rapidly waned under the blight of war. After a seven years' siege, the Sultan of Fez became master of the town, only to be expelled by another conqueror, who in his turn was driven forth by a fresh assailant. Ravaged in succession by Spaniards, Moors, as well as by the Turks, who finally became its masters, Tlemcen finally lost utterly, under the withering pirate rule, every feature of greatness and splendour; and is now almost a mere heap of formless ruins, a maze of crumbling walls, inhabited by a scanty and poverty-stricken population.

Still, even amidst the merciless havoc wrought by time and war, Tlemcen yet shows some traces of ancient power and splendour. Some beautiful arabesques still adorn the interior of the dilapidated grand mosque, and here and there, a minaret is seen exhibiting yet, a few of the bright enamelled tiles, with which its surface was once thickly covered.

Though the splendid palace of the kings has vanished, the towering walls by which it was encircled are yet uninjured; and, utterly ruined as are the ancient ramparts, their massive wrecks speak eloquently to the stranger's eye of byegone prosperity and strength.

A mile outside the present town, long lines of massive ruinous walls partially enclose a vast square space, whose desolation is made more striking by a lofty broken-down minaret tower which rises in the centre of the waste. Within that now almost empty space, the Sultan of Fez encamped his army for seven years before Tlemcen, and when he entered it, he celebrated his victory by converting the fortifications of his late camp into the ramparts of a populous town. How names survive to mock the triumphs they record! The long lines of ruined walls, amidst which one solitary mouldering architectural relic of the past is seen, still bears the proud exulting epithet of El Mansourah (the victorious), given to it by the conquering Sultan.

But while old Tlemcen lies a mouldering and almost formless wreck upon the shores of time, it nevertheless presents a chequered picture, for in the very centre of its ruined walls, the French have built a town, whose straight wide streets and tree-shaded squares look all the more bright and cheerful from their jostling contact with ruins and desolation. Within the lofty walls of the Mechouar, barracks and military structures of various kinds rise on the site of the vanished royal palace; and those ancient walls overlook a fine large square, whose numerous cafés and restaurants are daily filled with lounging officers.

Tlemcen enjoys great natural advantages in regard to situation. Shielded from the fiery desert blast by a chain of heights, at whose feet it lies, it is also protected from the fervent heat of an Algerian summer sun by the altitude of the small undulating plateau on whose verge it stands. But whilst snow is no rare sight in winter, the cold is never so severe as to injure the grove of olive trees by which the town is for the most part girt. Pure sweet water is plentiful, the soil is fertile, and the malaria fever is almost unknown. With such advantages, I found it difficult to reconcile the sight of the closed doors and barricaded windows of the deserted French village of Mansourah, within one mile from the town.

Tlemcen seems to have been most prolific in saints; for the whole neighbourhood is studded with koubbas, which are particularly valuable to the natives in a medical point of view, since the sick have only to lie for a night across the threshold or inside the dome of the maraboo's tomb, and if it is fated they are to recover, this means will infallibly achieve their cure. If, after this ceremony, they die, that result proves, not the inefficiency of the means of cure, but, that their time is come.

But of all the many koubbas that stud the vicinity

of Tlemcen, none can compare in dignity of aspect with that of Sidi Boumedin, which rises near the town in a small ruinous village bearing the revered maraboo's name. No vulgar foot, steps within that sanctuary without the special permission of its guardian, who kindly, however, allowed us free access to the interior of by far the most richly-decorated maraboo's tomb I had seen in Algeria. The walls were covered with inscriptions; lamps, coloured lanterns, and ostrich eggs were suspended in profusion from the vaulted ceiling as well as from the gaily-painted pillars that rose on high, whilst the gold-embroidered hangings, and large, bright, rich silk banners that hung immediately above the tomb, gave an air of costly splendour to the scene. One of the handsome banners which I saw, was a recent donation from a French General.

The adjoining mosque of Boumedin is the best preserved existing relic of ancient Tlemcen, and in the beautiful arabesques which decorate the vaulted ceiling of the interior, I saw the finest specimens of Moorish architecture I had ever beheld. Less fortunate in its fate is the tall minaret tower close by, for nearly all the enamelled tiles which once ornamented its surface have vanished, leaving a mass of rough mason work to affront the eye.

In a couple of days after our arrival at Tlemcen, the welcome sight at evening of a crescent moon in the sky announced to the Mussulman world that the long wearisome fast * of the Ramadam was ended, and on the ensuing morning the three days' feast of Aïd-es-Serir commenced by a profuse exchange of embraces amongst all classes of the community. The rich Moor had his turban kissed by his humble brethren; equals in station embraced each other in stage fashion; a kiss on cheek or lips was rare, and evidently the sign of particular friendship. An Arab woman with uncovered face touched hands with everyone she met, and kissed her own hands afterwards; but the Moresque *ennekabos* of Tlemcen gave no outward sign of being aught but the phantoms which they looked.

All the resources of each true believer's wardrobe were displayed in honour of the occasion. The rich Moor looked extremely picturesque in his handsome embroidered jacket and his snowy burnous, ornamented with rich white silk tassels. The caps of glittering gold coins which young boys mostly wore, gave them, in combination with bright coloured sashes and gay jackets, quite a radiant butterfly look. Even the beggar, who had no smart dress to wear, showed a very pleasing solicitude on the subject of his array, by a burnous whose colour evidenced that it had been lately subjected to the benign influences

---

* The Ramadam lasts a lunar month, and ushers in a feast called Aïd-es-Serir, meaning the little feast, in contradistinction to Aïd-el-Kebir, the great feast, which occurs at the beginning of the Mussulman year.

of soap and water. As to the ladies, they no doubt embellished themselves with koheul and henna to the best of their abilities; but my pursuit of knowledge on this subject was effectively checked by the nauseous festival cake, which was offered me by the first lady that I visited. To undergo the repetition of a similar compliment, was an idea from which I recoiled.

Besides smoking, eating, and drinking coffee, which form the staple enjoyments of the Aïd-es-Serir, there are other amusements of a religious character, belonging particularly to this season. Processions pass from koubba to koubba with banners and implements for making a noise, called music, and on their way they stop occasionally, and joining hands, they jump up and down in concert for a few minutes together, uttering the while the most dolorous of songs. Their greatest efforts in this line are, however, reserved for the interior of the koubbas which they visit, and where they address Heaven in such an amount of energetic steps, that before long they have to desist from weariness and lack of breath.

Being desirous of seeing a native fête which was to be held on the second day of the Aïd-es-Serir at a small village about a couple of miles from Tlemcen, I asked for a guide to conduct me there, and after the successive rejection of three Jews, whose sinister faces impressed me with the conviction that Israelites of the Nicodemus type were a rarity in Tlemcen, I engaged an Arab, a late Spahis, whose frank honest countenance was a pleasant sight after the visages I had previously reviewed. My guide had been on the eve of starting for the village, when his services were enlisted on my behalf, and in honour of the fête he had donned a new burnous, the hood of which was sumptuously ornamented with long white silk tassels.

After a pleasant walk through olive woods and fields, I reached the village of Aïn-el-Hout (literally 'spring of the fish'), a term derived from a sacred pond, the fish of which, my guide Mohammed informed me, were under the protection of a deceased maraboo, whose koubba rose close by, and who would certainly strike with death the sacrilegious wretch who dared to abstract one tenant from the pond.

The village was composed of a small cluster of low ruinous walls, overlooked by heights, crowned with two white koubbas. The male population sat in rows outside their doors, to watch the passers-by. Not a European but myself was visible, and though in native eyes I was unquestionably a kind of *lusus naturæ*, the exquisite good manners which seem innate in the Arab race, prevented me from being in the slightest degree annoyed by impertinent curiosity. In France, or England, a Tlemcen *ennekabo* would certainly be hustled and mobbed by the juvenile population of any country village, whilst I, as great a marvel here, as a Moorish lady would be there, had not a single shouting urchin following in my train. A low murmured 'Inglesa,' caught up from Mohammed's communication with his friends, was the only word that fell on my ear as I passed along.

After seeing some very vehement saltatorial devotions in the two koubbas on the height, I returned to the village, where a drumming noise led me onward to a large court, the far side of which was bounded by fragments of ruined walls, shaded by fruit trees. Under these trees, groups of Arabs sat cross-legged on the ground, whilst others, occupied an elevated position on the flat roof of a low house opposite. Several *ennekabos* in knots stood here and there along the walls bounding the enclosure, the centre of which was occupied by four young men who were performing a series of dancing evolutions, to the accompaniment of a music emanating from five instruments of a drum-like character.

Untrammelled evidently by any rules of art, each dancer gave free scope to the inspiration of the moment. One leaped upward, another crossed the court in a series of energetic jumps; a third raced backwards and forwards, yelling as he ran; and the fourth pirouetted round and round with extreme rapidity. Occasionally they joined hands together, and executed in concert some highly effective bounding movements; but for the most part, their energies were put forth in independant *pas seul* performances, which waxed so violent under the influence of the ever-quickening music, that, when it suddenly stopped, two dancers dropped down exhausted; a third reeled here and there like a drunken man; whilst the fourth, with maniacal looks and gestures, pounced upon a young lad who was standing near, and, flinging him over his shoulder as if he were a sack, ran round and round the court, roaring like a wild beast.

But startling as was this sight, it yielded in melodramatic horror to the next, for the apparent maniac suddenly cast the boy upon the ground, and, after rolling him over and over several times, yelling most fearfully, he gnashed his teeth, and made gestures and grimaces indicative apparently of an intention to tear the lad in pieces.

'The boy will be murdered by that madman. Go and save him,' I said to Mohammed, in alarm.

The placid smile with which my guide informed me that this startling scene was merely a portion of the dance, dispelled my fears. The seeming madman was only enacting the part of a jackal — nothing more — so I was told; but though I credited the assertion, it was a relief to me to see the boy rise up uninjured, whilst his late assailant, resuming his human character, went tottering round the court a truly pitiable object, groaning, moaning, and with his pallid face overhung by a top knot of long black streaming, dishevelled hair.

'Is this done for pleasure?' I said to Mohammed.

'Yes, and also in honour of the great maraboo

whose koubba you see upon the hill. I have often joined in it.'

'And do you like it?'

'Yes, very much; and when I get excited by the dance I can tear a live sheep to pieces and eat its flesh, which, by the power of the maraboo, tastes as if it were cooked.'

'Is it usual to tear a live sheep to pieces in this dance?'

'Yes, I have often done so. If you had come here some hours sooner you would have seen it done.'

The gentle, placid, amiable expression of Mohammed's countenance seemed so to belie the tenor of his words, that they would have appeared incredible had I not seen at Algiers, in the Aïssaoua dance, the maddening effects of fanatical excitement.

On the last day of the festival, as we passed through the village of Boumedin, I saw another strange devotional dance within a house, to which I was attracted by a drumming sound that issued from its interior. Passing through an enclosed court, we entered a small room, the several sides of which were lined with a row of women, whose eyes were fixed upon a girl of about eighteen, who, in a singular position in the centre of the floor, was executing an equally singular performance, to the accompaniment of three drums beaten with great vigour by female musicians.

In a crouching position that brought the knees in close proximity to the chin, the attitude of the girl somewhat reminded me of the byegone days when I performed the classical dance of cutchee-cutchoo around the nursery. But with the attitude, the resemblance ended, for instead of describing a circle by a series of jumps as was my custom, the girl was at first perfectly motionless, save for the violently tremulous movement of her arms, either hand of which was resting on the floor. Before long, however, her head joined in the performance, at first in a slow motion to and fro, which gradually quickened as time went on, into a rapid tossing backwards, forwards, and from side to side, whilst the rest of her body remained immovable, save for the slow circular movement which she gave it, by making pivots of her feet and her still rigidly extended arms. As, faster and faster, the drums were beaten, the girl flung her head from side to side with an ever-increasing violence, that evoked shrill cries of delight and applause from the lips of the spectators, till, nature giving way, she fell forward fainting on the floor. On this, the drumming ceased; and as I left the house, the apparently lifeless girl was lying across the knees of one of the musicians.

From this barbarous scene I gladly turned to visit the glen of Mafrouck, lying not far from the dilapidated village. Entering a wood, whose bright spring foliage was studded with hawthorn, broom, and jessamine, a rugged path conducted us onward along the brow of a steep hill overlooking a valley that, quickly assuming, as we advanced, the character of a glen, terminated before long in a magnificent amphitheatre of lofty heights, showing here, a wall-like range of bright red cliffs towering above precipitous banks of verdure, and there, the broken waters of the river Mafrouck as it dashed downwards in a series of fine cascades, whose snow-white spray sparkled amidst the rich overhanging foliage. Seated on the ruinous fragments of an ancient villa in the grassy hollow at the foot of the falls, and listening to their harmonious murmur, blending with the songs of nightingales, I thought, as I gazed on the rich walls of verdure that rose around, that I had seen few scenes of peaceful beauty that could exceed the glen of Mafrouck.

With the exception of this glen and the olive grove immediately without the town, the vicinity of Tlemcen presents a circuit of uninteresting bare hills; but one of the very bleakest and barest of these hills contains a beautiful cave, or grotto—as the French call it—which no tourist should fail to see. The first step necessary towards the accomplishment of this object is an application to the Bureau Arabe for a guide, and an order for torchbearers to be supplied by the Caïd of an Arab tribe living in the vicinity of the place, and on the payment of some twenty francs the application is granted.

Having gone through this necessary preliminary, we started one fine morning on horseback for the grotto, accompanied by M. Georges and his friend, a

Jewish gentleman. The bleak hills through which we rode for some eight miles or more, were so devoid of interest that, by the time I had arrived at the neighbourhood of the grotto, the influences of the route had made me well inclined to fancy that it was not worth the trouble of visiting. In this critical state of mind I dismounted at a very unattractive-looking cavity near the summit of a low hill, and our attendant Arabs having lit some of the numerous torches of coarse grass with which they came provided, we entered.

At first, I saw nothing distinctly, for, beside the blinding effect of a sudden transition from the bright light of day to subterranean darkness, our torches were not sufficiently numerous to do more than give us transient glimpses of a vast hall hung with stalactites; but as the grotto diminished in height with our advance, there burst in flashes on my sight a scene of the most exquisite beauty.

Stalactites, in every variety of size and form, closed in my view above, around, below. No ceiling of human work could exceed in varied beauty the deep fluted fringes and arches of pale yellowish hue that hung overhead; and not less exquisite were the clustering columns which, shooting up on every side, joined the vault above, or terminated midway in a group of glittering pinnacles. As we threaded our way through overarching aisles, with aisles and aisles seemingly extending into the darkness on either hand; the weird-like fantastic beauty of the scene conjured up my childish visions of fairyland — an illusion which our white-robed Arab guides was well calculated to foster, as, with flaming torches and uttering wild cries, they flitted around our way.

Though our path was very rugged, we had no difficulty in advancing; but the scanty supply of torches with which our guides were furnished, obliged us before long to retrace our steps. The Arabs said that no one had ever reached the extremity of the grotto, which, for miles on miles, as far as known, presents the same features as that portion which we had passed through. On our way back, the Arabs directed our notice to some of nature's artistic works, but I confess that the lion and the camel I was shown, taxed my imaginative faculties in as high a degree, as the well-known portrait of the man in the moon. As we approached the entrance of the cave, a very beautiful effect was produced by the filtration of the light of day through the fluted masses of transparent stalactites, that extended across the opening in a curtain-like drapery, from side to side.

The bare, bleak height near whose summit we emerged, was in striking contrast with the subterranean glories it contained, and so desolate and dreary was the scene around, that it taxed my faith in Monsieur Georges to credit his assertion that in five minutes' time we should be seated beneath the shade of a grove of fruit and forest trees, to which he was about to lead us. And no palm-tree oasis could contrast more forcibly with the parched lifeless sands of the desert, than did the bare bleak hills around, with the little isle of verdure in a neighbouring hollow, where, by the side of a clear brook we demolished with much satisfaction the contents of certain well-filled saddle-bags.

After a week's stay at Tlemcen we returned to Oran, bearing with us grateful recollections of the truly hospitable M. Georges and his kind family. The promise made on our arrival had been kept. The house, carriage, horses, placed at our disposal, proved no phrase of empty compliment.

CHAPTER XIX.

RETURN TO ORAN — FRENCH PROPRIETIES OF SEA LIFE — JOURNEY TO MARENGO — TIPAZA — AN ENGLISH COLONIST — A PANTHER TALE.

A LONG dreary day's journey brought us back to Oran, amidst a fierce storm, which made us almost recoil from the idea of returning to Algiers by sea, as we purposed doing; but the absolute necessity of economising our time determined us to proceed, if practicable, by the Government transport steamer that plied thrice a month between Algiers and the ports along the coast. Happily, the storm died out the ensuing night, and when we embarked from Mers-el-Kebir at an early hour on the succeeding morning there was scarcely any perceptible wind.

But, notwithstanding our luck in this respect, we were still very far from being in an enviable position. As ordinary passengers* in a transport steamer, we were condemned to take up our quarters in a small dark den containing three berths, one of which we

* Civilians can only obtain through official favour, first-class accommodation, such being ordinarily restricted to the exclusive use of officers and their families.

found, to our dismay, was the temporary property of a young burly Frenchman. As, fortunately, however, this startling discovery was immediately followed by the knowledge of the fact, that a French lady had been assigned a berth in company with two gentlemen in an opposite cabin, we stimulated her meek spirit to revolt against official ordinances, and succeeded in bringing the obnoxious Frenchman to acquiesce in an exchange. According to English notions, the arrangement which we effected, was only in accordance with that, which the commonest sense of propriety should have impelled the authorities to make.

But for one evil of our lot, there was no remedy save the philosophic resource of patience, as, lacking a fairy's wand, I could not change the 'tub' in which we were, into a swift-footed and steadily-conducted vessel. Had the sea been rough the unpleasant movements to which we were subjected might have been forgiven, but it was indescribably irritating to look on an unruffled expanse, only stirred by a slight swell resulting from the late storm, and to feel all the disagreeable sensations which had hitherto been connected in my mind with waves and wind.

If the sight of a fellowship in misery could have mitigated its weight, I had that in abundance, for as I lay rolled up in travelling rugs upon the quarter-deck, I saw a number of the many officers on board with countenances indicative of a state of the most abject wretchedness. Surely no Briton ever suffers in the same degree as a Frenchman from the terrible *mal de mer*. If he does, he undoubtedly hides his anguish better from public view. One wretched officer, who groaned and moaned as he lay prostrate on the deck, with his head resting on a travelling bag, might be, perchance, a great hero in the field of battle, but he was certainly a very small hero on board a ship. As for the coast scenery, I know nothing of it; the announcements of its grandeur that reached me from time to time, did not once stimulate me to lift my head above the bulwarks, at whose foot I lay. When darkness came, retreating to my den, I never emerged from it until the ensuing day at twelve o'clock, when we neared Cherchel, at which port, some thirty miles from Algiers, we desired to land.

From the dangerous character of the Algerian coast there are few ports along the shore at which a steamer ventures to touch in stormy weather. Fortunately for us, the moderate breeze which blew, did not interpose any obstacle to our disembarking at Cherchel. Leaving the steamer in a clumsy unwieldy ferry-boat which came alongside, a few minutes brought us to land, on which I stepped with a sensation of keen enjoyment.

Under any circumstances, however, the little town of Cherchel, where we landed, would be a pleasant sight, rising as it did, at the foot of a long range of brilliantly green heights, terminating far to the west in a noble headland, and merging immediately to the east in the dark masses of the Chenoua mountain, which rose up in frowning grandeur from the blue waters of the sea.

But though Cherchel is at this present day an insignificant mongrel French and Arab town, it can fairly lay claim to an illustrious pedigree. Whilst most Algerian towns cannot trace back their history beyond the ancient Roman empire, Cherchel claims Carthagenian Iol as an ancestor; and when Iol expired, it was succeeded by Julia Cæsarea, the large, rich, and handsome capital of Roman Mauritania. The relics and tokens of this era in the history of the place, are still abundantly scattered over a space of many thousand feet. In the very centre of French Cherchel arise the ruined but yet massive walls of the ancient palace of the Pro-consuls. Not far from it, are the remains of a theatre, which shares with a ruined circus the stigma of being the stage, where, many a Christian was torn by wild beasts or burnt alive; and the circuit of the ramparts can still be traced. Baths, a Pagan temple, a Christian church, a hippodrome, all in an utterly ruinous state, form the principal architectural remnants of the once splendid African capital of the Roman Cæsars.

A very superficial excavation in the ground that formed the site of the ancient town, is alone required to bring to view a profusion of broken columns, friezes, busts, and statues. Visiting a temple whose marble pavement had just been cleared of accumulated piles of earth and rubbish, I saw around me the remnants of some fine columns, a delicately sculptured frieze, and four large marble busts. The small museum of the town was full of fragmentary remains of various kinds, which, mutilated as they are, yet afford incontestible evidence of the splendour of the Mauritanian capital at a time when our Celtic ancestors, painted with woad, and clothed in wild beasts' skins, hunted for food amongst the primeval forests of Britain.

A violent earthquake, has evidently added to the ravages wrought by the hand of Time upon the architectural glories of Julia Cæsarea, for ruins of Roman buildings are visible beneath the waters of the port, and many columns have been found below, embedded in slime and sand. Not a town, indeed, along the whole Algerian coast but has suffered from a similar visitation, and though no earthquake of any magnitude has occurred since the French conquest, not a year elapses—it is said—without some warning shock being felt.

The mongrel French and Arab town of Cherchel is too insignificant to need description. A palm tree, opposite the hotel, presented its only striking feature, and with its desert associations, it looked quite a startling anomaly at the foot of a low range of heights of an emerald verdure. In the vicinity of the town

I saw a few settlers' houses, but the distant hills were indebted for their brilliant hue to the corn-fields and fruit trees of tribes of Kabyles.

A vehicle belonging to the gig species, conveyed us onward the ensuing morning to Marengo, a small French settlement, situated at the western extremity of the Metidja. Our course lay for the most part through a narrow and almost uncultivated valley, bounded on one side by the dark masses of the Chenoua, and on the other by ranges of hills, overtopped in the distance by the still snow-crowned Zakkar. On our way, we passed some broken, but still lofty arches of the magnificent aqueduct which had supplied the Mauritanian capital with water. One small French village, in the middle of a waste of brushwood, was the only sign of civilisation which we saw before gaining, after a two hours' drive, the settlement of Marengo. On arriving there, we exchanged our rustic conveyance for a vehicle of a still humbler description, to convey us to, and from, the ruins of Tipaza, a Roman town situated in the neighbourhood.

In a civilised country, a gardener's cart cannot be considered as a desirable conveyance, but I do not think that any vehicle of a more aristocratic character, could have borne us without accident across the network of holes and ruts, that formed the so-called road along which we journeyed to Tipaza. But meritorious as was our rural carriage in withstanding the violent shocks to which it was subjected, the narrow uncushioned wooden bench on which we were perched for an hour and a half, through a series of dislocating jolts, made us feel infinite satisfaction in arriving within sight of our destination.

From the height over which we passed to descend by a gentle slope to the ruined town, its aspect was grand and striking. Where, here and there, a broken arch or column is the sole surviving relic of an ancient city, fancy can only faintly and imperfectly bring back an image of the past, in its whole original grand proportions. But at Tipaza, the maze of low ruinous walls, that extended eastward along the shore far as my eye could reach, imparted a vivid sense of reality to the thought, that human life had once abounded amidst that now lone and desolate scene. Each mouldering heap of stones that rose up so plentifully amidst the glossy leaves of the abounding lentisk, was in itself an eloquent sermon on the transitory nature of all human greatness.

The dark precipitous masses of Chenoua which rose in a projecting point immediately to the westward of the ruined town, added in no small degree to the gloomy grandeur of the prospect. Time, that had spoiled the works of man, had left unscathed those beetling sea-lashed cliffs, as grand to-day, as when they successively overlooked the birth, maturity, decrepitude, and death of Roman Tipaza.

After a short drive amidst the ruinous heaps which strewed the ground, we came in sight of a cluster of most unpoetical-looking cottages, roofed with bright red tiles, and built in straight formal rows. This was modern French Tipaza, still in its babyhood, and the intended competitor in glory with that ancient Roman Tipaza, out of whose mouldering skeleton it is built. But though I hope the infant may arrive at a flourishing maturity, I confess that its vulgar, commonplace aspect, amidst such a solemn scene, inspired me at the time with an intense desire to see it razed forthwith.

Descending from our uneasy perch, at the door of a small tavern, I strolled amongst the ruins for some time. Here, as at Cherchel, the lapse of centuries had altered the relation of sea and land. Down through the depths of many feet of water, I saw an ancient pavement, and in several places, the waves broke against the base of mouldering walls. A hillock of sand, rising from the sea, was thickly strewed with large uncovered tombs of stone, filled to the brim with fine white sand. Amidst the ruins that littered the ground, I came, here and there, on a prostrate column, or on a ruined arch; but, for the most part, the formless heaps amongst which I passed, were simply mouldering walls.

Hearing from the landlady of the tavern that one of the settlers, an English lady, would be delighted to see me, I proceeded towards her house, which boasted the dignity of two stories. Judging from the expression of the lady's face, the first emotion that I inspired was one, partaking less of delight, than of bewildering surprise; but before many minutes had elapsed, I saw reason to believe that the landlady was right in her assurance.

Proffering herself as guide, she led me, through the brushwood, to the remains of a Basilica, the shape of which, was still perfectly defined; and the prostrate columns that lay in front, were, with the sculptured capitals by their side, the best preserved remains of Roman Tipaza I had seen. In our progress, we came upon several deep clefts and gaping fissures, evidently of earthquake origin. I much regretted that the approach of evening prevented me from visiting several ruins, of which my friendly cicerone spoke. On our way, she dilated on the bright prospects of the young settlement in which she lived, and on the happiness she found in a settler's life.

She was not lonely, she said, though she lived almost alone; for her husband, a Frenchman, would not leave Algiers. She warmly advised me to follow her example of obtaining a concession of land at Tipaza. The place was sure to prosper. The soil was immensely rich, and would grow magnificent crops of cotton, tobacco, and grapes, as well as corn. The malaria fever, consequent on the first cultivation of the land, had been of a mild character, and would soon altogether disappear. The Government was about to construct a port, between which and Algiers, there would be communication by steamer. As the

AN UNPLEASANT NEIGHBOURHOOD.

outlet of the rich west portion of the Metidja, Tipaza could not possibly fail to thrive. Under the influence of my energetic countrywoman's words, I looked with a considerable amount of tolerance on the previously abhorred formal rows of cottages, to which I reluctantly returned, to resume my uneasy perch in the gardener's cart, on a return journey to Marengo.

Owing to my somewhat undue delay amidst the ruins, the sun had nearly gained the horizon when we started, and our driver, a youth of nineteen, looking uneasily at the sky and murmuring 'it will be dark before we reach Marengo,' stimulated his horse to a pace that, under the circumstances, might be judicious, but, very decidedly, was not agreeable. In spite, however, of all the speed he tried to make over the miserable road, we were still amongst brushwood-covered heights when the shades of evening fell. As the twilight deepened, faster and faster the hapless horse was urged, till suddenly, after rattling down a slope ending in the plain, its speed was checked as the driver, turning round towards us with a joyful face, exclaimed, '*Je ne suis pas peureux, Mesdames, mais je n'aime pas d'être dans le voisinage d'un panthère qui fréquente un coin de la route en haut.*'

'Are we quite safe now?' I asked anxiously, for though not *peureuse*, I little relished the idea of making an intimate personal acquaintance with a live panther.

'Yes, quite safe now; we are out of the brushwood, where he lurks,' was the assuring answer. 'He is a dangerous fellow to come across when it is getting dark. Not long ago he sprang upon an Arab who was passing by on horseback, and made short work of him. He has lately killed ten cows, belonging to a Caïd living in the wood below. He is very cunning. No one can kill or catch him by gun or trap. He was like to have made an end of me not very long ago, on my return from Tipaza, when it was almost dark. My horse saw him first, and, trembling all over, suddenly stood still, and would not move. Then, looking round, I saw close by in the thicket two bright spots, which I knew to be a panther's eyes, and instantly lighting a match I had in my pocket, I set fire to some straw that lay in the bottom of the cart. The blaze frightening the panther, he slunk away, and the horse of his own accord galloped on.'

On hearing this story we felt very thankful to arrive safely at the comfortable little village inn of Marengo. 'To point a moral, or to adorn a tale' by falling into a panther's clutch, was an idea we little relished.

CHAPTER XX.

LEGEND OF THE TOMB OF THE CHRISTIAN.

WE had intended visiting, from Marengo, a curious Mauritanian monument known commonly by the name of Kouber-er-Roumia, an epithet signifying 'Tomb of the Christian;' but finding that neither mules or riding horses were procurable in the village, we could not carry our purpose into execution. However, for the edification of antiquarians, I append below* a French description of the structure;

* 'Un monument, d'un haut intérêt est le sépulcre des anciens rois de Mauritanie communément désigné sous le nom de Tombeau de la Chrétienne (Kouber-er-Roumia), situé au S. E. de Tipaza. C'est un édifice de 42 mètres (137 feet) de hauteur, dont la base polygonique a 60 mètres (196 feet) de diamètre. Des colonnes ioniques présentant des déviations de ce style, flanquent au nord un monolithe, sorte de fausse porte de 4 mètres (13 feet) de haut. Au-dessus, commence une série de 53 degrés, qui, en rétrécissant graduellement leur plan circulaire, donnent au mausolée l'apparence d'un cône tronqué. M. Berbrugger, conservateur du Musée d'Alger, l'a exploré à la fin de 1855. Il a pénétré de 14 mètres (45 feet), marchant de la circonférence vers l'axe du monument; dont le rayon est de 30 mètres (98 feet), et n'a rencontré que des assises de pierre de taille dont les caracteres d'appareillage inconnus aujourd'hui, peuvent induire à penser que l'architecture extérieure du tombeau, en complet état de ruines revêtait un édifice beaucoup plus ancien.' — VICTOR BERARD.

whilst to lovers of legendary lore—a far more numerous class—I present a fanciful Arab legend connected with the spot.

It is a long time ago since Youssef-Ben-Cassem lived, but even then the Tomb of the Christian rose on high in the vicinity of his home. He was rich; his wife was loving and beautiful; his children were healthy and obedient, his friends numerous; yet withal the abundant blessings of his lot, the fancy seized him to become a soldier. But taken prisoner by the Christians, and condemned to slavery in a foreign land, he then bitterly rued the folly to which he owed his fate. With bitter tears, recalling all that he had lost, he performed his allotted tasks.

'Oh, my God! am I indeed condemned never to see again my wife and children?' he exclaimed aloud, one day, in despairing accents, whilst engaged in out-door work.

Scarcely had the words been uttered, when he found himself confronted by a venerable-looking man, who said, 'Arab, of what tribe art thou?'*

'I am a Hadjout,' returned Youssef.

'Then thou certainly knowest the Kouber-er-Roumia.'

'Ah, would to heaven I might see it once more,' groaned Youssef, 'for it is but an hour's walk distant from the spot where my family dwells.'

---

* The Arabs generally use the second person singular in conversation.

'If thou desirest to return to them, I will restore thee to thy native land, on one condition.'

'Name it, oh, Christian!' exclaimed Youssef, vehemently; 'if it be not contrary to the words of Allah, and the teaching of his blessed prophet, I will do it joyfully.'

'Be easy on that point. In return for ransoming thee and sending thee back to thy native land, I only ask thee to take a certain scroll of paper and burn it in a little fire to be lit at the entrance of Kouber-er-Roumia. Swear that thou wilt do this on the fourth day after thy return, and I will procure thy freedom and restoration to thy native land.'

Youssef joyfully assented to these terms, and the Christian giving him a scroll covered with unknown characters, he embarked that very day in a vessel bound for Algiers. Arrived at home, he did not forget his oath, for on the fourth day after his return he repaired to the Tomb of the Christian to do as he had sworn.

The fire being kindled in the appointed place, the mysterious scroll was thrown into it, and scarcely had it touched the flames when thousands of gold and silver coins flew forth from every portion of the Tomb, and darted off in a straight continuous line towards the country of the Christians. For a minute or two, Youssef watched that marvellous sight in motionless surprise, but recovering from his bewilderment, and anxious to obtain some portion of the riches which were passing high above his head, he took off his burnous, and flinging it upward, it struck the precious stream, and brought down one hundred and twenty gold and silver coins. No sooner, however, did they touch the ground, than the jet of riches ceased.

The tidings of this marvel having reached the Pasha, he immediately sent labourers to demolish the Tomb, in order to obtain possession of the riches it contained; but with the first blow struck, the workmen recoiled in terror from their task, at the sight of a phantom woman, who, standing on the summit of the Tomb, shrieked out in an unearthly voice, 'Alloula,* Alloula, come to my help; they are going to carry off my treasures.' On this appeal, the lake poured forth swarms of enormous gnats, whose furious attacks, made the workmen rush frantically from the spot.

Such is the legend of the Kouber-er-Roumia, but I could not obtain the slightest information on the subject of the Christian lady, who still keeps in death a watchful guard, that her buried treasures will not pass into any Mussulman's hands.

This ancient monument is a striking object from every portion of the Metidja, for though it is not more than 137 feet high, its form, alone, breaks the continuity of the wall-like outline of the low Sahel range, bounding the western side of the plain.

* The Lake Alloula lies immediately below the Tomb of the Christian.

CHAPTER XXI.

HISTORY OF MARENGO — A VISIT — KOLEAH — A GARRISON GARDEN — SIDI FERRUCH — MILITARY RECREATIONS — MATRIMONIAL EXPERIENCES — RETURN TO ALGIERS.

THE well-tilled fields which extend around the tree-shaded village of Marengo combine, with its clean white cottages, to give it now a very cheerful and flourishing look; but what its past has been, may be best narrated in the words of the civil, intelligent landlady of the inn where we passed the night.

'My husband, myself, and three young children, formed part of a band of 850 colonists, who were sent by Government in 1848,[*] to establish an

[*] In 1848 the National Assembly voted fifty millions of francs in furtherance of the colonisation of Algeria. The depression of trade at that period made the idea of emigration thoroughly popular with the needy working classes of Paris. Bankrupt shopkeepers, tailors, shoemakers, jewellers, watchmakers, musicians, and artists, and tradespeople of various kinds, composed the band of 13,500 emigrants who, consequent on the Assembly's vote, were sent in successive detachments to Algiers. Revelling in the idea of having a house, land, cattle, agricultural implements free of cost, and a daily ration of food for the period of three years, the colonists landed on the Algerian shores amidst dances, songs, and shouts. But once drafted to the interior, to live in wooden huts amidst a waste of brushwood, in an atmosphere laden with miasma, and utterly unfitted for

agricultural settlement in this spot. Little any of us thought, when we left Paris, what fate we were going to face. At first our dwellings were only wooden sheds, that let in at many a chink the poisonous air that reeked from the brushwood and the newly upturned soil. Unaccustomed to handle a spade or axe, scarce a man amongst us could stand the toil of cutting down the brushwood, by which the land was covered. From poor and scanty food, from insufficient shelter, and from the terrible fever which raged in autumn, more than half the settlers were dead in eight months' time; in twelve months, few remained. I lost all my children, every one. I was nigh following them myself, so was my husband. But it pleased God to spare our lives for the enjoyment of that better time which, after years of terrible suffering, has now come.'

Such is the history of Marengo, which, like Boufarik, owes its present flourishing look to a population several times renewed.

Starting from Marengo at an early hour of the morning, we drove along an excellent road, through the most prosperous-looking portion of the Metidja

hard out-door work, despair entered into their souls. To detail their subsequent fate, I shall borrow the words of a French writer: 'Ces malheureux ont été décimes par les fièvres, par les maladies et la misère, les plus heureux se sont faits débitants de boissons, quelques uns ont trouvè, à s'employer de leur état, quand a ceux, qui perseverent dans l'idée du cultivateur, la science agricole leur faisait défaut. Des masures en ruines, entourées de terres incultes, voilà, ce qu'offrent à chacque pas, les colonies agricoles de 1848.'— ÉMILE CARDON.

that I had yet seen. In truth, the cheerful tree-shaded villages, and large fields of corn through which we passed on our way to Blidah, were worthy of a highly civilised land. In this portion of the plain, French colonisation is at this present day, an evident success.

We arrived at Blidah in time for breakfast, and as the diligence to Koleah, our next halting place, did not start till the afternoon, I employed some of my spare time in visiting a Moorish lady of high rank, whose illness had prevented me from making her acquaintance during my former stay at Blidah. Being personally acquainted with many members of her family living in Algiers, I had no hesitation in presenting myself to her notice without any introduction. Both as an acknowledged beauty in her world, and as a prince's daughter, the lady whom I visited is deserving of a particular description.

A wall some eight feet in height, and pierced by a small door, was all that was visible from the native street of the Caïd her husband's house. On my knock, the door was speedily opened by a youth of about seventeen, who, addressing me in fluent French, asked me to walk in. He was exceedingly sorry, he said, that the Caïd, his brother, was not at home to receive me, but Madame would be most happy to make my acquaintance. Passing through a small court, in which orange trees, in full blossom, loaded the air with an overpowering fragrance, I was ushered into a long, low, narrow room, of which the unpainted rafters overhead, contrasted somewhat strikingly with the presence of a costly Parisian timepiece, a rich carpet, handsome china cups, and some pictures. A table and chairs, were the only European drawing-room features absent from the scene.

The young gentleman having left me to announce my arrival to his sister-in-law, speedily returned, and sitting down beside me on a divan, in a Christian-like manner, warmly expressed his regrets that Madame had not received previous notice of my intended visit, so that she might have had time to dress herself suitably for my reception. 'You know, ladies always desire to make themselves look handsome,' he added, with a gravity befitting the announcement of a philosophical dogma; and with equal solemnity I assented to the great truth.

In a few minutes, a very young and strikingly handsome Moorish lady entered the room, but her faultless features lacked the beauty of expression, a defect probably made more than usually perceptible, by the pallor consequent on her recent illness. According to Moorish fashion, her brows were joined by a broad streak of koheul. Her black hair was almost concealed by the folds of a light blue silk handkerchief; a striped silk scarf was thrown loosely round her shoulders, and figured calico trousers, met just below the knee by a pair of long brown stockings, completed her costume.

With earnest apologies for her dress, Madame began the conversation. I tried to relieve her mind upon the subject, but my endeavours were evidently fruitless, for every few minutes she re-introduced the topic. With a kind of stunned and bewildered look, she heard me speak of my late travels; and she did not apparently recover her faculties until I communicated the exciting intelligence that one of her cousins was soon to be married. A wedding was evidently quite as important an event in Mohammedan, as in Christian lands.

From the wedding, we merged into a discussion on mutual acquaintances — ever a highly valuable acquisition, in a conversational point of view. On taking my leave, Madame once more expressed her deep regrets on the subject of her dress, and begged, if I returned to Blidah, to give her notice, so that she might attire herself fittingly for my reception. The visit was finally wound up by the truly touching request of Madame and the young gentleman, that I should give them a place in my memory.

Koleah lies directly opposite to Blidah, on the Sahel range of heights which bound the Metidja on its westward side. The distance between the towns is only about thirteen miles, and our course for the most part lay through a well cultivated tract of country, studded with large comfortable-looking houses surrounded by trees. Shortly before we commenced the steep ascent leading to Koleah, we passed through a narrow strip of the forest of Massafran, amidst whose swampy recesses the panther lurks.

Like other Algerian towns, Koleah exhibits a mongrel French and Arab aspect. Almost utterly destroyed by an earthquake in 1825, the evidence of this calamity is very conspicuous at the present day by the number of ruinous and utterly ruined houses that meet the view. But the earthquake which destroyed the town, religiously spared a mosque, a lofty minaret, a tall palm tree the produce of a seed from Mecca, and the koubba of a great maraboo, who sometimes, it is said, presents himself under the form of a black lion to the pilgrims to his tomb.

In Christian eyes, an adjoining deep ravine is a more attractive feature of Koleah than the cluster of sacred objects so precious in the Mussulman's sight. Amidst the varied and luxuriant vegetation which clothe the steep banks of this ravine, a very beautiful flower garden has been made by the French soldiers stationed at Koleah, and which is entirely laboured and kept up by them. It was truly pleasant to see the interest they took in their occupation. Not a weed was visible amongst the bright flower beds, and the intelligent young soldier who conducted us through the grounds, led us exultingly to a half finished grotto, tastefully decorated with shells, the work of a talented *camarade*. Everywhere the garden evidenced that it was a garrison pet.

The whole ravine was in itself a natural garden,

of extreme beauty. On every spot to which the sun had free access the ground was carpeted with marigolds, larkspur, trefoil, lavender, and blue pimpernel, whilst the abundant yellow broom and white asters were wreathed with the beautiful blossoms of the pink convolvulus. A little stream that ran through the ravine was fringed on either side by almond, orange, lemon, and fig trees, amongst which, here and there, the pomegranate showed its brilliant flowers. I had never witnessed a scene of such luxuriant beauty.

The very few natives whom we met greeted us with the utmost cordiality, and, amidst their reiterated assurances that the English and Arabs were brothers, they besought us to visit their gardens, where they unmercifully stripped orange and edible lemon trees of their few remaining fruit, to present them to the representatives of the great English nation.*

After passing one day at Koleah, we started early the ensuing morning in one of the two diligences

---

* Two causes may be assigned for the popularity of the English with the Arab population of Algeria. One arises from a belief, often confided to my ears, that the English would conquer the French, and then give Algeria back to its rightful owners. The second cause originates in an idea that the English may, some day or other, become good Mussulmen; for they say that the envoys sent by the blessed prophet to ask the Christian nations to become believers in the true faith, met with a downright refusal in every case save that of England, which returned for answer, 'We will consider about it.'

which daily run from Koleah to Algiers. Wishing however, to visit Sidi Ferruch, the place where the French landed in Algeria, we told the *conducteur* to put us down at the point where the road to it branched off from the main line, intending to return in time to catch the afternoon diligence to Algiers.

Though only some two and twenty miles from Algiers, the neighbourhood of Koleah shows still great tracts of brushwood, dotted only very rarely with a plot of corn. At a small French village at which we halted, a woman, with a sad, care-worn face, entered the diligence, and the account she gave me of her experiences of colonial life tallied in every sad particular with the many I had previously heard. In about an hour's time we were set down at La Colonne, a pillar raised by the French to commemorate their landing at Algeria. A pleasant walk of about a mile and a half in length brought us to the isthmus of Sidi Ferruch.

Surely, if the ghost of the holy Sidi does not haunt the spot where he dwelt in life, he must be truly a philosophic spirit; for his koubba, which crowns the point, has been converted into a Christian church, in which, for many years, a *Te Deum* was sung on the anniversary of the landing of the French in Algeria. Perhaps, however, the saint avenges the desecration of his tomb by blighting the French village which bears his name; for the few small, humble cottages of which it was composed seemed for the most part empty.

Before long, however, the village of Sidi Ferruch is likely to emerge from its present insignificance, as a large body of soldiers, encamped close by, were busy at work constructing a fort and barracks, large enough to contain 2,000 men. The works were carried on under the direction of an engineer officer, who, happening to overhear our enquiries in regard to shells, advanced to answer our questions, and very politely offered to show us a chandelier made by the soldiers from their gatherings on the beach. Accepting his civil offer, he conducted us to a small, wooden house, in which, on entering, we found ourselves in a room tastefully ornamented with coloured drapery and garlands of leaves, as well as by the really very pretty chandelier we had come to see.

'This is all the soldiers' work,' the officer said; 'sometimes the place serves them in the evening for a theatre, at other times for a concert room, just as they may feel inclined.'

As at Koleah, so now here, I compared in thought the influences respectively moulding the character of the soldiery of France and England. The Algerian soldier, who works by day in making roads or building forts, and passes his evening in rational recreations, can scarcely fail to be a far more refined, enlightened, and better man than the English soldier, whose days of weary idleness, unenlivened by harmless amusement, goad him into dissipation. The truth in regard to idle hands, which good Dr. Watts, in well-known lines, strove to impress upon the infant mind, is one applicable to every phase of human life.

After partaking of some refreshments which the courteous officer offered us, we wandered for several hours along a beach strewed thick with small bright-coloured and delicately-marked shells. The day was beautiful—just such another day, most probably, as that memorable 14th of June, 1830, on which the French first set foot on the shores of Algeria. As I reclined on a bed of sparkling sand and shells, fancy called up the picture of that bygone period— filling the blue waters of the curving bay with the snowy canvas and tapering masts of a fleet of vessels; dotting it over with boats that gleamed with the flash of bayonets; peopling the beach with file on file of the invading army; and, amidst an array of waving banners, flashing swords, and nodding plumes, mingling the sound of drum and trumpet with that of the harmonious roll of the breaking wave.* It would be a dull world to live in if the bodily eye were the only organ of sight we had. Reality pales beside the rich colouring of an ideal picture.

Leaving the shore, we returned to La Colonne to catch the afternoon coach, and whilst waiting for its appearance, an Arab woman, twirling a distaff,

---

* However calm the air, I never saw the Mediterranean at rest on an Algerian beach. Even when there was not a breath of wind, the sands were ever marked by the broad trail of sparkling foam left by the breaking wave.

approached me. Having ascertained that I was unmarried, she proceeded to give me her views on married life. She considered that I was a highly blessed woman in not having a husband, for all husbands were terrible and cruel tyrants to their wives. They beat and they scolded, and when they had done scolding they commenced to beat again. No wife would have any joy in this world if it were not for her children, and yet they were also a heavy grief, if it happened, as it had done to her, to lose them all by fever. Such were poor Fatima's experiences and opinion of matrimonial life.*

The diligence arrives at length, and we take our seats inside, beside two young women, one of whom, wearing a conventual dress, is evidently in the last stage of consumption. The country through which we proceed is covered with brushwood, till we reach the immediate neighbourhood of Staoueli, a small malaria-scourged French village. As we advance, the country improves in look, and the brushwood finally gives place to corn fields, houses, and groups of trees, before even we have gained the picturesque suburban village of El-Biar, where the convent to which the dying nun is going, rises conspicuously above white villas gleaming amidst luxuriant masses of varied foliage.

Leaving El-Biar, and advancing along the summit

* I heard, on excellent authority, that it is no rare thing for an Arab wife to revenge herself upon her tyrant by poisoning him.

of the height on which it is built, we pass onward amidst white villas and gardens, where the dark leaves of orange and lemon trees enhance the brilliant spring foliage of the almond, pomegranate, and fig. As Mustapha comes in view, its villas sparkle brilliantly amidst the mass of verdure that rises up on high above the magnificent curving, foam-fringed bay of Algiers. The snow-crowned Djurjura, and the range of mountains above which it lifts its wintry head, show loftier and loftier in the quick deepening shades of evening; whilst ever brighter and brighter grows the glorious disc of a full moon, whose silvery light enhances the loveliness of a scene, from which we turn only to skirt the brow of a deep ravine, rivalling Mustapha in verdure, and overlooked by the precipitous height of Bouzareah. Gaining the city walls, we pass the Sahel gate to dash onward through the once formidable citadel of the Casbah, and ever rapidly downward we proceed, till the steep descent, terminating in the French street of Bab-el-Oued, we advance between its long arcades to the Place du Gouvernement, amidst trumpet flourishes not unworthy to herald the approach of some crowned head.

Gaining the hotel, we talk about the eastward journey through Algeria, which is to succeed the westward expedition now just ended.

CHAPTER XXII.

THE FEAST OF BEANS — NEGRO DANCING — AN EXEMPLARY VICTIM — THE FEAST OF THE CHRISTIAN — A TALE WITH A MORAL.

THE Algerian negroes celebrate by an annual religious fête the commencement of the bean harvest. Owing to the cold spring, the Aïd-el-Fould (Feast of Beans), usually held in April, did not take place till after our return to Algiers in the beginning of May. We were thus enabled to be present at the festival.

The first portion of the ceremonial took place in the French street of Bab Azoun, in which the negroes assembled in numbers at an early hour. Guided by the din of drums and castanets, accompanied by some vocal performances of a very inharmonious character, we made our way, amidst a throng of ebon faces, to the interior of a circle formed round a diminutive bull, standing amidst the uproar as quiet as a lamb. The red handkerchief which draped his head, the strings of cowries that dangled from his neck, the wreaths of flowers which ornamented his horns, and his gay trappings of gauze and calico, evidently exercised no exciting influence on his feelings. After the singers and the drummers had apparently reached the climax of their power, the musical performances broke off abruptly, and the circle, melting away, formed into lines behind a tall negro, who advanced along the street carrying a large banner bearing the inscription 'Vive la France—l'Abolition de l'Esclavage.' The bull marched onward immediately behind the banner, with a sober dignity quite in keeping with his previous demeanour under trying circumstances.

The site of the negro festival is a certain place upon the beach, distant some two miles from Algiers. Having, through the means of an omnibus, arrived long before the procession at the spot, we awaited it there in the vicinity of a few tents, in which some elaborately attired young negresses were visible. The most effective toilette I saw was that of a young woman, who had encircled her head with a wreath of faded artificial flowers, whilst a striped red and yellow scarf hung in petticoat fashion from her waist. Pink, yellow, and more especially red, seemed the colour most in favour with the ebon belles, who were evidently quite as proud of their array as any French or English ball-room queen could be of hers.

The procession, consisting of some four hundred blacks, made its appearance on the beach in about half an hour. Advancing across the sand in the same order it had left Algiers, it halted at length close to the bank on which the tents were raised;

and the bull, as meek as ever, was tied by the horns to an aloe that grew close by. This done, the procession resolved into a large circle, at one side of which a number of drummers and castanet players squatted on the sand; and in the midst of the uproar which they made, three negroes and a fraternising Moor, bounding towards the centre of the open space, commenced to dance in African fashion.

The attire of the performers was as varied as their evolutions. A bare-headed negro, wearing a long green robe descending to his feet, did little more at first than shake his head and sway his body from side to side. Another negro, very conspicuous by a yellow turban, put forth his whole energies in upward jumps. A third, wearing a striped burnous, went round the circle in a series of zigzag movements, whilst the fraternising Moor, in an elaborately patched and darned white burnous, flourished a short stick aloft in accompaniment to the slow attitudinising evolutions he performed.

With the accelerated beat and clink of drum and castanets, the performances increased in animation, and the dancers in number. The yellow turbaned negro desisted now and then from his aërial jumps, to turn head over heels from one extremity of the circle to the other. The wearer of the striped burnous made rapid races to and fro, until he tripped and fell prostrate on the sand. Two dancers, grasping each other's hands, whirled round and round so fast in the same spot, that, when they loosed their hold, they staggered like drunken men. One negro broke through the circle and rushed off madly towards the sea, but before he reached the water he suddenly turned, retraced his steps, and celebrated his reappearance in the circle by a series of summersaults. But not one of the performers indulged in such extravagancies as the green-robed negro, for, after evidently shaking every particle of reason out of his cruelly-tossed head, he sprang round the circle uttering loud cries, and, with face contorted by horrible grimaces, he rolled his eyeballs fearfully, and at times put out his tongue. A more hideous, revolting object never met my view.

But the ebon company thought differently, for when the music suddenly ceased, I saw a number of negroes and negresses throng around him to enjoy the privilege he willingly conferred, of twisting their heads from side to side, and wrenching their shoulders. Doubtless the frenzied state of the wretched man was considered to be the evidence of an inspiration from on high, or from below—which, made little difference, since the Algerian negroes most impartially address their prayers, now to Allah, now to Chitan (Satan).

This interlude was followed by other dances in the same place, of a similar character to that described; and a little way apart, a circle formed round a young woman, who tossed her head from side to side, and bounded upward, and turned heels over head, until, utterly exhausted, she sank back moaning into the arms of a negress beside her. Before I left the barbarous scene, the patient bull had terminated his existence. I have little doubt that he met his death with the stoic calmness which distinguished his life; but having turned away when I saw him conducted towards the sea for immolation, I ignore the details of his last moments, save that his final breath was drawn amidst vocal performances, accompanied by the beat and clink of drum and iron castanets. Immediately after his decease, many butchers set to work upon his carcase, to provide the materials for the entertainment which was to form the last act in the Aïd-el-Fould.

On the night succeeding the Feast of Beans, I was as involuntary, and as passive also, an actor in another festival, as was the poor animal who had enacted such a conspicuous rôle in the ceremony of the day; and, like it also, I played the part of victim. I did not die, however; happily, the sacrifice stopped short of that consummation—a fact not wholly unnecessary to mention in these days of familiar intercourse with the spirit world. To what order of revellers I served as victim during a warm May night, will be readily guessed by such of my readers as have passed a summer in a southern clime; and no less readily will they sympathise with my feelings of dismay, when, on waking up at morning from a deep sleep, I found that one eye utterly refused to open, whilst the other only permitted me a blinking vision; and, as this was accompanied by the discovery that my nose and mouth were utterly unfamiliar to my touch, I felt inclined to cry out, like the renowned little old woman in the nursery tale, 'Goodness mercy on me, sure this is none of I.'

What her little dog was to that remarkable female, a mirror was to me, and having seen sufficient evidence to convince me that I was really myself, memory so vividly recalled the booming hum of mosquito horns across my head before I fell asleep, that I was at no loss to trace my calamity to its source.

An Arab sowed a field of wheat, and when the wheat was just in ear and giving promise of a splendid crop, it was utterly devoured in a few minutes by a swarm of locusts. On seeing the ground, so lately green, as bare as a new ploughed field, the philosophic Arab exclaimed, with uplifted head and hands, 'Glory to God, who has given such marvellous powers to an insignificant insect.'

On looking at my swollen and distorted features, and considering the fragile form of my tiny foes, I fear my state of mind was very different from that which had prompted the philosophic Arab's exclamation, since I looked on, with a feeling of vindictive pleasure, as the housemaid's avenging broom flitted here and there along the mosquito-dotted walls on an exterminating mission. Few of the late revellers at my expense would ever have an opportunity of enjoying again an *Aïd-er-Roumia* (Feast of the Christian).

Every tale ought to have a moral. That no traveller should sleep in Algiers, in the month of May, without the protection of mosquito curtains, is the instructive lesson to be deduced from mine.

CHAPTER XXIII.

ACROSS THE PLAIN TO DELLYS—CHANGE OF PLAN—FRENCH COURTESY—A PRIMITIVE MODE OF TRAVEL—A BEAUTIFUL VIEW—FORT NAPOLEON.

WHAT has not been done, cannot be done, and should not be attempted, is a logic so popular in respect to ladies, that our proposition to proceed by land to Constantine evoked in Algiers a shower of assurances that the project was either wholly impracticable or highly dangerous. Audacious as our journey by land to Tlemcen had been thought, it was considered to be a mild specimen of '*la hardiesse Anglaise*' in comparison with the project to travel through Great Kabylia, a country yet destitute of French roads. Having often proved how ignorance is prone to create bugaboos, we were far from feeling assured that the project was as '*impossible*' as it was termed; but, yielding to public opinion, we agreed to adopt the usual mode of going to Constantine, by availing ourselves of the Government transport steamer which plies between Algiers and Philippeville, from whence to Constantine there is a French road.

But though it was '*impossible*' to travel through

Great Kabylia, yet, as no one disputed the propriety of our journeying by land as far as Dellys, a small French port at which the steamer touched, we availed ourselves of this concession to start early one morning from Algiers to Dellys in a public conveyance, that plied at certain intervals between the towns. The idea of another long voyage in a Government transport packet was deprived of some of its terrors by the consideration that a letter, kindly furnished us by Mr. Bell, the English Consul, to Captain Adeline, the Director of the Port of Dellys, would probably secure us first-class accommodation.

The features of the country through which we passed do not merit any detailed description. After leaving the bright Moorish villas and brilliant verdure of Mustapha, we traversed a dreary and, for the most part, brushwood-covered portion of the Metidja, to enter amidst a hilly country, cultivated here and there by a native population. The small inn at which we stopped for breakfast was the only European house I saw in this district; and it was the afternoon before we reached the next, a French caravanseraï, situated in the centre of the narrow valley of the river Isser. Here, the condition of the road necessitated a change of conveyance, and we were transferred from a species of diligence to a small char-a-banc. In this, we followed, through a somewhat picturesque valley, the course of the river Nessa, to the sea; then, turning directly towards the east, we proceeded along the side of a range of precipitous hills, which, as we neared Dellys, were clothed with the luxuriant verdure of a variety of fruit trees, whilst the roadside banks were lined with ferns and mosses, and overhung by roses and honeysuckle. We had left Algiers at the break of day, but the sun had almost set, when, after a long series of trying jolts, we entered the Hotel de la Colonie in Dellys.

Dellys is very finely situated on the rock-bound Algerian shores of the Mediterranean, at the foot of a lofty cliff that merges immediately towards the west into a long, narrow, precipitous point, to which the town is indebted for the usually safe harbour it enjoys. The ruined koubba, which rises on the summit of the natural mole, is surrounded on all sides by tombs—fit emblems, in their decay, of the forms they cover. A lighthouse, built on the extremity of the point, commands, towards the east, a magnificent view of a rock-bound coast, showing many a bold projecting headland. As for Dellys, it presents the usual Algerian features of a new French and old Arab town, which latter possessed the not very honourable distinction of being the dirtiest labyrinth of ruinous walls I had ever entered.

The Director of the Port, to whom we brought the letter, received us most politely; and, promising to convey us on board, said, that he had no doubt that his friend, the captain, would give us first-class accommodation.

We visited many native houses in Dellys and its vicinity; and, however poor the dwelling might be, the women inside wore massive silver ornaments, and in several instances, their eyes were encircled by an elaborate pattern, neatly executed with brown paint. Many of the girls and young women were very handsome; but some of the middle-aged and elderly were absolutely hideous. The mass of luxuriant foliage that overhung the paths leading to native dwellings in the country, rendered a visit to them a highly agreeable occupation; but in the town, the case was somewhat different, for, after daintily picking our way through crooked alleys reeking with vile odours, we had invariably to pass through a foul cow-house or stable, before entering the dwelling.

Here, as elsewhere, the natives received us with the utmost hospitality, and not a man with whom we spoke but assured us in the most earnest manner that the English and Arabs were brothers. Natives who looked sternly at us when they thought that we were French, held out their hands at once when they discovered we were English. On one of these occasions, a Moor, in the service of Government, made an observation that exercised an important influence on our proceedings.

'If you like to see high mountains and fine trees, you should visit Fort Napoleon and the country of the Kabyles.'

'We heard it would be dangerous to venture.'

A disdainful smile, and an assurance that we would be as safe from harm in Great Kabylia as in the Place du Gouvernement in Algiers, renewed our strong desire for a land journey to Constantine; and after a consultation on the subject, we determined to apply to the Director of the Port for his opinion on the question. Here, on the frontiers of Great Kabylia, reliable information was likely to be obtained.

The result of our application was highly satisfactory, for Captain Adeline's opinion as to the perfect safety of the proposed journey was confirmed by the words of an officer who had just arrived from Fort Napoleon. The affair having reached this stage, Captain Adeline proposed and undertook to submit the project to Colonel de Neveu, a high Government functionary, then at Dellys, who, in answer, sent us word that he would not only sanction, but facilitate the accomplishment of our scheme in every way he could. Knowing that a Government sanction carried with it the protecting power of some 80,000 soldiers, we no longer hesitated in carrying out our strong desire to visit Great Kabylia.* In an interview the succeeding day, the Colonel confirmed in person the message he had sent, and most courteously desiring his *chaoush* to assist us in making arrangements with a Caïd for the hire of mules and guides, we left

---

* Government holds itself responsible for the safety of every person who travels through the country under the sanction of the authorities. Certain routes are proscribed as dangerous.

his presence, bearing letters from him to the commanding officers of Tiziouzou and Fort Napoleon, and to the Bach Agha, Ben Ali Cherif, the chief of the district through which we were to pass.

Strong, however, as was my wish to visit Great Kabylia, my enthusiastic desire to explore its recesses underwent a chill, as, at an early hour on the ensuing morning, the mules provided for our use arrived at the hotel, for their meagre sides and rough hides, overhung by a pair of panniers, were infinitely more agreeable in a picturesque than a locomotive point of view. But, the first shock over, we proceeded undauntedly to smother, with rugs, cloaks, and shawls, an offending coil of ropes around the panniers, and on which it was intended we should sit. Our equipment thus completed, we mounted, and I found that it did not require a large amount of stoic philosophy to look benignly on the assemblage which, despite the early hour, had collected at the hotel to witness our departure. Jews had stepped forth from their just opened shops close by, to fix their keen glance on us and our arrangements. Arabs, with cord-girt heads, looked on with solemn wondering faces. Frenchmen, with expressive shrugs, spoke in low undertones of the incomprehensible travelling mania of the English; and little boys, French, Jew, and Arab, stared at us with wide-opened eyes, and sucked their fingers after the fashion of ingenuous youth in every clime.

Beside the mules on which we rode, we had a third to carry two travelling bags—our whole amount of luggage; and our retinue consisted of two Arabs, whose dress was somewhat obnoxious to criticism, but as we heard that they had been specially selected for our service from their estimable qualities, we looked with lenient eyes on the dilapidated burnous, the soiled haïk, and the goat-skin sandals, which formed their livery.

After leaving the town, we entered on a bridle track that wound up the side of a rugged hill thickly covered with brushwood, that gave place towards the summit to fields in which an Arab was here and there scratching the ground, by means of a plough formed out of the rudely chipped hooked trunk of a young tree, tied at one extremity to the centre of a long log that was fastened by straw ropes across the necks of a pair of bullocks, and guided at the other by a straight upright handle grasped by the ploughman's two hands. I saw in this primitive implement the probable facsimile of the plough used by my forefathers in the days of Julius Cæsar.

The track through which we passed was destitute of trees, except here and there, where a sheltered hollow amidst the hills showed a small grove of figs. The unattractive features of the scenery around our course enhanced, however, the effect of the beautiful prospect which suddenly burst upon our view, as, after a ride of about three hours, a turn round a projecting crag brought us to the brow of a richly-wooded gorge, backed by hills of varying height, that rose loftier and loftier in the distance, until they merged into the dark towering masses of the snow-crowned Djurjura.

Descending a steep path winding amidst fig and olive trees, we soon arrived at the Arab village of Beni Attar, perched midway on the height. The miserable cluster of dwellings, amidst which we passed, were constructed of interwoven reeds, whose interstices were filled up with mud and a cement composed of the sweepings of cattle sheds, whilst the structures were completed in a very suitable style by conical roofs of sticks thatched with coarse grass. A group of men reclining together in attitudes of indolent ease, seemed to think it too great a trouble to even raise their heads to look at the Christian strangers. The women, on the contrary, rushed forth to see us, and, staring as if we were apparitions from another world, afforded us the sight of an array of ugly, dirty, tattooed faces. As both hands and arms were elaborately embellished in a similar manner, the ladies of Beni Attar must be well qualified to recognise the correctness of the French saw, '*Il faut souffrir pour être belle.*'

After leaving the rich gorge, a couple of hours' ride over hills covered with gorse and fern, brought us to the banks of the river Sebaou, which, as we forded, benevolently gave me a contribution to fill my panniers, whilst the dark clouds that had gathered overhead, not to be outdone in generosity, added to their contents by a torrent of rain. Soon after passing the river, a cluster of white walls, with red-tiled roofs, which came into view, wore such a European civilised look, that I was greatly surprised to find that the village was inhabited by a Kabyle tribe. In point of architecture, it was very evident that the Kabyles were far advanced beyond the Arabs in civilisation.

A short ride through a treeless, but cultivated valley, brought us to the French settlement and military station of Tiziouzou. Thinking that we should stop here the night, Colonel de Neveu had furnished us with a letter to the commanding officer of the garrison, to bespeak his services on our behalf; but the small inn at which we halted was so dirty, untidy, and comfortless in look, that, hearing we could readily gain Fort Napoleon before nightfall, we determined to rest ourselves and mules for half an hour and then resume our journey. Whilst the Arabs munched bread and the mules ate barley outside the house, we sat within in a clothes-hung kitchen, partaking of a *déjeuner* consisting of bad *café noir*, brown bread, and a greasy omelet.

On leaving Tiziouzou, we proceeded along an imperfect carriage road which has been made between Algiers and Fort Napoleon; but as the old mule track was considerably shorter than the new highway, we soon abandoned the civilised route for a rugged path, which, after leading us through a shallow stream and along the side of a wide valley, conducted us up a lofty, precipitous, and richly-wooded hill, crowned with the white walls of a Kabyle village. The ascent was very steep, and as we advanced between hedges of cacti, overshadowed by the intermingling foliage of fig and olive trees, we got a glimpse every here and there of an emerald green glade of sprouting corn. Gaining, at length, the summit of the hill, there burst upon my view a scene whose varied features combined to form one of the most magnificent pictures I had ever beheld.

Sheer below me lay a deep ravine, whose precipitous banks, richly clothed with trees, were dotted with brilliantly green plots of corn, or grass. A range of lofty and well-wooded hills that rose beyond the gorge, was backed by the undulating verdant crests of ridge on ridge of still loftier hills, until their wavy outlines stood out in sharp relief against the soaring, bare, dark rocky masses of the snow-crowned Djurjura. A brilliant burst of light from the almost setting sun, enhanced the exquisite beauty of the scene, and in the golden radiance which shed a glow on the sparkling snow and dark lifeless crags of the towering Djurjura, and steeped the richly-wooded hills in a flood of lustrous light, the white walls of many a Kabyle village, perched like an eagle's nest on the summit of lofty peaks, gleamed out amidst an embowering mass of foliage.

Warned by the brilliant sunset glow that we should not dally, I reluctantly turned away from the glorious view, to proceed along a tree-shaded path that wound in and out amidst the projecting crags of the ridge of hills to whose summit we had ascended.

As the shades of evening commenced to fall, and dark clouds to gather overhead, we began to look out anxiously for Fort Napoleon, and we had mistaken for it many a Kabyle village that came into view, before we heard the welcome cry: '*Tchouf* (thou seest) *Souk-el-Arba*,'* as, winding round a projecting peak, I saw several rows of undoubted European buildings covering the brow of a near height. In ten minutes' time we had gained a fine military gate, which, passing through, we dismounted close by, at the door of a small house bearing the imposing title of Hotel d'Europe.

In civilised lands we should certainly not have been altogether satisfied with the accommodation afforded by the Fort Napoleon Hotel d'Europe; but as, immediately after our arrival, a heavy shower of rain dashed against the cracked panes of my one pigmy window, I looked up with much satisfaction to the low raftered ceiling which gave us effective protection from the storm.

* Souk-el-Arba, literally, market of Wednesday, the Arab name or Fort Napoleon.

CHAPTER XXIV.

GREAT KABYLIA—KABYLE AND ARAB CONTRASTED.

BEFORE proceeding further with the narrative of our journey through Great Kabylia, it may be well to give some information respecting the inhabitants of this region.*

Some historians trace the origin of the Kabyles to Canaan, the grandson of Noah. Other writers are contented to identify them with the ancient Numidians; but all agree in stating that this people are the descendants of the Berbers, who occupied a large extent of North Africa, at the period of the invasion of the Arabs. Previous to this era, their history is very obscure; but it is believed that the part of the Little Atlas mountains which now bears the name of Great Kabylia, was peopled at the epoch of the Roman conquest by fugitives from the rich plains of the sea coast, on which the conquerors seized. Roman ruins, so abundant in other parts of Algeria, being

---

* The greatest portion of the details contained in this chapter, have been derived from a work of General Daumas on Algeria.

almost absent from this district, it would seem as if the authority of Rome was never really established there. In subsequent centuries, though nominally subject to the Arab sway, the Kabyles were virtually independent, governing themselves in their own way. The Turks, on their arrival, raised some forts on the northern and southern slopes of the Djurjura, but obtained little more than such recognition of their authority as was implied by an assent to pray for the Sultan in the prescribed form. It was not till 1857 that the Kabyles of the Djurjura were brought really into subjection to a foreign rule.

The period of the adoption and the origin of the term Kabyle, are controverted points. At one time it is known that the inhabitants of the Djurjura were called by the Romans the *Quinque Gentii*; but no epoch can be fixed for the conversion of either this term or that of Berber into Kbäil—the word from which the French and English appellation of Kabyle is derived.

Except in the neighbourhood of the Djurjura, the Kabyles are thinly scattered along the seaboard range of the Atlas mountains, which extend from east to west in numerous chains, running parallel to the Mediterranean. Of the 800,000 Kabyles who inhabit Algeria, some 250,000 live amidst the group of mountains of which the Djurjura is the centre. Hence, the name of Great Kabylia given to this region by the French—a wholly modern term, as the Kabyles do not designate the country they inhabit by any special name. Each tribe, taking the name of the mountain on whose sides they live, are only linked together by the common individual designation of the term Kbäil.

Converted to Christianity in the early ages of the Church, the Kabyles adopted tenets which were considered so unorthodox at Rome, that attempts were made to convert them to sounder views, by the forcible argument of the sword; but, secure in their mountain fastnesses, the Emperor Maximilian and his legions vainly essayed to make them change one article of their creed. Strangely enough, however, what Rome could not do, was effected subsequently by the Arabs in the eighth century, though the Kabyles never gave any but a nominal submission to Arab rule; for, renouncing Christianity, they unanimously accepted the religion of Mohammed.

Still, though the Kabyles are nominally Mohammedans, they are but lukewarm Mussulmen, and, as a general rule, neglect to conform with most of the positive injunctions of the Koran. Though enjoined to pray five times a day, the Kabyle will probably not perform his devotions even once. He scruples not, in the holy month of Ramadam, to break his fast before the sun has set. He eats the flesh of the wild boar without compunction. He is an habitual drinker of brandy made from figs. Chiefs, maraboos, and tolbas (learned men) alone conform, amongst the Kabyles, with the requirements of their faith.

Little, however, as the Kabyle concerns himself about the due observance of his religious rites, he has a profound veneration for the saints whose koubbas crown his hills; and to their descendants, the maraboos of the present day, he yields willing homage. When quarrels occur between two tribes, it is the maraboos who adjust their differences. To the maraboos also belong the unquestioned right of directing and controlling the public choice in the matter of the election of a chief; and the chief himself must bow, in all emergencies, to the maraboos' decision. Lodged and fed at the public expense, the maraboo, amongst the Kabyles, is in every respect a highly-privileged man.

The Kabyle, like the Arab, is superstitious, but their superstitions differ. The talisman in which the Arab has unlimited faith as an averter of misfortune, is an object of contempt to the Kabyle, who, however, eagerly applies to old women with reputed witch-like gifts, for a charm that may render him beloved and his rival hated by some girl he desires to marry. He firmly believes in lucky and unlucky days. The journey commenced on Monday and Thursday may be accomplished safely, but that begun on Saturday will assuredly prove prosperous. No prudent man should set out on any expedition on a Wednesday, Friday, or Sunday. Tuesday must be avoided as a day of battle; and a blessing rests upon a house into which the bride has entered on a Thursday. A jackal seen on rising, or two crows at the commencement of a journey, are favourable auguries; but the sight of a hare in the evening, or of a solitary crow, is ominous of misfortune. Happy are those who die during the Ramadam, for then the gates of hell are closed, and those of heaven stand always open. Except in that sacred season the demons are to be greatly feared, and they are likely to assail the man who leaves a house at night without invoking the protection of Allah and the Prophet.

The Arab and the Kabyle are totally dissimilar in character. The indolent Arab, hating labour, and working only from the stimulus of necessity, looks on it as a degrading action; whilst the Kabyle, considering idleness a shame, not only diligently cultivates the soil, but applies himself to various branches of industry. With the waters of a mountain stream he irrigates his glens. The abundant oil yielded by his carefully grafted and tended olive trees, is sold in every town and market throughout Algeria. Woodsman and turner, amidst the declivities of his forest-clothed mountains he manufactures looms and platters, and labours as jeweller, smith, or armourer, in districts where the almost naked rock will produce neither corn nor trees. The tribe of the Beni Abbês make guns; the Flissa, sabres, ploughshares, knives; the Kboula, gunpowder; the Beni Sliman work iron mines; and the Kabyle, who lacks the means of profitable employment at home, readily leaves his mountains in search of fortune, to return at some future time with his hard-won earnings to his native village, where, building a house and buying a gun, cow, and wife, he enacts the gentleman.

The Arab has little regard for truth, but the Kabyle considers falsehood shameful. Arab tribes will attack each other without warning, and conquer by stratagem, if such be practicable; but the Kabyle tribes never engage in hostilities without an open declaration of war, and they scorn all trickery to advance their ends.

If the Arab has more money than suffices for his present wants, he hides it in the ground, whilst the Kabyle lends at interest, or buys cheap to sell again at a higher rate. Though the Arab loves the sound of music or the sight of dancing, he regards with infinite contempt such persons as thus minister to his pleasure; but the Kabyle loves to play on his little flute, and gaily dances in the company of his friends.

The Arab murderer who pays the *dia* (price of blood) to the family of his victim, escapes all further punishment under native laws; but amongst the Kabyles no money compensation is accepted, and the murderer is abandoned to the law of the *vendetta*, which imposes on every man the obligation of revenging the death of a near relative, and if the victim has neither a father, brother, or son, to discharge the debt of blood, the mother, wife, or sister will hire some man to avenge her loss. If too poor to pay from her own means the sum required to obtain a deputy-avenger, she begs from tribe to tribe until the amount is gained. Rarely does the murderer fail to forfeit his life in expiation of the one he has destroyed.

The Arab woman, even though she is allowed amongst Saharian tribes to go about with uncovered face, never joins in male society, is never free from espionage, and never shares the meals of her nearest male relative; but the Kabyle wife eats with her husband, goes unattended, with unveiled face, to market, to buy and sell, and sings and dances in the company of his friends. Sharing, too, in his industrial tastes, she spins and weaves; the burnous he wears has been altogether fashioned by her hands.

The difference between the two races extends to the government and organisation of their respective tribes. The Arab's code of law, founded on the Koran, is administered by a despotic chief, to whom the land occupied by the tribe belongs; but the Kabyle, the secure possessor of the soil he labours, is governed by a chief, who, elected by universal suffrage, can be deposed, if he fail in administering justice according to the traditional laws which have been handed down by father to son from a remote generation. From amongst the village chiefs a superior chief is elected to lead in war, when hostilities have been declared. Except when for any particular purpose they contract to form a league, the tribes are independent of each other.

As the Kabyle has retained his national laws, so likewise he has remained faithful to his national language, which is spoken with least admixture of foreign words by the tribes of Great Kabylia, but the Berber alphabet has been lost, and there does not exist one book written in that language. In the absence of a national literature, Arabic is taught in village schools, through the medium of which, the Kabyle youth learns half a dozen prayers, a few verses of the Koran, and to repeat in Arabic the formula of Islam, 'There is no God but God, and Mohammed is the messenger of God.' When, in some instances, the knowledge of reading and writing Arabic is added to these acquirements by a more prolonged term of study than is usually devoted to educational purposes, the proud possessor of such attainments acquires the name of *thaleb* (learned), and is qualified to become a teacher. The Kabyle school forms generally a portion of a group of public buildings bearing collectively the name of *Zaouia*, and consisting, in addition to the school, of a mosque, a koubba, a house for pupils, and another for travellers and beggars, to whom gratuitous lodging and food are furnished. Governed and superintended by maraboos who live there at public cost, the *Zaouia* presents a strong resemblance to the ancient monastic institution, and may possibly indeed have originated in Christian times. The ascetic practices adopted by one of the religious orders in Great Kabylia, afford also a striking analogy with those that prevailed amongst the Christian fanatics of an early day. Nor did the recluses of the Thebaïd mortify their bodies more than do the disciples of Cheik-el-Madhy, as each, enclosed in his little cave or cell, which permits him scarce room to move, and diminishing day by day his food until it reaches the minimum amount on which existence can be maintained, passes his life in prayer, meditation, and ecstasies. The known derivation of this sect from Egypt strengthens the likelihood of a Christian origin.

When such differences of character exist between two people inhabiting the same land, it is only natural that a mutual antipathy should be entertained; but bitterly as the Kabyles and Arabs hate each other, this feeling did not prevent them, under the inciting influence of a keen sense of a common danger, to co-operate vigorously to resist the French conquest of Algeria. But the Arab had long laid down his arms before the Kabyle gave up the unequal contest, and it was not until the fortifications of Fort Napoleon rose up amidst the rugged strongholds of Great Kabylia that the warlike tribes of the Djurjura made a real submission to the conquerors. From that day to this, a refusal, here and there, to pay the tributes imposed upon each tribe, has been the only sign displayed of a hatred of foreign rule; and on such occasions the appearance of a French detachment amidst the refractory tribes has sufficed to crush every evidence of an insurrectionary spirit.

CHAPTER XXV.

A KABYLE VILLAGE—A MARABOO HOST.

THE unprecedented apparition of two English ladies at Fort Napoleon, added in no small degree to the excitement caused by the anticipated arrival on the ensuing day of the Governor-General from Algiers. These two remarkable events, almost coincident in point of time, must have proved a most grateful *distraction* to the civil and military inhabitants of a secluded spot, destitute of theatre, fashionable promenade, and restaurants.

With the view of making arrangements for our onward journey through Great Kabylia, we left the hotel immediately after an early breakfast, to deliver our letter of introduction from Colonel de Neveu to the commanding officer of the garrison. On approaching his house, we saw signs of preparation for his expected guest, the grass before the door being strewed with litter, amidst which lay several large deal boxes, some empty and some unopened. We had no difficulty in procuring the desired interview, and, after reading the letter which we had brought, the Colonel very politely expressed his desire to aid us as far as he could.

'I expect the Bach Agha, Ben Aly Cherif, here this evening to meet the Governor-General,' he said. 'I will send you on through Great Kabylia, under his escort. He speaks French fluently, and is a well-educated man.'

'We are desirous to start as soon as possible,' we said.

'Arrange your own time, ladies; and I shall see that the Bach Agha accommodates his movements to suit yours.'

After stating that we desired to start on the ensuing morning, if practicable, we ended our visit, leaving the Colonel doubtless to meditate over the strange ideas of enjoyment entertained by English ladies.

And, assuredly, to such as fancy that ease and luxury constitute the great blessings of life, our project might well seem strange; and as, with rare exceptions, Frenchmen think that social pleasures, balls, concerts, theatres, are all-sufficient to satisfy the aspirations for happiness of the human heart, to them especially does the English propensity to court hardship as an enjoyment, appear more like the impulse of a deranged than a rational mind. The romance which leavens the English character is absent in theirs. Hardship with them has no pleasant side, the mastery of difficulty no charm. To them life is a prosaic thing. To live well, talk, dance, sing, to amuse oneself from youth to age, that is the French ideal of happiness. If such an ideal also exists in England, it is the ideal of but a few.

As to this projected journey of ours through Great Kabylia, it commended itself, I believe, to both our minds by the romance attaching to the unknown. Assured of safety as we emphatically had been, we were well satisfied to undergo a few days' hardship for the sake of journeying through a fine mountainous region, where no guide book would authoritatively prescribe the sensations that we were to feel. Unimaginative people like to be told the train of ideas suitable to each sight they see. Not lacking imagination, I prefer to pronounce for myself as to whether this or that scene and object is to be admired, or the reverse. To one whose life has been passed far more in the realms of fancy than in the real world, the faculty of judgement comes easily. And the unknown has, from my earliest years, had a great charm for me. Even to that unknown land 'beyond mortal ken' my thoughts have ever willingly soared. The glittering stars in the midnight sky, the roar of the breaking wave, the voice of the tempest, and every grand scene and sound in nature, fill my heart with a solemn joy, and an ardent longing to penetrate the mystery of infinity.

The Colonel's dwelling was magnificently situated on the very crest of the lofty hill on whose summit the town is built; and the prospect from this height was still more beautiful than that I had seen the preceding evening, by the golden light of the setting sun. For though, in the main, the features of the scene were much the same, our closer vicinity to the Djurjura gave an added majesty to his snow-crowned head, as it towered aloft over high precipitous wooded hills, whose every peak was crowned with a cluster of white gleaming cottages. The brilliant spring verdure of the deep semicircular gorge I immediately overlooked; the undulating crests of mountain chains, fading one behind another into the haze of distance; and the pure transparent air of a lovely May morning—all combined to form a truly magnificent scene.

The site on which Fort Napoleon stands was not in the occupation of the French until the end of May 1857, when the tribes of the Beni Raten, who live amongst these heights, were finally conquered after a long and fierce resistance. To maintain the supremacy which had been so arduously gained, Fort Napoleon was built with a marvellous rapidity. In five months after the first stone was laid, the small citadel town, with its imposing array of numerous military buildings enclosed by walls, pierced by two handsome marble gateways, was completed as it now stands. A road by which it is approached from the vale below was made by the troops in the heat of the conflict with the resisting tribes. The civil population, whose scanty numbers occupy one half-built line of street, are merely camp followers. Encircled by precipitous and already populous hills, Fort Napoleon can never be anything more than a military station.

Being anxious to see a Kabyle village, we resolved to visit one of the many visible in the immediate neighbourhood of the fort. A market that was being held immediately outside the Djurjura gate, afforded, at the commencement of our walk, a good opportunity of observing the appearance of the inhabitants of this region, and the favourable impression produced by a distant view of their dwellings was somewhat reversed by the dirty and scantily-clothed figures amongst whom we passed. If the Arab shaves his head, he has the good taste to conceal his bare poll by a picturesque cord-bound haïk; but these Kabyles, with bristling hair scarce an inch in length, wore no other covering on their heads than a diminutive black leather cap, fitting closely to the crown, and many wore none at all. A loose woollen tunic, descending to the knees, was the sole garb of many; others added to this dress a large greasy leather apron; and the small number of burnouses which I saw, evidenced in their stains and rents a respect for antiquity that was far from pleasing. Such as were not barefooted, wore sandals of goat skin, and had rags swathed by cords around their legs by way of stockings. Squatted around bags of grain, wool, corn, dried figs, and pepper pods, they talked together with animation; but I saw few faces that did not wear a somewhat stern, and occasionally fierce expression. The listless Arab look was nowhere visible. Passing onward through the assemblage, we proceeded along the narrow crest of a richly-wooded hill, on whose summit rose the village we desired to visit.

Looking up on one side to the snow-capped Djurjura, and down on the other into a deep gorge, clothed with the most brilliant verdure, we wound along the height through a thicket of lavender, cistus, and thorny broom. It was not long before we reached the village, where our arrival was proclaimed by the angry barks and growls of some fierce-looking dogs, which at once arrested our progress, as we well knew that such demonstrations of hostility were not to be disregarded with impunity.* Waiting patiently for the alarm to produce its invariable effect, we soon saw a woman issue from a house close by, and after a well-aimed fire of stones had sent the dogs howling to their homes, she signed to us to follow her. Gladly complying

* Algerian dogs are the fiercest of their kind. A wild-beast nature seems ever to prevail amongst them. Their bite is horrible, for they tear out the flesh in which they have once fixed their teeth. During my winter at Algiers, two children were each dreadfully bitten by a house dog. No Arab will approach his neighbour's house without a previous call to secure the dogs.

with her summons, we proceeded onward, down a steep short winding descent amidst a cluster of houses, into a long straight street, bordered with substantially built dwellings of stone and mortar, roofed with red tiles.

The throng of women that soon gathered around us, plied us evidently with eager questions; but as we did not understand a word of what they said, we could make no response but a shake of the head, which, however significantly it may be done, is not quite sufficient for conversational requirements. Under these circumstances, it was highly agreeable to have the assembly increased by the addition of a young man, who, rushing forward to shake hands, called out exultingly—

'*Moi saper Français. Francais buono. Toi Français?*'

'*Non; Anglais.*'

'*Kif-kif* (alike) *buono; Anglais buono, Français buono; tout buono,*' returned our accomplished friend—'*Moi maraboo, moi Turco,** *moi saper Français. Venir mon casa, venir; Anglais buono; venir—venir.*'

Yielding to the urgent invitation, we followed the

---

* The term Maraboo, as has been previously stated, is now, for the most part, a mere title of nobility, and Turco is the name given to a body of native infantry in the French service. The term Zouave is derived from the name of the Kabyle tribe who first yielded submission to French authority.

maraboo, who exultingly led us onward to his house. In comparison with the Kabyles I had seen in the market he was sumptuously arrayed—a distinction he probably owed to his noble birth. A blue jacket and trousers were visible underneath the folds of a very white burnous, whilst the largest portion of his cropped head was covered with a fez. A small leather bag, suspended at his side by a long leather strap hung round one shoulder, completed his attire. His smiling jovial face contrasted pleasantly also with the stern expression of those of his countrymen I had lately seen.

Informing us that he was not yet married, the maraboo ushered us into his dwelling, which consisted of one small room, with a square unglazed aperture for window. A few cooking vessels, a water pitcher, a palm brush and basket, and a roll of mats in the corner, constituted the whole furniture of the interior. Giving the brush to one of the many women who followed us in, the maraboo directed her to sweep away some ashes lying upon a broad ledge of mason-work projecting from the wall. This done, the mats were dragged forth from a corner to be laid upon the newly cleaned spot, and on the mats, our host spread out his own burnous, covering that again with two coloured cotton handkerchiefs. The seat of honour being thus prepared, we were requested to sit down on it.

All the women present were elaborately tattooed,

but however varied the pattern imprinted upon their faces, each showed a small cross on cheek or forehead, probably a relic of the forsaken creed of their forefathers. If it had not been for these disfiguring marks, the young women and girls would have been very well-looking, for they had mostly fair complexions and regular features, combined in general with an intelligent expression. Both young and old wore large, rudely-fashioned, clumsy ornaments, composed of coral and silver, and from under a coloured scarf flung round their shoulders a long white skirt descended to their feet. As the room was too small to contain conveniently more than a few spectators at a time, our host most considerately made our numerous visitors take in turn the honour of admission to our presence, and when he failed to keep a flock of little boys at bay, by assailing them with grimaces and French oaths, he finally put them all to flight by a threatening rush into their midst. With the exception of the maraboo's young brother, the assemblage was composed of women, one of whom the maraboo specially introduced to our notice as ' mon frère,' after having introduced the youth in the same manner.

From the specimens that have been given of the maraboo's style of speaking French, it may be readily supposed that we found some little difficulty in the interchange of ideas. Indeed, the construction of his sentences was so very peculiar that they often altogether baffled our comprehension, and we generally said '*oui*' and '*non*' in answer to his observations, without having the smallest idea what it was we were negativing or affirming. The words '*les montagnes*' stood, I believe, in his vocabulary for half a dozen meanings; and as to the signification of the phrase '*les montagnes venir moi beaucoup*,' no subsequent reflection has ever enabled me to discover, and it is my opinion that no amount of reflection ever will enable me to solve the question. Whatever it was, I assented to it most emphatically, after finding that a '*non*' produced rather a look of disappointment.

As the maraboo seemed to have quite as much difficulty in understanding our French as we had in understanding his, he quickly renounced his conversational attempt for a new method of entertaining us. Producing pen, ink, and a small blank book from his leather bag, he wrote his name in very neat Arabic characters, in return for which attention I wrote mine underneath, but as he knew as little of the characters in which I wrote as I knew of those he used, the result was not particularly satisfactory; and closing his book he demanded eagerly, '*Toi mangiar tabac?*'

Some very emphatic negatives having apparently convinced the maraboo that we did not relish this luxury, he next demanded, '*Toi mangiar couscousou?*'

Decidedly, however, as we also negatived this proposition, the maraboo, after begging of us to await his return, went off to the dwelling of his mother, to get her to prepare the proffered dish; but no sooner was he gone than, after agreeing it would be well to escape the menaced feast, we left the house also.

Proceeding along the central street, amidst houses quite as substantially built as those we had seen before, we soon arrived at a small mosque, built on the brink of a tremendous precipice. Thus compelled to retrace our steps, we had not proceeded more than a few yards, when we met the maraboo, and after a pathetic reproach for our desertion, he entreated us to return to drink the small can of milk that he was carrying in his hand. Hearing no farther mention of the dreaded couscousou, we allowed the maraboo to conduct us back to the seat of honour we had clandestinely quitted.

Having resumed our seats, the maraboo brought forth and placed between us a dish of dried figs, after which he rushed about from corner to corner of the room, as if in search of some missing article, and at length, with an exulting shout, he waved aloft a small white delft cup, which, on being washed, was placed with the can of milk beside the figs. Then whilst we ate, or rather feigned to eat, he produced a short wooden pipe, and whilst the young brother stamped his feet alternately, and chanted '*deb a deb, dig a doo, deb a deb, dig a doo,*' in a monotonous cadence, the maraboo, playing upon his pipe, commenced to dance in a most energetic manner, till suddenly varying the entertainment, he dropped the pipe, and after seizing his brother's hands and whirling round and round with marvellous rapidity, he finally turned a somersault by way of climax to the performance.

Thus does a noble of Great Kabylia entertain his guests!

On our rising to leave, the maraboo, much disappointed to find that the figs had but little diminished in quantity, insisted that we should fill our pockets with the remainder, and declaring vehemently that we did not '*saper le route*,' he marched on before us through the village. Picking up on his way a handful of olives spread out upon the ground to dry, he offered them to us, and after our refusal of the proffered delicacy, he began to eat them with much apparent relish. Shortly arriving at a well-beaten path leading to the Fort, the maraboo stopped, and looking regretfully at his oily hands, he happily seemed to be impressed with the conviction that the parting salutation must be limited to the exchange of a '*bon jour*.'

As a gorgeous sunset shed a glowing light upon the magnificent scenery round Fort Napoleon, the roar of cannon reverberating amongst the heights announced the arrival of the Governor-General of Algeria.

CHAPTER XXVI.

A TRYING ORDEAL — ROUGH RIDE — ROUGH QUARTERS — ON TO AKBOU — A DELIGHTFUL SURPRISE — A CURIOUS SCENE — A CIVILISED DINNER.

EARLY the ensuing morning the Colonel notified to us that, as the Bach Agha had not arrived, he had arranged to send us onward towards Akbou, under the escort of a Kabyle caïd, in whose house we would pass the night. We might start forthwith, if such was our desire. Mules and guides from the Bureau Arabe could be furnished instantly. Agreeing on the propriety of a speedy departure, we were soon prepared to resume our journey; and, in a primitive style, similar to that in which we left Dellys, we started from the hotel.

Our departure from Fort Napoleon took place under very trying circumstances, for, after slowly progressing, in market-woman fashion, through a street swarming with officers and soldiers in their smartest uniforms, we had scarcely passed out of the Djurjura gate, and escaped from the scrutinising glances of the lounging throng, when the Governor-General and his glittering staff came into view, advancing directly towards us. A high bank on one side, and a steep descent on the other, cut off all means of evading an encounter, and as we ran the gauntlet of a long line of doffed plumed hats, accompanied by a dropping fire of '*bon voyage*,' Colonel de Neveu, who was amongst the cavalcade, had the malice to follow up his hearty English 'good bye,' with the assurance that we were quite fit to make our appearance in the Bois de Boulogne.

At a village close by, we were joined by the Kabyle caïd, a lean, sharp-featured, stern-countenanced, elderly man, dressed in burnous and fez. Unlike the ever-courteous Arabs, he passed on before us without the slightest greeting, and I was confidentially informed by one of our Arab attendants that the caïd was a 'donkey,' who did not understand one word of French or Arabic. The jargon in which this intimation was conveyed was a fine specimen of the critic's own lingual attainments.

Winding along the ridge of a precipitous and well-wooded chain of village-crowned hills, each deep ravine that opened on our view showed, in its hollow and on its slopes, the signs of careful cultivation. The bright green foliage of the fig was visible in every sheltered nook, amidst the abounding olive which clothed the heights. Passing at times under a thick canopy of over-arching trees, we emerged from shade, to wind through thickets of broom, and of exquisitely fragrant white heath. Our rugged path became still more rugged, as, rising upward by an occasionally interrupted series of short sharp ascents, we reached, at length, an elevation considerably greater than that on which the Fort is built, and commanding, a still more extensive view of the billow-like crests of olive-crowned hills, gleaming here and there with the eyrie of a Kabyle tribe.

It was late in the afternoon before we reached the vicinity of the village in which our escort and destined host, the caïd, lived. Built on a low conical hill, rising in the centre of a deep well-wooded glen, I remarked regretfully, whilst admiring its picturesque position, that it showed no gleam of white-washed walls. Bad as our path had hitherto been, it was a triumph of engineering skill compared with that by which we descended, amidst the luxuriant foliage of the glen, to the village in its centre. Dismounting, as did the caïd also, we stumbled onward over a deep bed of loose rubble stone, leaving our guides to concentrate their energies on the task of preserving the mules from broken knees. Gaining the banks of a small stream that ran through the glen, we remounted, and a short steep ascent soon brought us to the caïd's village.

Entering amidst a cluster of un-whitewashed walls, we threaded our way along a narrow street, overarched here and there by the projecting second story of a house. As these archways were invariably very low, whilst my mule was tall, I felt thankful to find myself at length in the small paved court of the caïd's house, with my head uninjured.

Whilst waiting in the court, in accordance with our guide's directions, until a room had been prepared for our reception, we became the centre of a group of women, who, emerging from the various doors which opened off the court, flocked with eager faces round the wonderful strangers. All showed elaborately tatooed faces, each bearing the impress of a small cross, as in the Kabyle village near Fort Napoleon. A large massive silver brooch was stuck in front of the coloured handkerchief that girt each head, and another silver brooch, precisely resembling in form the ancient Irish fibula, fastened a scarf worn round the shoulders. Some of the young women were very well looking, but it seemed to me that both their persons and attire would have been much embellished by the application of soap and water.

On an intimation being speedily made that our room was ready, we turned towards our allotted quarters, and with sundry misgivings we entered a dark, low, but rather spacious apartment, in the centre of which was a carpet covering a portion of a large mat, that had been spread out upon the recently swept earthen floor. No other furniture was visible, but feeling assured that we would have an ample amount of fresh air to breathe, we forgave the deficiency. A second glance, however, having showed us a low stake partition on either side, bearing a suspicious likeness to stalls for cattle, we exchanged somewhat rueful glances, and in the midst of our uneasy speculations on the subject, four cows marched in to occupy the partition to the left, whilst a mule took up his quarters on our right hand with an air of indisputable authority.

After the first shock of discovery, we immediately rallied, and acting on the admirable philosophic principles of Mark Tapley, we agreed that to have four-legged companions in a large room was better than to be huddled into a small nook with the far from cleanly women who thronged around us. Besides, only a few hours' discomfort was before us, as the nights were short, and at break of day we could resume our journey.

The caïd's brother, a well-looking young man with fair complexion and sandy hair, devoted all his energies to our service. After bringing us figs and milk, he was able, by a few words he possessed of Arab French, to make us understand that later in the evening we should partake of couscousou: and when we expressed a desire to explore the village, he led the way with an air of exultation, bearing aloft my parasol, which he seemed to consider in the light of a state canopy. The houses amidst which we passed were all well-built structures, showing externally good walls and roofs, but the interiors were dark and dirty, and almost destitute of furniture.

The shades of evening were thickly falling when we returned to our Hôtel de La Grand Kabylie.

Before very long, the promised dish of couscousou arrived; and, whether or no influenced by hunger I cannot say, but I thought it a very commendable specimen of Kabyle culinary art. After dinner, regally dismissing the numerous company that had formed at a little distance in a circle round us, we prepared to try what amount of sleep was procurable.

The result of my night's experience does not warrant me in advising any lady or gentleman, with Sybarite tendencies, to follow our steps through Great Kabylia; for although the cows proved quite inoffensive neighbours, the mule had a highly unpleasant fashion of snorting and shaking himself continually. With our leather bags for bolsters, and an animated carpet for beds, we were truly rejoiced to see the light of dawn begin to penetrate through the crevices of the door. After a toilet, that was limited to washing hands and faces with the contents of a small water pitcher, we were ready to start forward on our journey.

Our parting with the caïd was somewhat stormy; for, having stoutly resisted his desire to substitute other mules and guides for those which had been furnished us by the Bureau Arabe at Fort Napoleon, he waxed indignant at our defiance of his authority, and he had not recovered his equanimity when, after distributing some gifts amongst his household, we rode off. His young brother, however, with unabated evidence of good will, accompanied us down the steep descent up which we had come the preceding evening, and intimated his willingness to accompany us to Akbou, if such were our desire. Whilst declining his offer, and bidding him '*bon jour*,' I regretted that I could not conveniently present him with my parasol, which he evidently considered a masterpiece of mechanism, and a triumph of civilisation.

After crossing the stream which ran through the glen, our mules had a most arduous scramble up a precipitous wooded bank to the summit of a hill, crowned on either hand by a wall of light grey crags, thickly streaked with lines of deep red hue. Looking towards the lofty Djurjura, I saw regretfully that its snowy peak rose now so far behind, that it would probably soon altogether vanish from view; and in a very short time it ceased to be visible.

Entering on a bleak, bare, uncultivated mountainous tract, the scenery through which we rode was utterly devoid of interest until, after a couple of hours, we reached a point from which there broke upon our view a cultivated and well-wooded valley, bounded by high hills extending in parallel chains, ridge behind ridge, in the distance, and dotted here and there with a white village.

'Akbou!' exclaimed our guides simultaneously, as they pointed to a cluster of red-tiled roofs, only a few miles distant. Advancing towards the village by a steep descent, we began to speculate somewhat anxiously on the subject of our quarters for the ensuing night; as we little relished the idea of a repetition of our late experiences. Naturally, a Bach Agha, and moreover a descendant of the Prophet,* would live in a style of greater luxury than a village caïd; and, meditating on the matter, we permitted ourselves to hope that Ben Ali Cherif would give us cushions for a couch, and a room unshared by four-legged tenants.

A near view of the village of Akbou somewhat dimmed our hopes; and as we halted at the Bach Agha's house, its exterior blighted them completely, till one of our men, who had entered the house, returned to say that, although the Bach Agha's family dwelt there, we were to proceed onward down the hill to another house of his, where he ordinarily lived; and in about half an hour after leaving the village, our guides, directing our notice to a large isolated white building, rising near a river which ran through the valley, gave us the cheering information that this highly respectable looking structure was the Bach Agha's house. From that moment we considered the cushion question as satisfactorily decided.

Soon reaching our destination, we skirted two sides of a high white wall, to arrive at a lofty arch-

* The word Cherif, attached to the name, signifies that its proprietor is descended from Fatima, the daughter of Mohammed.

way leading underneath a high range of buildings into a large courtyard, at whose farther side was another goodly range of buildings. The sight seemed so unreal in the heart of an uncivilised land, that I felt as in a dream, even before a Frenchman hastily advanced with a polite bow, to greet us with a cordial ' bon jour.'

'We bring a letter for the Bach Agha,' I said; 'is he at home?'

' Unfortunately, ladies, he is absent. Summoned to Constantine by the General of the Division there, he left this morning. But as far as your accommodation is concerned, his absence will make no difference. Pray alight; you must have need of rest and food. You can have immediately a cup of coffee, and in half-an-hour I shall have a *déjeûner* prepared.'

The whole force of human eloquence seemed to be concentrated in the Frenchman's words. Coffee and a *déjeûner* were verily exquisitely harmonious sounds to persons whose preparation for a six hours' ride had been a breakfast composed of dry bread and a draught of sour milk.

Dismounting amidst a number of Arab retainers, the Frenchman ushered us into a lofty saloon, furnished with a mahogany dining-table and chairs, whilst the painted walls were hung with pictures. Begging us to sit down till he brought us coffee, he left, to return immediately with the welcome beverage; and, whilst we were drinking it, two Arabs, dressed in snowy haïks and burnouses, entering the room, sat down a short way off. Hearing from the Frenchman that the one was the nephew and the other the Arab secretary of the Chief, we handed to them the letter with which we had been furnished by Colonel de Neveu.

After drinking our coffee, which was poured into china cups out of a silver coffeepot, we followed the civil Frenchman up a wide flight of stairs, and then along a gallery into a room, whose aspect made me more and more imagine that I was truly an inhabitant of the land of dreams. Cushions, and the exclusive occupancy of a room to ourselves, being the highest limits to which our most glowing hopes had reached, it was positively quite bewildering to find myself in a large and lofty room, furnished in a style of luxurious Parisian splendour. From the soft carpet on which I trod, I raised my eyes to a large tent bed and two lofty windows draped by crimson damask curtains. A costly wardrobe here, confronted there a high pier glass ; and, as my sweeping glance took in every luxurious feature of the scene, I sank down on the soft crimson sofa by my side, with the sensation, of having realised that fairy tale in which the wandering stranger, through desolate wilds, arrives at the door of an enchanter's palace. Truly, our preceding night's quarters had a salt olive-like power in giving zest and flavour to the sometimes palling luxuries of civilised life.

After a rest and an excellent *déjeûner*, I examined curiously the interior of the Bach Agha's house. Amidst the civilised splendour of its general aspect the influence of barbarism was visible in its details. Though only six years old, the house showed symptoms of decay, and disorder was rife within the walls. Our bedroom door had lost its handle, and several other doors were in a similar plight. Scarce an uncracked or unbroken pane of glass was visible in the windows which lit the inner court. The handsome balustrade extending around the gallery off which the bedrooms opened was draped with blankets and soiled burnouses, and immediately below our luxuriously furnished chamber, a group of Arabs squatted cross-legged on a mat, in the midst of vacancy, bounded by bare walls.*

Outside, civilised and uncivilised life met together in curious contrast. Here, I saw a French cook presiding over a French *cuisine*, and there, a group of women, with tatooed faces, busily engaged in the manufacture of couscousou. In an arbour erected in the centre of a small garden, laid out in formal beds and walks, the Agha's secretary prostrated himself in prayer, whilst we stood close by conversing with the French gardener; ourselves, amidst the swarming retainers of the Chief, formed, perhaps, not the least incongruous features of the picture.

* From Bougie, the nearest sea-port town, the furniture was brought some sixty miles by mules, over a mountain path.

In answer to a question, the Frenchman told me that as this house was the frequent halting place of French officers on their way through Great Kabylia, it was considered not to be a sufficiently private residence for ladies belonging to the Bach Agha's household; and on my speaking of the visible dilapidations going on, he said that already a considerable portion of the original furniture and decorations of the rooms had been pilfered by the Chief's dependants.

The Bach Agha's nephew and secretary joining us at dinner, sat down, plied knife and fork in Christian fashion, and, in defiance of the Koran, drank wine. The nephew, a rather coarse-featured and dull-looking young man, did not seem altogether at ease in dispensing the rites of hospitality towards his unwonted guests; but the far better looking secretary was perfectly self-possessed, and acted, I observed, by looks and undertones, as a Mentor to the evidently raw youth beside him. As neither could speak a word of French, I was obliged to labour painfully in Arabic to do the polite in conversation.

We had an excellent dinner, entirely French in character, save for a dish of couscousou that closed the entertainment; after which, followed by our hosts, we went upstairs to a very large and handsomely decorated drawing room, where, amidst rich crimson damask draperies, painted walls, large mirrors, luxurious sofas, and easy chairs, we were served with coffee poured from a richly chased silver coffee-pot into delicate porcelain cups.

Before we went to bed, we made arrangements for the continuation of our journey on the succeeding day. The nephew promised to furnish us with guides and mules, and a letter to his father, the Caïd Ahmed Ben Jeddo, in whose house we were to pass the ensuing night. Hearing it was a long day's journey from Akbou to that place, we begged that the mules should be ready to start at dawn.

CHAPTER XXVII.

THROUGH GREAT KABYLIA — BEAUTIFUL SCENERY — A LONG DAY'S JOURNEY — CAÏD AHMED'S HOUSE — SCENES IN ARAB LIFE — A HOSPITABLE CAÏD — ENTRY INTO SETIF.

DAWN broke amidst a drizzling rain, which was still falling when, after waiting some time for the expected mules, they at length arrived. The nephew was at the door to see us off, and to give the promised letter to his father into the hands of an Arab retainer, whom he sent with us. When we found that our escort mounted our baggage-mule, on which on former occasions our two guides had ridden in turn, we regretted not having at our disposal an extra mule, unprocurable now without a loss of time that we could not possibly spare. The civil Frenchman, adding to the benefits he had already conferred, furnished us with a store of bread, meat, and wine, which would render us entirely independent of native fare until our arrival, on the ensuing day, at the French town of Setif.

A short steep descent bringing us to the bed of the river Akbou, we forded it, to ascend a rugged path winding along the side of a range of hills, which, with an opposite chain, bounded the valley.

A KABYLE INTERIOR.

As we advanced, village after village came into view, each perched on high, and often crowned by a white *koubba*, that gleamed forth brightly amrdst the luxuriant foliage of the abounding olive; whilst, lower down the heights, bright plots of corn intermingled with groves of figs and pomegranates. The dark clouds, from which a heavy rain poured down, altogether hid the distant prospect.

After a ride of several hours, the rain cleared off, just as we gained a conical peak crowned by a village, at which our escort proposed we should halt for breakfast; and on our assent he led the way to a caïd's house, through the cleanest and best built cluster of Kabyle dwellings with which I had yet made near acquaintance. Dismounting at an archway, flanked inside by stone benches, we passed through a court to enter a clean, lofty, airy, and well-lit room with brilliantly white walls, two of whose corners showed large bottle-shaped earthen vessels for holding grain. A small shallow basket, hung from the ceiling by long cords, served as a cradle for an infant, whom a young woman was swinging to sleep as we entered. Two other women were also present, and, but for their tatooed faces, would have been very well-looking, besides exhibiting the merit of being cleanly in dress and person. As I sat down on a leather-cushioned bench, I indulged the hope that the Caïd Ahmed's house would present as agreeable an aspect.

Declining the proffered couscousou on the plea of inability to wait for its preparation, we breakfasted from our private stores, whilst our escort, reclining on the floor, munched figs and bread with much apparent satisfaction. But the thought of the long day's journey that was before us, made him soon give the signal for proceeding; and after a short halt, we remounted and went onward.

The bright gleams of sunshine that now broke through the still dark clouds above our heads, gave added brilliancy to the rich verdure of the numerous deep glens that lay around the height on which the village stood; and on every side the undulating outlines of mountain-chains that rose, ridge behind ridge, in the distance, formed a grand framework for the scene. Descending by a steep and rugged path to a river running through a valley immediately at our feet, we entered on the wide gravelly bed of a then insignificant stream, fringed with oleanders, whose beautiful pink flowers were just beginning to show amidst the dusky foliage. The chains of hills that rose on either side were thickly dotted with olives, which in many places sprung from a bright red earth, entirely destitute of any other vegetation. Ever as we advanced along our primitive road, village after village came into view, crowning the heights above.

After a short mid-day halt by the river's side, we again proceeded onward, and, leaving the gravelly bed through which we had long been travelling, we wound up a steep hill through a thicket of white cistus in full bloom. As a magnificent view was opening out with our advance, down from the horizon rushed a mass of storm clouds towards us, and as the wind and rain swirled round our heads, my mule stumbled, fell, rolled over, and though happily drawn unhurt from a somewhat perilous position on the brink of a steep bank, I rose up ignominiously covered with mud.

The storm soon passed off, and by the time we arrived at the summit of the height, the heavy clouds were resting in dark billow-like masses on the tops of distant mountains, whilst bright gleams of sunlight streaked the sides and crests of the nearer hills, whose varied forms were indescribably picturesque and beautiful. Here, they turned towards us sharp angular sides, all richly wooded; there, they were grouped in chains, whose undulating ridges and conical peaks were crowned with white gleaming villages, whilst the recesses of the deep glens around, were clothed with the brilliant emerald vegetation of early spring.

A steep descent, followed by an abrupt ascent, brought us before long immediately opposite to the dark rocky masses of a mountain called Beni Yala, over which we had to cross; and the path we followed led upward through the centre of one of the many villages which clung to its steep sides. This, Ginzet, as our escort called it, had quite the look of a small European town, save for the stony rugged lanes that formed its streets. A high round fort rose up above a large cluster of well-built houses, and to a long low structure with an arcaded front, our French-speaking Arab escort gave the imposing epithet of *college*.

Our progress through the village created a deep sensation, but whilst most of the Kabyle men we met saluted us with a friendly *buono*, the juvenile population of the town, which speedily congregated in our train, soon began to rend the air with shouts which, I felt assured, were not of a complimentary character, from the deprecating tone in which our Kabyle guides exclaimed several times 'muchecho * maboul' (children are fools). Soon tired of following up the steep ascent, our juvenile enemies, halting in the outskirts of the village, uplifted their shrill voices in an uproarious parting shout, accompanied by a general upward toss of caps and handkerchiefs.

As we proceeded up the rocky heights of Beni Yala, the eastern boundary of Great Kabylia, we entered into a mist, whose density rendered us unable to see beyond the distance of a few yards, and on reaching the summit, instead of the glorious parting view of the Kabyle country which we would

* *Muchecho* is a Spanish word in general use amongst the Arabs of Algeria. Many other words of similar, or of Italian origin, are grafted on their language. Algerian Arabic is at the present day a mongrel language, almost unintelligible in Syria or Egypt.

have assuredly seen on a clear day, stone walls were not more impenetrable to the eye than the thick darkness which hemmed us in. After a steep descent, we emerged from mist and fog to traverse narrow, uncultivated, uninhabited shallow valleys, between low hills, scantily dotted with juniper and evergreen oak.

The sun had almost set, when we gained a point from which we could see the white walls of the Caïd Ahmed Ben Jeddo's house, rising in lonely dignity on the conical summit of an eminence in a narrow valley. Its distant view was satisfactory enough to raise pleasant anticipations in regard to the character of our night's quarters. Our visions were not so glowing, however, as to make us expect we should find another fairy-like palace in Algerian wilds.

Our mules having had but little time to feed that day, we shortly dismounted amidst some luxuriant grass, for which they unequivocally showed a strong inclination, and, accompanied by our escort, to whom a sore foot gave a hobbling movement, a short ascent brought us in a few minutes to a low range of buildings, enclosed by a white wall. After exchanging a fraternal kiss with the Arabs who came forth to meet us, our escort, begging us to wait outside, entered the court to deliver his letter to the caïd.

Speedily returning, the Arab, telling us to follow him, led the way through a large court to a low building; on entering which, I found myself in a small room, showing a ceiling of rafters, begrimed with smoke, and lit by a diminutive window destitute of glass. A large chest confronting a carpet, edged along the walls by a long bolster-shaped cushion, and some cooking vessels, formed the whole amount of furniture I saw. Taught by experience, we were somewhat alarmed by the sight of a low partition at the far end of the room.

A middle-aged man in a blue burnous, and a handsome young woman, decked out with silver ornaments, were in the room; and the man, instantly applying his natural bellows to the task of blowing up some charcoal embers, smouldering in a small round hole in the earthen floor, speedily manufactured two very excellent cups of coffee, thoroughly to be appreciated after our long day's ride. Whilst drinking it, we were greeted by the welcome appearance of two large mattress-shaped cushions, which, deposited on the carpet, formed, with the adjoining bolsters, a very presentable-looking couch; and in a few minutes afterwards, this arrival was followed by the entry of a couple of chairs. Quite contented with the present aspect of our fate, we looked with perfect equanimity on the small flock of goats that entered the room, to vanish from view behind the partition which had raised our fears.

We had no lack of visitors, and amongst them there rushed in a little woman, who, after shaking hands with us and saying '*bon jour*,' rushed out again before I had time to distinguish her features in the deep twilight. From an enquiry I made as soon as she had darted off, I found that we had been honoured by a visit from the caïd's wife. As for the caïd, he was probably too sorely troubled in spirit as to the proprieties of conduct to be observed towards two such unprecedented guests, to venture on the very un-Mohammedan proceeding of entering our unveiled presence; but as he walked past the door, his head surmounted by an imposing turban, I saw him cast a sharp furtive glance into the interior.

After dining off a dish of couscousou, we lay down upon the cushions, which made a very far from despicable substitute for civilised beds, and promised us a sufficiently comfortable night. Our example was soon followed by the three members of the caïd's household, into whose apartment we had been introduced. Making a nightcap of the hood of his blue burnous, our coffee-maker and his young wife and child lay down upon a mat in our vicinity, and disappeared from view beneath the folds of a large red counterpane. Except for a sickly kid, which, by the light of an oil lamp, I saw wandering disconsolately around the red heap upon the floor, I should not have been aware of the presence of any four-legged companions.

Shortly after I awoke, at dawn, from a sound and refreshing sleep, the red heap showed signs of life, and, the owner of the blue burnous having risen up, performed his toilet by flinging back his hood. Then, after opening the door and window, he applied himself diligently to the task of manufacturing coffee; whilst his wife, rising up, completed her toilet by a process scarcely more elaborate than that of her husband. Our own was not less primitive, for it simply consisted in bathing our faces, and having water poured upon our hands in Oriental fashion. After drinking our coffee, we were ready to start.

But our departure was delayed by an unexpected difficulty. Seeing that our Arab escort was suffering much from his inflamed foot, we told him the preceding evening that we would dispense with his further attendance, and that he could wait at the caïd's until the baggage mule he rode would return from Setif; but to our annoyance we found that he had started off for Akbou at break of day on this very mule, leaving for ourselves and baggage only the two we rode. Whether he had mistaken, or wilfully disobeyed our orders, we could not tell.

Agreeing that the frequent stumbles of our mules, the day before, rendered it very undesirable that they should carry any extra weight, we requested another mule in the place of the one that had been taken away.

'The caïd has none to send,' replied several of the chief's dependents who had assembled to witness our departure.

Satisfied that the assertion was false, we said we

must speak to the caïd himself on the subject, on which we were informed that the caïd would not be visible for some time.

'No matter, we can wait till he appears,' we said, resolutely; and to show that we were thoroughly in earnest, we sat down in a deliberate solemn manner on our baggage, which, by a simple pluck at the primitive equipment of our mules, we tumbled on the ground.

The strategy was most effective, for scarcely more than a minute had elapsed before one of the Arabs advanced and said, 'There is the caïd's brother, you can speak to him.'

Instantly rising to address the young man thus indicated, and who had stood somewhat aloof, I immediately received from him the satisfactory assurance that we should have a mule forthwith. The promise was kept; and in a few minutes we set off, accompanied by a guard of honour in the person of a tall negro, draped in a picturesque blue burnous, and mounted on a fine-looking horse, with embroidered trappings.

The scenery of our morning's ride was destitute of interest. Not a tree was visible amidst the grassy and monotonous undulations of the country through which we passed, and the absolute desolation of the prospect was only very rarely relieved by the sight of a small group of tents rising amidst a few plots of corn. After a cheerless ride of many hours, we halted at noon at the small stone-built house of a caïd, to which we were conducted by our negro escort.

Greeted with the most cordial welcome from the chief, we were conducted by him into a very small but perfectly clean whitewashed room, whose furniture simply consisted of a small mat upon the floor, and a long gun suspended from the walls. His heart evidently fixed on the desire of doing us honour, he seemed greatly distressed when we told him we could not wait for the dish of couscousou he declared he would prepare for us. Why should we hurry away? he urged. It was not necessary we should proceed to Setif that night. His house was entirely at our disposal, so long as we might be inclined to honour him with our company. Were not the English and the Arabs brothers? Let the *Inglese* stay and take couscousou with him.

But though we were obdurate to his solicitations in regard to the proffered dish of couscousou, he had the pleasure of seeing us thoroughly enjoy the eggs, new milk, and wheaten cakes, which, at our suggestion, were furnished in lieu of the more honourable dish which we declined. After we had finished eating, he insisted on our pocketing the solid remnants of the entertainment, and wound up his hospitable zeal by pouring water over our hands. In requital of his attention, we gladdened the hearts of his wives and children by donations of tiny mirrors and penny trumpets. On remounting our mules, the friendly and hospitable caïd warmly expressed his hope that we should revisit him.

Shortly after we left the caïd's dwelling, the grassy hillocks amidst which we had journeyed the whole morning died away into an extensive plain, sparsely dotted in the distance by small groups of whitewashed cottages, with red-tiled roofs; a sight which, beyond the limits of Great Kabylia, was an unequivocal evidence, in Algeria, of our approach to a civilised region. Except in the immediate vicinity of these villages, not a tree was visible, nor was any brushwood to be seen.

The mule track we followed merged into an imperfect road, as we gained the European settlement of Messaoud, which looked the embodied idea of desolation, from showing almost every door and window blocked up by stones. A few miles further on, we reached the kindred settlement of Aïn Arnat, whose desolation was made still more striking by the presence of a church of imposing dimensions, and an untenanted *école* and *mairie*, rising high above a silent grass-grown street. French colonisation was, evidently, a most unequivocal failure in this portion of the plain of Setif.

We met very few Europeans, until we reached the immediate vicinity of Setif; and there, to our great dismay, we found that we were obliged to pass along a fashionable promenade, swarming with French officers and smartly-dressed ladies. Fortune had truly played us a malicious trick, both at the commencement and end of our rough ride. Trying as had been our meeting, at Fort Napoleon, with the Governor-General and his glittering staff, we were now exposed to a far longer, and therefore more painful, ordeal at the gates of Setif. The guise in which we made our reappearance in civilised life was calculated, unquestionably, to shock its delicate sensibility; and the poignancy of this conviction was sharpened, in my case, by a knowledge that my dress bore very evident traces of my previous day's fall.

Even when we had got clear of that terrible promenade, our tribulations continued; for, after threading our way, through swarming soldiers, to the Hôtel de France, we heard that the house was filled to overflowing with the officers belonging to the newly-arrived *colonne*; but it was mercifully suggested that we might possibly find a vacant room in the Hôtel de Paris. With decidedly very unfriendly feelings to the *colonne*, we proceeded towards the indicated hotel, where our ominous anticipations were most pleasantly dispelled by the '*Oui, Mesdames*,' which answered our appeal for accommodation.

Thus ended our rough ride through Great Kabylia, a journey rich in recollections of beautiful scenery and quaint pictures of native life.

CHAPTER XXVIII.

SETIF — AN ECCENTRIC GAOL — A DREARY DRIVE — LOVE IN A COTTAGE.

THE ruins of the large Roman city of Setif strewed the ground when the French, in 1847, reared the modern town of Setif on its site. The traces of ramparts which remain, evidence the importance of the ancient capital of Setifian Mauritania.

But although Setif affords a rich field for antiquarian research, it wears on the surface a completely modern aspect. Such ruins, or ruinous relics, as are now in existence hide themselves from observation, except outside the town, in the Promenade d'Orléans, where the statue of the late Duke presides over a goodly array of broken columns, fragments of friezes, mutilated statues, and busts that made me sensibly feel that a nose is decidedly a highly ornamental appendage to the human face. Straight, wide streets; fresh, well-built houses; and spacious squares, ornamented with trees, form the characteristic features of modern Setif.

The departure of the *colonne*, the ensuing day, reduced Setif to its evidently habitual state of chronic stagnation, which, in combination with the absence of all picturesque scenery in the neighbourhood, rendered it well adapted as a resting-place, after our long ride through Great Kabylia. But uneventfully as two days passed on, we found, just at their close, that we had ignorantly been face to face with a danger, which, if known, might well have justified a considerable amount of disquietude.

The bedrooms which we occupied at the Hôtel de Paris were in a back return, and opened off a wooden gallery, extending along the wall, at about nine or ten feet above a small court beneath. This court, enclosed by walls not more than eight feet high, communicated by a door with another small court, that opened on the street by a covered passage, through the front building. A sentinel soldier in the front court, and a group of lounging Arabs in the court below our rooms, were such familiar Algerian sights that I never thought of asking why they were there. A general officer staying in an hotel, as was constantly the case, would account at once for the presence of the soldier; and as for the lounging Arabs, such an everyday sight gave rise to no speculation of any description.

But at the close of our last day at Setif, I chanced to see, amidst the lounging Arabs, a dark-browed scowling European, who paced to and fro across the court, with the air of a man in bondage; and as, just at that moment, I observed the soldier peering through a small grating in the low door between the courts, it suddenly flashed upon my mind that, marvellous as it might seem, we had been living for some days in the immediate vicinity of a prison. On application to the mistress of the hotel, she confirmed the correctness of the supposition, and informed us, with the utmost coolness, that one of the men we saw was accused of committing a dreadful murder. That a gaol should exist in the heart of an hotel was a still less greater marvel, to my mind, than that prisoners should remain one hour in a most imperfectly guarded court, overhung by a gallery almost within reach of an active jump, and enclosed by walls that any ordinarily active boy could readily scale.

Whilst at Setif, I learned the history of the two deserted villages in its neighbourhood, through which we had passed. Built in 1856, with some other adjacent villages, by a Genevese company, to whom the Government granted a large concession of land, the Swiss emigrants established there fled, in a couple of years, from the malaria scourge which fast thinned their numbers. Destitute of swamps and brushwood, and at an elevation of more than three thousand feet above the sea, the table-land of Setif has yet, it seems, the same death-dealing power as the low, marshy, brushwood-covered plain of the Metidja.

From Setif to Constantine, a distance of eighty

miles, we journeyed in a diligence, through a country utterly destitute of picturesque beauty. In the vicinity of Setif, a bare expanse, bounded in the distance by low unwooded hills, was scantily dotted here and there by a colonist's house; but, for succeeding miles on miles, an occasional cluster of Arab gourbis alone relieved the desolation of the scene. An almost deserted European village, which we passed through in the afternoon, afforded another evidence of the present failure of French colonisation in this region. The lights from the camp of the *colonne* gleamed picturesquely on the heights of Constantine, as, at early night, we gained the town. Hearing at the Diligence Bureau, on our alighting there, that we should have to start the succeeding morn for Batna — if we would profit by the diligence going that week from thence to Biskara — we resolved to prosecute our journey there without delay, in hopes of preceding the summer heat, of which a French authority gave an intensely terrific description.*

The sun had not yet risen, when, leaving Constantine by a steep descent, we entered upon a narrow,

* ' Il fait tellement chaud à Biskara, que les chiens n'osent pas sortir en plein midi, et que les bougies fondent à l'ombre. L'eau des ruisseaux est si chaude, que bien des personnes ne peuvent s'y baigner. Les militaires composant le garnison allégent peu à peu leur uniforme aux heures où le service ne les réunit pas, et se montrent dans le costume primitif du père Adam.' — *Indicateur-Général d'Algérie.* (The private reunions of the French officers at Biskara must present a somewhat primitive picture.)

treeless, and but partially cultivated valley. After passing the still grand remains of a Roman aqueduct, the scenery became utterly dreary and uninteresting. Not one of the very few French villages along our course but wore a malaria-cursed aspect, that fully confirmed the account of the unhealthiness of the country given to us by a young Frenchwoman, our companion in the *coupé*. Advancing along a road that was almost nothing better than a carriage-track, we journeyed on through a desolate and uncultivated valley, except where very rarely a cluster of Arab gourbis rose in the midst of a plot of fast-yellowing corn. The chain of bare arid hills that rose on either hand, was quite in keeping with the other features of the prospect. It was a marvel to me how the little Frenchwoman's gay spirit and blithe looks had survived a four years' residence in such dreary solitudes.

'Well, it is a dull enough country to live in,' was her answer to a remark I made; 'but for all that, we might be worse off in many a pleasanter-looking place than on the borders of the salt lake where we live, for it is quite free from fever; and Pierre, who farms the salt, and I myself, have had right good health since we came there. Besides, we little care for any society but our own, and we have many a pleasant hour with music, for I sing to Pierre's accompaniment on the flute, which he plays well. I intend to buy my pardon, by this new *morceau* I am bringing home, for having exceeded my allotted time at Constantine' — she concluded jestingly, glancing at a roll of music in her hand.

It was the afternoon before we reached the young Frenchwoman's home, and as the diligence stopped to put her down in the vicinity of a dreary-looking two-storied house, rising up amidst a waste of yellowish grass, on the borders of a small lake encircled by desolation, I thought that 'love in a cottage' could never be exposed to a more trying ordeal than in the present instance. Scarcely had the Frenchwoman left her seat, than a stout-built, middle-aged man with a shaggy beard, issuing from the house, quickly advanced to meet her, and kissing her fondly, he exclaimed in tones not altogether in unison with his words, '*Perfide, traître! pourquoi m'as tu dit un mensonge?*'

With a laugh for answer, the little Frenchwoman put her hand on her husband's arm, and they walked off together on such amicable terms, that it was evident the new *morceau* was not required to win her pardon.

It was almost evening before, emerging from amidst the bare arid heights through which we had been travelling since dawn, we entered upon a narrow plain, bounded by hills partially clothed with the dusky foliage of the evergreen oak and cedar. The white walls of Batna were nigh hand before we saw one colonist's house, and in a very short time afterwards we were driving along the straight, wide, but partially completed streets of a small French town.

Set down at the door of the goodly-sized Hôtel d'Europe, we instantly secured seats in the diligence, which was to start the ensuing morning for the Saharian oasis of Biskara.

The idea of camels and the Sahara were so connected together in my mind, that it seemed to me quite unnatural that we should be conveyed to a palm grove in a lumbering diligence. But, at the advanced period of May at which we had arrived, all poetical and sentimental objections to such a means of transport were effectively overcome by the luxurious ideas of ease and coolness suggested by the vision of a Saharian journey in a civilised four-wheel carriage.

CHAPTER XXIX.

A STARTLING INCIDENT — TOURISTS IN DISTRESS — A JOURNEY UNDER DIFFICULTIES — A MIDNIGHT WALK — EL KANTARA — A SAHARIAN SCENE.

THE *coupé* having been preengaged, we could only obtain seats in the less comfortable *intérieur*, which was, however, roomy enough to afford most ample accommodation to us and three mechanics, our fellow-passengers. The sun had not yet risen when we started, and the air felt so fresh, that I felt little alarm in regard to the temperature that might await us, some eighty miles south, at Biskara.

All symptoms of French colonisation soon died out after leaving the immediate vicinity of Batna, and the arid-looking plain through which we travelled was only very rarely dotted by a patch of verdure, girdling the miserable group of tents of an Arab tribe. The low chain of hills on either side were too scantily clothed with diminutive evergreen oak, and juniper, to counteract the bleak and lifeless aspect of the narrow plain they bounded. Had it not been for the almost incessant jolts to which we were subjected, I would have certainly yielded to the soporific influences of the scenery and an early start.

A STARTLING INCIDENT.

Having become habituated, on Algerian roads, to a ship-like mode of progression through a rough sea, I had ceased to regard heavy lurches with alarm, but my sense of security was destined before long to be rudely dispelled, by finding myself hurled forward on my head, as, after a heavy lurch, the toppling diligence fell crashing on the ground.

Raising up my head, and combining a vague idea it was fractured with an intense desire for extrication, I sought an exit through the door window, relying, not unwarrantably as it proved, on my slender dimensions and unfashionable dress. Standing amidst the avalanche of luggage which littered the ground, I had come to the satisfactory conclusion that I was the proprietor of an unfractured skull some minutes before my companions in the *intérieur* had emerged from it by the legitimate mode of an opened door. An eager inquiry into each other's experiences, led to the pleasant information that I was the only one who had even a bruise to show.

After the *intérieur* had given forth its contents, the driver, hastening to deliver the occupants of the *coupé*, hauled out a tall, gaunt, middle-aged gentleman, wearing a light-coloured linen blouse with pockets that most ludicrously dangled on either side far below the garment. To him succeeded a younger gentleman, who was followed by a very stout but comely lady in a high state of excitement. Sinking down amidst the pile of baggage upon the ground, the late occupants of the *coupé* vented their feelings by a torrent of '*mon Dieu's*,' intermingled with appalling '*aiyahs*' from the tall gentleman with the remarkable pockets, who filled up each interval between his groans by execrating the destiny which had subjected him, as he alleged, to the affliction of a terribly damaged shoulder. The other gentleman more heroically confined his demonstrations of suffering from an almost imperceptibly bruised wrist, to an occasional grimace and groan. Madame, his wife, declared she was quite unharmed.

By the united efforts of the driver and the mechanics, the diligence, being raised, was found to have sustained no serious injury. But the driver, vowing that the conveyance — a new one — was unsafe, declared that he would return to Batna for the old diligence to take us on to Biskara.

'I told the *administration* that this diligence would never do for a road like this; if they had heeded my warning this would never have happened.' So saying, the driver set off on a two hours' drive to Batna, leaving us to guard the luggage until his return.

This parting speech served Monsieur Poches as a text for vociferous denunciations of the *administration*. '*Les coquins!—les scélerats!*' he shrieked forth, '*c'est vraiment une infamie de nous envoyer dans une voiture dangereuse. Ils méritent d'être pendus comme des chiens. Oh, mon Dieu! comme je souffre. Aiyah! aiyah! — quel douleur affreux.*

Une telle canaille doit être citée devant les autorités — aiyah! aiyah! Oh, mon Dieu! mon Dieu!'

To listen for probably nearly four hours to an alternation of groans and denunciations of the *admi-ministration*, was a prospect so little to our taste that we soon agreed to walk onward, and, if possible, to reach a caravanseraï, where it was intended we should halt for breakfast. But with our very leisurely advance under a hot sun, frequent pauses on the road, and a visit to Arab tents in quest of milk, we had scarcely gained the caravanseraï when the diligence arrived.

On rejoining our fellow-passengers, we found Monsieur Poches still intermingling groans of anguish with denunciations of the *administration*; and whilst his injured member was supported by a handkerchief hung round his neck, the other gentleman had his almost invisibly damaged wrist suspended in a similar manner.

On resuming our journey in the diligence, I looked with much dissatisfaction on the sharp corners of the hinged windows, which were fastened back against the low roof, and as, with every severe jolt, an iron bar above gave a sharp rebuke to my head for rising to an undue elevation, I felt the most earnest hope that the veteran conveyance would bear out the driver's assurance of its trustworthy character. As the *coupé* had but seats for two, the gentlemen were ungallant enough to send Madame to be our companion in the *intérieur*. Her company, under existing circumstances, was not particularly agreeable; for with every one of our many lurches from side to side, she shrieked, whilst with her brows contracted into an expression of intense alarm, she uttered from time to time, in a bitterly repentant, despairing voice, '*Oh, mon Dieu! mon Dieu! une mère de famille ne doit pas voyager en Algérie.*'

I had never seen, even in Algeria, such a mockery of a road as that over which we advanced. Huge stones often littering the track, and projecting rocks alternating with deep ruts and holes, soon made every passenger prefer a toilsome walk to a dangerous drive; and, following in the wake of the staggering diligence, we arrived in about three hours at a very small roadside inn, from which, after a short halt, we started onward with the disagreeable certainty of not being able to reach before dark our night's destination of El Kantara. The want of food, for the horses, alone prevented us from insisting on remaining at the inn that night.

The hilly country through which our course now lay, added to the dangers by which our progress was beset. Sharp descents, followed by abrupt ascents over slanting or projecting rocks, tried the driver's skill to the uttermost degree; but with all his care, the two wheel horses soon lay prostrate on the ground, and one was so tightly wedged beneath the pole that he was raised with difficulty. As daylight faded the road grew worse and worse, and the empty diligence, which we followed on foot, had many a narrow escape from being upset. But for the mechanics, our fellow-passengers, the diligence would have certainly committed suicide on the steep bank of a shallow stream, which we crossed and recrossed perpetually. Utterly wearied out at length by my day's exertions, I reentered the diligence in a state of mind which made my desire for rest predominate over my fear of being overturned; but fear gained the upper hand, as after a heavy lurch, accompanied by a loud cry, I sprung through the hastily opened door to see, by the light of a bright crescent moon, the two near horses lying prostrate in the river, on whose banks we were.

By dint of vigorous exertion, amidst a hurricane of oaths and cries, one horse was quickly raised; but nearly half an hour elapsed before the other was dragged out from beneath the pole, under which he lay in imminent danger of being drowned. On his release, it was discovered that his partner in misfortune had taken advantage of the confusion to walk off; but having had the indiscretion to stop to graze on his way to El Kantara, he was speedily recaptured on our advance.

Somewhat rested by the halt, I joined my fellow-passengers on foot. The moon having set, the only light we had to guide our way was from the stars, which sparkled brilliantly in a cloudless sky — a light so insufficient for the exigencies of our position that we gladly accepted the workmen's proffer to carry us across the stream which we had perpetually to cross. Even tall, gaunt Monsieur Poches, and stout Madame, were ferried over in the same primitive manner.

Midnight found us still plodding wearily onward, but when, worn out with fatigue, I reentered the diligence, I had scarce been two minutes there when I was startled by a woman's piercing shriek. As the thought of a prowling wild beast flashed across my mind, I was inexpressibly relieved to find that the alarming sound only denoted Madame's involuntary plunge into the shallow river, by whose banks she walked. As her husband, with commendable heroism, had jumped in to rescue her, he was quite in as moist a state as was the lady when she arrived, in a state of violent agitation, at the diligence, into which she entered, followed by Monsieur, who, petting his stout wife as if she had been a child, endeavoured to conquer her gasping sobs and exclamations of despair by beseeching his '*petite colombe*' and his '*petite pigeonne, d'être tranquille.*'

Ladies who weigh some twelve or thirteen stone should decidedly have no nerves, I thought.

Feeling as if our nightmare-like journey would never end, it was a happy moment when, as an unwonted steadiness of movement made me look out, I saw beyond the bridge we crossed an indistinct vision of palm trees rising up at either side of a wall of rocks, between which we advanced. The joyous cry of 'El Kantara!' that broke from my lips was echoed by my fellow-passengers in full as joyous a tone. Soon passing some Arab houses, before which several men lay sleeping on the ground, we gained, immediately afterwards, a large caravanseraï, whose gate was speedily opened for our reception. After a cup of coffee, I lay down on a clean soft bed in an airy room, with a sensation of intense enjoyment; and, with a very vivid conviction that a diligence journey to the Sahara was not at all to be considered a luxuriously enervating mode of progress, I fell asleep.

It seemed to me as if I had but just closed my eyes, when I was suddenly awakened by a loud knock; but seeing that I was in broad daylight, I sighed over the transitoriness of human bliss, and, rising up, made a hasty toilet, followed by a hasty breakfast, for our driver was urgent we should start forthwith. Our poor horses had still more reason than ourselves to quarrel with a scanty allowance of rest and slumber.

But, hurried as we were, I managed to avail myself of a few spare minutes, to wander beyond the high walls of the caravanseraï, to get a view of the palm grove of El Kantara,[*] and a scene as beautiful as it

---

[*] El Kantara, signifying 'the bridge,' derives its name from an old Roman bridge, over which we crossed the preceding evening.

was striking burst on my sight, as I looked down upon an islet of brilliant verdure rising at the entrance of a deep narrow gorge, which cleft in twain a rampart-like chain of red precipitous arid crags. That gorge, a natural gateway between the Tell and Sahara, bears, as the Arabs say, the hue of perpetual summer on its southern side. Turning from the palms that overshadowed the mud-built native village of El Kantara, I glanced towards the south over a narrow, undulating, and parched-looking plain, bounded by low, bare, sunburnt hills. In the peculiar transparency and oppressive heat of the air, and in the colouring of the landscape, the vicinity of the burning sands of the Sahara spoke plainly to the eye. Here was Africa, at length, as my fancy had imagined it to be.

Before starting onward, the driver gave us the welcome assurance that our road would be infinitely better than that over which we had for the most part plodded on foot the preceding day. The improvement, however, was not so great as to relieve our minds altogether from apprehensions of being overturned. Madame suffered in spirit from at least a dozen upsets, and every now and then a terror-stricken cry announced her full conviction that her last hour was nigh, whilst from time to time she reiterated her strong conviction that *'une mère de famille ne doit pas voyager en Algérie.'*

After leaving El Kantara, we proceeded across an

undulating plain, bounded to the left by bright red crags, whose jagged peaks and pinnacles assumed, in many instances, the form of ruined castles or towers. Some plots of stunted yellowish corn were visible near El Kantara, but the vegetation, dying out as we advanced, was soon limited to a small thorny shrub dotting the arid soil, except along the channel of a shallow stream whose course we followed, and which showed the rich pink blossoms of the oleander rising above its stony bed. As we advanced, we met several tribes of pastoral Arabs proceeding northwards, with camels, sheep, and cows.

Near the southern extremity of the plain, the scenery was diversified by the salt which strewed the ground over which we passed, and glittered on the side and summit of an adjacent hill. Winding through a series of hillocks into another small plain, still more arid than that which we had just left, it was a pleasant sight to see a green islet in its centre, and pleasant news to hear that we would find there, for an hour or more, protection from the sun, whose rays poured down on us with a true Saharian fervour. Arriving before long at a diminutive palm grove overshadowing the Arab village of El Outhaïa, we alighted at a French caravanseraï in its immediate neighbourhood. On entering the house, I for the first time in my life felt thoroughly impressed with the conviction that coolness and shade were to be reckoned the greatest luxuries of existence.

After a good rest and *déjeûner,* we set off again; and, on leaving the oasis, we approached a chain of hills that formed the southern boundary of the small plain of El Outhaïa. These hills were low, but on either hand the higher ranges into which they merged were backed in the distance by mountain chains, steeped in the indescribably rich glow of the lustrous light, poured down through the limpidly-transparent air. No silvery haze, nor filmy violet veil, obscured the brightness of the bold red crags, whose radiant masses rose against a sky which melted gradually from a brilliant azure overhead into a tint of the most delicate pearl grey towards the horizon. Not a shadow, far off or near, was visible. The Sahara was well worth a visit, even if it had nothing else to show than that radiant glow and translucent atmosphere.

Winding by a pass through the southern chain of heights, the cry of 'Biskara!' soon broke upon our ears; and looking towards the south, I glanced from a palm forest, that rose immediately above the heights, to an apparently unlimited plain, extending in unbroken expanse to the far horizon. The sterile, desolate, and sun-scorched Sahara lay before my view.

After a steep descent, and a short drive amidst arid hillocks, we arrived at the gate of a walled-in town. Driving through a yet unbuilt space, we soon gained a handsome *place,* flanked on two sides by tall French houses. The isolated palm trees which adorned the *place* alone reminded me that I was in Africa, as I entered the large Hôtel de Sahara, French in all save name.

CHAPTER XXX.

BISKARA — A NEGRO VILLAGE — PALM GROVE — MERITS OF DATE PALM — INTENSE HEAT — AN UNDESIRABLE RIDE — BATNA — LAMBESSA — A WISE JUDGE.

THE oasis of Biskara contains seven villages within a circuit of about seven miles, fertilised by the never-failing waters of the Oued Zeyour, which rises in the low chain of hills immediately above the spot. Too small in summer to do more than supply the wants of the inhabitants of the oasis, through which it winds by many an artificial channel; the stream in winter becomes a torrent, which, after furnishing to various neighbouring tribes of pastoral Arabs the means of creating artificial meadows for their flocks, wanders onward through the desert for thirty miles to join another stream.

The French town of Biskara rises at the distance of about half a mile from the mound of ruins marking the site of native Biskara, which the conquerors destroyed. The Biskara of the present day is therefore a thoroughly modern creation, and, like other French Algerian towns, has a clean bright look. The soldiers which garrison the spot form nearly the whole of its European population, and its commerce is confined to the traffic carried on across the counter of a grocer's or spirit-dealer's shop.

The small native population, denizens of the place, is composed of Arabs, negroes, and of dancing girls, who, with painted faces, and persons laden with tawdry ornaments, form conspicuous objects in the streets, whilst in the evening the Arab cafés resound with the monotonous music to which they perform their equally monotonous dances.

A crow or magpie's nest might well challenge comparison, in architectural skill, with a cluster of negro dwellings which rise in the outskirts of the town. With walls of branches converging from a small circle into a cord-girt point not five feet from the ground, these structures seemed to me to render the act of standing upright an impossible performance for their tenants, and I had come to the conclusion that they must belong to a pigmy race, when my theory was upset by seeing an ordinary sized negress creeping forth on hands and knees through a small aperture curtained with rags. The lady who made her appearance in this primitive manner, was resplendently dressed. Ears distended by large heavy gold earrings, arms encircled with bracelets, a neck hung with chains, and fingers and ancles laden with rings, formed, in combination with her home, as ludicrous a picture as I ever saw.

Immediately beyond these wigwams, we entered the palm forest of Biskara, and with a sensation of keen disappointment I found that imagination had invested the scene with a false and delusive splendour. Instead of the clustering lofty plume-crowned columnar stems I thought to see, I beheld palm trees of inconsiderable height, scattered so thinly over the surface, that they formed no protection against the sun; whilst the ground beneath them, in many places newly upturned, and in others wearing a parched look, lacked verdure; and, worst of all, the streams, which fancy painted as clear sparkling brooks, showed as narrow drains filled with liquid mud. The numerous fruit gardens, where the fig and pomegranate mingled with the palm, were to me the most attractive feature of the oasis.*

The villages, built of unbaked bricks, were all dirty, and some in a very dilapidated condition. The interiors which we entered were in keeping with the exteriors of the dwellings, and the dirty women who received us were in perfect harmony with the whole scene. The enormous red or green woollen plaits which they wore in monstrous hanging loops at either side of their heads, made me reflect on the high amount of feminine ingenuity universally exhi-

* From information subsequently obtained after my visit to Biskara, I have reason to believe that we were ill advised in not visiting, in preference, the Saharian oasis of Laghouat, in the province of Algiers. The palm-trees there, I was told, were infinitely loftier and finer than those at Biskara, to which we had been recommended to go, by one we thought a very competent adviser. This hint may be of use to any contemplating Algerian tourist.

bited, in civilised or uncivilised lands, in the art of self-disfigurement.

In one house we were ill-bred enough to refuse partaking of a dish that looked like a decoction of mud and treacle, encircled by a border of stewed pepper-pods. In another, however, we were presented with a juicy mass of candied dates, that formed, with a jug of excellent new milk, a most welcome repast, which I would have thoroughly enjoyed, if enjoyment had been possible in a sweltering atmosphere, alive with flies.

The date harvest was long past, for in Algeria it begins in October and ends in winter. Though the date, simply dried, forms the staple food of the inhabitants of the oasis, it is also eaten boiled, stewed, or simmered into a kind of pulp with honey. The young tender leaves of the palm afford a salad, and the trunk when pierced yields a mild beverage called date milk, convertible by distillation into a potent spirit. The sap produced by cutting off the crown becomes, after fermentation, toddy, or palm wine; and on distillation turns into arrack, a highly intoxicating spirit.

The date palm is said to grow in size for seventy years, and to flourish for seventy more; and when it falls, towards the end of its second century, the withered trunk sends forth a shoot, which, after going through the same career, is succeeded by a young scion from the old stock; and so on, for ages.

Owing to this peculiarity of growth the date palm has acquired the botanical term of *Phœnix dactylifera*. If well watered, its sucker will produce fruit when only four years old.

Not unnaturally, the date palm is to the Arab an object of peculiar veneration. A harbinger, amidst scorching sands, of the spring where he may slake his fiery thirst, it supplies him at all times with a pleasant and nutritious food, whilst three hundred and sixty uses to which this invaluable tree can be applied have been celebrated, by Arab writers, in prose and verse. Some Oriental authors have even ascribed to the date palm the honour of being a sentient creature, grounding their statement on the uncontrovertible fact that, like an animal, it cannot survive the loss of its head.

The Prophet, fond of dates, recommended them to the faithful, and from him they learned that the date palm was formed in Eden of the superabundant tempered dust remaining after the creation of Adam. Twice in the Prophet's life, the date palm testified to an unbelieving world the sacred mission of the messenger of Allah. When the sceptics of Medina mocked his words, they were put to confusion by seeing a lofty fruit-laden palm spring from the spot where the Prophet, one moment before, had placed a seed; and on another day, as he sat down to rest beneath the shade of palms, they greeted his presence with a shout, and a loud *salaam*.

But, however fully I might be impressed with the transcendant merits of the date palm, I soon discovered that a residence in their vicinity, in the latter end of May, was the very reverse of pleasant. The heat was beyond all that I had ever experienced in the height of summer, in southern European latitudes. In two hours after the sun had risen, its scorching beams seemed to pierce my brain. Before eight o'clock each morning, we had to return from our early stroll, or ride to seek the protection of the hotel; where, to escape the pest of flies, I lay simmering in a room too dark to admit of any other occupation than that of sleep, which the stove-like air prevented. A prisoner till the sun had set, the time passed so wearily, that minutes seemed to lengthen into hours, and hours into days.

Beside the fervid temperature for which Biskara is famed, it possesses the equally disagreeable distinction of being infested with scorpions. Opthalmia is general; and a peculiar disease, called the *bouton d'Alep*, is very prevalent in the dog days. In comparison, however, with the alleged sanitary condition of a native town in an oasis some few miles off, Biskara may be considered healthy; for it is said that one-fifth of the population of Sidi Okba is totally blind — nearly all suffering from opthalmia, whilst many are lepers.

But, intense as I found the heat, I was assured that the great heats of Biskara had not yet begun.

With the commencement of the dog days, the swarming flies, I heard, died off — an alleviation, certainly, of the misery of living in an aërial furnace; but I felt strong doubts as to my ability to survive a temperature fatal to my insect persecutors. Far from desiring, however, to test that point, I felt an inexpressible longing to get away from Biskara; and, for the first time in my life, I thought of walrusses and arctic bears with a feeling of envy.

Under the influence of the vivid remembrance of the misadventures and danger of our late diligence journey, we resolved, on our arrival at Biskara, to return to Batna on mules. Notwithstanding, however, our dismal experiences, the diligence, after a day's stay in the oasis, started back with a fair supply of passengers, one of whom, a young Parisian tourist, declared he was ready to face any danger rather than to endure exposure to the Saharian sun. After a two days' stay at Biskara, I was strongly inclined to admire the wisdom of his choice; but as to wait for the next diligence starting from Biskara would involve the residence of a week in the vicinity of the palms, we applied to the Bureau Arabe for mules and guides. We proposed to travel by night; but the authorities negativing this idea, we arranged to start as soon as dawn arrived, in company with our late and now sympathising fellow-travellers — Madame, her husband, and the gaunt gentleman with the remarkable pockets.

Poor Monsieur Poches! his visit to Biskara had indeed been a sorrowful enterprise for him. Refusing to be comforted by the assurance that a strained sinew or muscle would soon get well of its own accord, he insisted on having his injured member bled in quick succession by two regimental doctors, who both agreed that they could see nothing wrong. Gaunt as he was before the performance of this process, he stalked about with quite a spectral look after the loss of blood had robbed his long, thin face of all the colour it previously had. Anxious to impress an unsympathising world with the intensity of his sufferings, he frequently withdrew his arm from its sling, to raise it aloft, amidst heartrending groans and appalling grimaces — at which the unsympathising world only laughed in its sleeve, and vowed that M. Poches was an arrant fool. He would never get well, he said — never! even if he lived to the age of Methusaleh. The *administration* of the Biskara diligence were a *canaille* — a set of villains, deserving to be hung. I verily believe that he would have seen with pleasure the infamous *administration* chained to a burning pile.

After a two days' stay at Biskara — a week, seemingly, in length — we started off, on mules, at dawn, whose delicious coolness infused a sensation of energy and enjoyment into my heat-enervated frame; but long before we had gained the caravanseraï of El Outaïah, the sun was pouring down upon our heads its scorching beams. A long rest, however, under a protecting roof, nerved us to resume our journey, after the midday heat was past; but the approach of evening brought us little relief, for, near sunset, a fiery wind sprang up, which, parching my mouth and lips, produced a consuming thirst. My intense craving for water, and intense enjoyment of the bowl I drained on reaching the caravanseraï of El Kantara, will never fade from my remembrance.

After a night's rest in this very clean, comfortable caravanseraï, we again set off at dawn. As I crossed the old Roman bridge, which spans the gorge in its narrowest part, I could well understand how the first French columns which gained that spot halted, and gave vent to their admiration by a spontaneous shout and a burst of music; for the vivid verdure of the palm grove, heightened by contrast with arid crags beyond, and with the precipitous bare rocks, which rose, in wall-like masses, on either hand, formed a scene of the most striking beauty.

Though no longer exposed to the influence of the scorching Saharian glare, the heat of the Tell sun was yet sufficient to make our long day's ride extremely fatiguing. The mules furnished us by the caïd of El Kantara were, without exception, miserable; and mine, which exhibited ears eaten into shreds by dogs, could not be prevailed to abandon, for even the shortest time, its habitua snail-like pace. The aridity and desolation of the scene through which we travelled aggravated the wearisomeness of our journey. Long before the walls of Batna greeted our wistful eyes, I had arrived at the conclusion that I had paid a heavy price for a glimpse of the palm groves of Biskara.

The site of Batna was a marsh previous to the French occupation of that district in 1844. The scarcity of water, and the sudden changes of temperature to which the elevated plain of Batna is exposed, render its neighbourhood ill adapted for colonising purposes. A very scanty European population extends around the yet unfinished walls of the small town. Situated in the centre of an arid-looking desolate plain, overlooked by low mountain chains, for the most part destitute of trees, Batna has no claim upon a tourist's notice save that it derives from its vicinity to the ruins of Lambessa, an old Roman town, but better known in Europe as the site of a prison, to which political offenders in recent times were sent.

An hour's drive from Batna brought us to the entrance of a huge building, at which alighting, we entered a court, destitute of all sights or sounds of life; and, after a glance into the interior of a number of small empty rooms opening off the court, we were about to give up a search for the official whom we had been told to seek, when he appeared, and civilly granted our request to let us have a glimpse of the interior. Telling us what we had heard before at Batna, that the building was now altogether empty, he conducted us into a huge gaol, constructed on the silent, separate system of punishment.

As I looked at the multitude of doors opening off the long corridors of the building, I wondered at the motive which could have inspired the utter abandonment of a structure raised evidently at a very large cost. The subsequent transportation of the political criminals there, to the pestilential marshes of Cayenne, forbade the idea that the change effected in their place of exile arose from a humane desire of removing them from the influence of the Algerian malaria fever.

The finest Roman ruin I had yet seen in Algeria rises at a few yards' distance from the gaol. A vast square building, some fifty feet in height, shows walls which have for the most part braved the assaults of time. Adorned by columns, and pierced by high arched gateways, this still fine structure presents a striking sight amidst the surrounding waste.

Some doubt exists as to the particular purpose for which this edifice was reared, but the name of Prætorium is generally assigned to it by French authorities. The open space inside, converted into a museum, contains a number of antique remains, collected within the circuit of the ancient town. Numerous inscriptions, bearing the name of Antonino, Aurelian, and Germanico, mingle amongst stone coffins, delicately sculptured friezes, fragmentary capitals and columns, and mutilated marble busts and statues. One gracefully-draped Roman lady had lost her head, another confronted posterity with a pair of stumps where there ought to have been a pair of hands; and it was a rare exception to see one of the illustrious assembly who had not altogether or partially lost the nose — a want highly inimical, in my opinion, to beauty or majesty of aspect. Better not to confront posterity at all, than to meet its gaze with a countenance shorn of its central feature.

A shed close to the Prætorium encloses a small circular mosaic pavement, showing heads representing the seasons — Winter in a hood, Spring with flower-wreathed hair, Summer garlanded with ears of corn, and Autumn crowned with vine leaves — were ranged round a central head encircled by grapes. But beyond the merit that this group possessed of showing unfaded colours and an uninjured surface, I could see no other; and though I was assured on guidebook authority that the five mosaics were '*d'un travail exquis*,' I irreverently pronounced them to be a rude coarse piece of workmanship — as inferior to the mosaics that adorn St. Peter's, as the Berlin wool screen pictures in an English drawing-room are to the beautiful creations of the Gobelin looms.

Two triumphal arches in a state of good preservation

rise amidst formless piles of stone, scattered over a surface more than two miles square, forming the site of the Roman town reared by the Third Legion in the proudest days of imperial Rome. Most of the ruins of Lambessa bear the numeral sign of its military founders. Wandering over the desolate expanse, I sat down at length on the crumbling walls of an amphitheatre, to muse on the vicissitudes of time, and to muse joyfully, too, over the thoughts suggested by the mouldering heaps around.

For surely joy, not sorrow, was the fit emotion for any reflecting mind in such a scene as this. Lambessa, the offspring of imperial Rome, and doubtless a reflection of its venality, profligacy, corruption and brutality, deserved no sigh or tear in its hoar decay. Meditating on the civilisation of the days in which the now utterly ruined city was upreared, and contrasting it with the civilisation of the present time, I exulted keenly in the consciousness of the progress that the world had made. And even as I looked down with pride upon the mouldering relics of a civilisation far inferior in moral and material attributes to that amidst which my lot is cast, so, in another two thousand years, the sight of the mouldering heaps of London may possibly give rise in some tourist's mind to similar feelings of exultation.

We parted at Batna with our French fellow-travellers. M Poches, as doleful as ever, eased his mind, however, in some slight degree by a complaint to the Commissaire of Police of the infamous conduct of the *administration*; whilst we eminently deserved the gratitude of all future English tourists by successfully reclaiming, through that functionary, a goodly number of francs which this same *administration* had overcharged us for our seats.

'Give back the ladies their money,' said this second Daniel to the awe-stricken *administration*; 'and from this time forward let the prices of the *coupé* and *intérieur* be written up inside the diligence.'

'Never take seats in a diligence office without enquiring previously from some French gentleman or lady what is the proper fare,' was Madame's kind and wise advice to us. 'No Frenchman, having any dealings with you English, but thinks himself justified in securing a few pickings to himself out of the mine of gold that you are deemed.'

A list of prices, duly affixed inside, greeted our sight, as we took our places in the *coupé* of the night diligence to Constantine.

CHAPTER XXXI.

CONSTANTINE—EFFECTIVE PICTURES — LONGEVITY OF ANCIENT INHABITANTS — LADIES OF CONSTANTINE — CASCADES — TARPEIAN ROCK — GARDEN OF SALAH BEY — RAILROAD ENTHUSIASM.

REAR up in fancy a huge quadrilateral mass of rock, with a summit rising to the height of 2,000 feet above the sea; encircle that mass from east to west by a profound ravine, and face its north-eastern side by frowning cliffs, rising up in beetling precipices out of a luxuriantly-wooded valley far below; streak those cliffs with the glittering waters of a river, which, springing from the dark recesses of the ravine, gains the bright vale beneath by a series of fine cascades; join, on the west, that precipice-girt block to an adjacent height by a bridge-like neck of land; cover the sloping summit of the rock with clustering white houses, interspersed here and there with a dark cypress or tall minaret, and—behold the city of Constantine, in bygone days the magnificent Roman capital of Eastern Numidia!

But except for its glorious site, which has known no change, the magnificence of imperial Constantine has utterly vanished. The temples, arches, and columns that once fitly crowned those frowning heights, have disappeared, leaving nothing but ruinous fragments as mementoes of ancient splendour. Half French, half Arab in architecture, the modern city presents the usual incongruous aspect of an Algerian town. Here, tall French houses rise in formal lines; there, low red-tile-roofed native dwellings overarch dark winding alleys. Here, European shops courting the bright light of day; there, Arab stalls half buried in obscurity. Such is modern Constantine; the mongrel creation of a civilised and half-civilised race.

If Algiers had not made me familiar with every feature of native life, I should have felt much interest in exploring the native portion of Constantine, and even as it was, I highly enjoyed a stroll through the rue Combe, the principal native street, underneath whose rude wooden roof, a long line of stalls extending on either hand presented a motley collection of varied trades. Here, the blacksmith in a tiny forge manufactures a reaping-hook; there, a saddler fashions a high-peaked saddle; here, an embroiderer is at work on a dark crimson jacket — there, a shoemaker sews a clumsy round-toed shoe; here, a seller of rancid butter and sour milk is tranquilly sleeping — there, a fruit merchant is apathetically smoking; and ever and again the way is cleared, by warning shouts of *balek*! for long files of donkeys, whose projecting goat-skin bags of oil fill up the whole breadth of the thoroughfare.

A palace built by the last Bey, and now the residence of the governor of the province, is the only native building of any size or beauty in Constantine, and though its style of architecture is not imposing, its long arcaded galleries rising above courts laid out in flower-beds overhung with shrubs and trees, gave it a very attractive look under a hot Algerian sun. These galleries, decorated with frescoes by a Turkish artist, are calculated to give high pleasure to the admirers of the old China style of art. The pictures of the chief towns of Islam, which the walls present, cannot be excelled, in originality of conception and boldness of handling, by the most venerated and cherished of porcelain jars; and houses slanting upwards, trees growing in the air, ships sailing on clouds, cannons floating on waves, had their striking effect enhanced by a liberal expenditure of red paint.

The mosques are numerous, and much more ornamented than at Algiers. Wreaths of painted flowers, on the walls, adorn that belonging to the religious fraternity of Mouley Taïeb. A multitude of gay-coloured lanterns suspended from the ceiling decorated another, and the ordinary matting was, in many cases, replaced by bright carpets. The grand mosque was in the hands of workmen, employed by government to remodel and beautify the building, at a considerable cost.

A native Government college which we visited showed the pursuit of knowledge carried on in a very primitive style. The students, amounting in number to thirty-five, had each a cell-like room, furnished simply with a mat or carpet—his bed by night, his seat by day. Here, pursuing his studies for three years, he learns to read the Koran and to write; having gained this knowledge he departs a *thaleb* (learned man), and a new student is installed in his vacated cell. The youths, selected by government from different tribes, receive each twelve sous a day to supply the cost of food. Caïds are subsequently chosen from this stock of *thalebs* that the college sends forth.

The Arab citadel, or Casbah, has been so altered by the French, that it has the air of a modern building. In despite, however, of its youthful looks, it dates its existence from Roman rule, and the still perfect large vaulted cisterns beneath the walls, filled by a subterranean canal from an adjacent height, are a valuable legacy of those days. But, notwithstanding the supply of water from this source, it becomes a highly prized luxury in Constantine in the hot months of the year. The picturesque, unhappily, is not often allied with comfort and convenience.

Pending the construction of a museum, a little garden serves as the receptacle for the Roman antiquities found in the neighbourhood. Under the guidance of the learned antiquary, M. Cherbonneau, we traced back by fragmentary remains the history of Constantine to a far distant era. A lion with a mutilated tongue, and broken slabs on which the figure of a moon was rudely carved, spoke of Numidian Cirta, the first town which crowned the precipice-girt rocks. But, amidst the varied remains of its successors, Julia Sittiana and Constantine, which met my view, none interested me so much as the monumental inscriptions, which testified to the peculiar longevity of the ancient inhabitants of the now unhealthy town and neighbourhood. In days when centenarians seemed to have been a very numerous class, the autumnal fever scourge must have been unknown. A good omen for the future I thought.*

A visit to an ancient palace inhabited by the descendants of Salah, the most illustrious of the Beys of Constantine, presented us with a melancholy picture of the ruined fortunes of the native aristocracy; and

---

* Through the kindness of M. Cherbonneau, to whom we were furnished with a letter of introduction from Mr. Elmore, Vice-Consul at Algiers, I give the following list of centenarians, whose tombstones have been found in Constantine or its immediate neighbourhood:—

Marcus Julius Abaeus lived 131 years; Julia Getula, 125; .... ca (name illegible), 125; Creptabula, 120; Marcus Cassius, Gracilis, 120; Caius Julius Pacatus, 120; Fittav Feriusis, 115; Umbria Matronica, 115; Granius Neptunalis, 110; Cornelius Crescens, 107; Sempronius Januarius, 101; Publius Agatopus, 101; Licinia, 100; Julia Rogata, 100; Lucius Pompius Sabinanus, 100. All the monumental stones were inscribed in this fashion.

D M
M IVLIVS
ABAEVS
V-A-CXXXI
H S E.

In English thus: To the Gods mānes, Marcus Julius Abaeus has lived 131 years. He rests here.

the dejected looks and plain dress of our hostess, an aged Turkish Princess, was quite in keeping with the long series of large, empty, faded rooms, through which we were conducted. Coffee, as at Algiers, was offered to our acceptance.

Far differing in appearance from the Turkish Princess, was the wife of an *Adel* (a Cadi's assessor) whom we subsequently visited by invitation of her husband. Prepared for our appearance, the lady had arrayed herself in all her gala splendour to do honour to her company. Instead of the short trousers worn at Algiers, she was clad in a long robe of green and red cheneé silk, edged by a broad yellow border. From beneath a brilliant coloured handkerchief which covered her head, a red gauze veil hung down around her shoulders. A band of small gold coins invested her chin in bridle fashion, whilst another similar band encircled her throat in company with a vast variety of chains. Wrists laden with bracelets, ears distended by heavy gold earrings, brows and eyelids lined with koheul, hands dyed with henna, altogether combined to form an undoubtedly most striking toilet.

The Adel, in waiting to receive us on our entrance, conducted us up a narrow flight of steps to a small room, where, seated on the floor in Moorish fashion beside our host, we were served by his radiant wife with dates and coffee. This duty done, she stood before us with her crossed hands, mute and motionless, like a servant, debarred by her creed from the honour of sharing her lord's repast. Did she wonder why he did not consider himself demeaned by eating in company with us? I think not, for her young dollish face was utterly devoid of any expression indicating that she thought at all.

The outdoor costume of the Moresques of Constantine consists of a large, blue, sheet-like shawl, in which she is enveloped from head to foot, with her face concealed in the *ennekabo* mode; her feet are the only portion of her person visible as she walks. The Jewesses dress as in Algiers, and the negress here, as there, wears gold and silver rings around her arms. A portion of the black population of the town are said to practise the rites of Fetish worship, and the native inhabitants of every class have the reputation of being extravagantly superstitious. Shops for the sale of amulets and talismans have a flourishing trade, and I might have become the possessor of an infallible safeguard against misfortune at a very moderate cost. The talisman-seller's weird-looking shop—its walls all covered with cabalistic characters—was the only unfamiliar native sight I saw in Constantine.

But though Constantine, as a town, cannot compete in interest with Algiers, it commands the stranger's admiration by the magnificent pedestal on which it stands. Except for the neck of land which on the west connects the quadrilateral rock with the heights of Coudiat Ati, the stupendous natural rampart of the town would be complete. But grand as is the ravine, whose high precipitous walls of rock gird it on south and east, their grandeur is far surpassed by the magnificent beetling cliffs which extend along the northern side, and from whose foot the river Roumel, issuing from the ravine, leaps downward in sparkling waterfalls to the green valley of the Hamma. Standing amidst the luxuriant verdure of the vale into which the river plunged, and glancing from fall to fall of foaming water up to the towering town-crowned cliffs beyond, I thought that the grand, solemn beauty of the scene could scarcely be surpassed.

The dread memories connected with the precipice which forms the north-east angle of Constantine enhance the effect of its awe-striking look, for under Turkish rule it was used as a Tarpeian rock for suspected or faithless wives. The ancestors of the kites which soared above my head in the ravine had, doubtless, feasted on many a victim of jealousy. Hurled from the ledge of such a dizzy height, death, if it came in a form terrible to the fancy, could have proved no lingering torment, and consciousness of life must have passed away, ere the poor wretch was dashed against the rocks below. Moorish women may well rejoice at the substitution of French for Turkish rule.

The ravine which extends along the southern side of Constantine presents the character of a rent, for the confronting walls of rock, rising almost to a similar height, are separated by an interval that in its widest part does not exceed 300 feet. Down in the depths of this dark abyss, into which no gleam of sunlight ever penetrates, the hachiche smoker has a favourite nook which he frequents to inhale the fumes which are both his hell and heaven—and here, reclining on a small plot of bright green grass, with which a hot spring has carpeted the flat surface of a projecting rock, he passes the sultry noontide hour in twilight gloom, and in a silence only broken by the gurgling river.

Amidst the arid hills which surround the town, the garden (as it is called) of Salah Bey possesses something of the charm belonging to an oasis in the desert. A favourite residence of the Bey whose name it bears, his palace has dwindled into formless heaps of stone amidst a tangled maze of luxuriant vegetation—a doom which the true believer thinks is a Heaven-sent judgement on the impiety of a ruler who dared to execute a blessed maraboo. How Sidi Mohammed's spirit, appearing to mortal view in a raven's form, rose upward in the air from the place of execution—how, uttering ominous croaks, it darted off to the country palace of the Bey, where, having uttered another series of awe-striking croaks, it vanished—and how the contrite Bey, mourning for his impious deed, raised a koubba to the saint on the spot where the raven had disappeared, forms a tale whose truth no Mussulman questions; nor should

Christians either, since I can testify there rises up in Salah's garden a koubba bearing a title signifying My Lord Mohammed the Raven. In my eyes, however, the magnificent palm which grew near the spot was a more interesting object than the maraboo's white-domed tomb. If the groves of Biskara had shown such towering trees, I should not have thought my visit to the oasis dearly purchased.

On the eve of our departure from Constantine, the French town was thrown into an ecstasy of joy by the arrival of the intelligence that the French Legislature had decided on granting money to make railroads in Algeria; and as this decision would give Constantine an iron highway to its port of Philippeville, the cannons of the Casbah celebrated the joyful tidings by many a thunderous roar. These promised *chemins de fer* were destined, it was said, to inaugurate a golden era of prosperity throughout Algeria. To the nearly bankrupt trader they brought a vision of thronging customers in his now almost empty shop; and the sickly colonist hoped for the extermination of malaria through their means. I was but the embodiment of the jealousy of '*perfide Albion*' when I ventured to doubt if the *chemins de fer* would realise these glowing visions.

It was late in the evening when we started in a diligence for Philippeville; night travelling being the rule in summer, to escape the noonday heat. Having neglected a timely engagement of places in the *coupé*, we had to occupy seats in an uncomfortable *intérieur*, in company with a priest, a mechanic, his wife and two children. The mechanic looked very sickly, his wife had a thoroughly worn face, and the two children were both suffering from opthalmia. After ten years in Algeria, they were on their way home to France. The priest told them they were unwise in leaving Algeria at a time when the country was on the point of being enriched through the means of railroads; but, with a sorrowful glance at his pale wife and children, the mechanic answered that, it were better to starve in France than to live in luxury in Algeria.

Night soon closed in our view, whilst we were journeying through a valley dotted here and there with a settler's house, in the midst of fields, whose neglected look spoke of the presence of malaria fever.

CHAPTER XXXII.

MISANTHROPY CURED—PHILIPPEVILLE—HEADLAND OF STORA—JEMMAPES — FUTURE PROSPECTS — ANOTHER MULE RIDE — A RICH COUNTRY—A SETTLER'S WIFE—AN ORNITHOLOGICAL SITTING-ROOM.

A NIGHT journey has never, under the most favourable circumstances, exhilarating tendencies; but, combined with a hard high narrow seat, incessant jolting, and stifling clouds of dust, its effect was such, that when I alighted at break of day at the Hôtel de France in Philippeville, I was altogether impressed with the conviction that life was a grievous burden. A bowl of excellent *café au lait*, followed by a few hours' sleep in a comfortable bed, having, however, considerably modified my sentiments, it needed but a glance at the view visible from my window, to wholly reconcile me to existence.

For before me lay a magnificent curving bay, whose bright blue waters marked with a trail of shimmering foam the several silvery sandy coves, which edged here and there the base of a long range of cliffs, extending from a precipitous wooded headland immediately on the west, to a lofty promontory in the far distance. A sky all cloudless, save for a few silvery streaks that flecked its surface; a waveless ocean, that flashed here and there with the winglike sails of a felucca; and a brilliant African sun, that shed a lustrous light on high beetling crags, on wooded heights, and on the unbounded expanse of azure sea that bathed their feet, formed altogether a scene that might well cure misanthropy of a much deeper seat than mine.

But though, from a tourist's point of view, Philippeville is entitled to high praise, its merits as a French settlement and seaport are very inconsiderable. As a settlement, it was, up to the last few years, a charnel-house for its inhabitants. In spite of the fresh north sea breeze which blows through the narrow valley along whose sides it rises in tiers on high, it was scourged with malaria fever to a degree beyond that of any other French Algerian town, with the exception of Bona. Little more than ten years ago, the mortality amounted to ten per cent. in the population. Sheltered from the sirocco blast, built on the very shores of the Mediterranean, and with no swamps or marshes in its immediate vicinity, the unhealthiness of Philippeville is a fact that seems to set at defiance every recognised sanitary principle.

As a port, Philippeville has only a nominal existence; for, exposed to the full brunt of the north wind, its vicinity would be shunned by every craft, were it not for the high wooded headland of Stora, two miles distant towards the west, and which forms, with a cluster of rocky islets that lie off its projecting point, a safe harbour at every season of the year. The only marine structure of which Philippeville can boast is a short·rude wooden pier, *fort tourmenté* (as I was told) by the sea in winter time; and the tormenting process is often finished off by the waves in a truly feline manner.

Like other French Algerian towns, Philippeville shows lines of wide, well-built streets, and squares ornamented with flourishing trees. The long rue Impériale, flanked by arcades, contains fine large shops, which, from the apparent dearth of customers, made me marvel at the great array of finery their windows displayed. From the results of my own observation, I should say that the keepers of cafés and restaurants were far more likely to make fortunes than any other class of tradesmen in the town.

Philippeville stands upon the site of the large Roman city of Rusicada, of which many vestiges still remain. The fine cisterns that supply the French town with water are a legacy of the past; and the ground in the neighbourhood yields up innumerable fragments of art. Rings, coins, and engraven stones are said to be sometimes cast upon the beach after a storm; a circumstance which seems to indicate that some portion of Rusicada, like Julia Cæsarea, has been swallowed up by the sea.

Stora, the real port of Constantine, exhibits at this present day a scanty number of small French houses at the foot of the precipitous wooded headland of the same name, rising some two miles to the west of Philippeville. The small poor French village, redolent of fishy odours, was very unworthy of its beautiful situation on the edge of the grand cliff-girt cove in which it lies. Here, also, are the ruins of an old Roman town; and as I toiled, panting, up the precipitous height, on whose side its mouldering walls are seen, I felt most forcibly that its inhabitants had need of limbs and lungs of no ordinary strength, to enable them to find enjoyment in their place of residence.

The road which connects Philippeville with its port of Stora, is a fine specimen of engineering skill, and commands views of exceeding beauty. Hewed out of the side of a precipitous cliff, clothed from base to summit with luxuriant vegetation, the thickets of myrtle, arbutus, cistus, and lentisk, through which it winds, enhance by their rich beauty the stern grandeur of the long rampart-like wall of rock towering eastward above the bright blue waters of the Mediterranean, and terminating in the long promontory of the Cap de Fer. More exquisite combinations of wood, rock, and water cannot well be seen than those which every portion of this fine road commands.

After a brief stay at Philippeville we started for Jemmapes, in a nondescript kind of public vehicle belonging to the car species. A French lady, a fellow-passenger, spoke with enthusiasm of her *campagne*, to which she was going. The soil produced magnificent crops of every kind; tobacco brought her a clear profit of five hundred francs per hectare.* The malaria fever had almost vanished from the neighbourhood, and she found that, with the extended cultivation of the land, the great heats of summer were very perceptibly diminishing. Her *campagne*, at which she speedily arrived, turned towards the road a picturesque looking, cheerful cottage front.

Our road, in the neighbourhood of Philippeville, traversed a narrow cultivated vale between hills thickly covered with lentisk, arbutus, and myrtle. Cultivation, however, quickly ceased with our advance, and after passing through the thriving looking settlement of St. Charles, at ten miles distance from Philippeville, nearly every sign of civilised life disappeared from view, until, in some two hours' time, we arrived in the vicinity of Jemmapes. Emerging from a wilderness of brushwood, and passing through a luxuriant belt of cornfields and vineyards, we entered a small French town, which the commendable strong horticultural tastes, of its inhabitants, had made gay with gardens filled with flowers.

Jemmapes, situated on an eminence in the centre of the valley of the river Fendeck, is at this day one of the most thriving French settlements in Algeria. Sharing in its infancy in all the calamities which

* About 10*l.* the acre.

befell the French Algerian settlements founded in 1848, it is now the most prosperous of a group whose early history is a dismal tragedy. The low walls which enclose the little town are still unfinished and destitute of gates, and it has neither military buildings nor soldiers. The colonists are mostly French, with a scanty sprinkling of Germans, one of whom amused me by his pertinacity in insisting that I had come to survey the country for railway purposes.* All spoke with enthusiasm of the future prospects of the place. Every kind of crop flourished in the rich soil of the valley; vineyards yielded excellent wine, and fig, pomegranate, and fruit trees of various kinds, mingled with the valuable *chêne liége* that clothed the surrounding hills, abounding in minerals, the source of future wealth. As a climax to these blessings, the malaria fever had vanished from the spot. Such is Jemmapes. Should Algeria thrive, the valley of the Fendeck will, doubtless, before long become a rich tract of cornfields and vineyards.

A Sunday halt at Jemmapes afforded us the opportunity of assisting (as the French would say) at the procession of the Fete Dieu, which happened to take place at that period. The improvised chapels with which the streets were decorated for the occa-

* In another place we were set down as Commissioners employed by the Emperor to enquire into the wants of the people; in another, we were considered to be searchers for hidden treasure; in another, speculators in cork;—in short, there were no end of ingenious solutions of the cause which led us to travel through Algeria.

sion did great credit to the artistic tastes of the inhabitants. Laurel branches, flowers, lights, coloured paper, and bright hangings, arranged in every instance in harmonious combinations, formed a striking evidence of the innate perception of beauty with which the Gallic race seem peculiarly gifted. Through streets thus decorated, the procession passed late in the afternoon, and as the long lines of girls which followed the Host passed before my view, I scarcely thought that any portion of the Circassian race could have presented such a congregated mass of youthful ugliness.

Guelma, the next French town through which we were to pass on our way to Bona, is nominally connected with Jemmapes by a carriage road, but from the account we received of its character, we resolved to hire mules for the day's journey, rather than to pay an exorbitant sum for the privilege of being well jolted, and not improbably overturned, during our progress.* An Algerian sun in the month of June had become sufficiently hot to render the prospect of our ride not particularly attractive, but by starting at dawn we hoped to be able to enjoy a long midday rest.

As invariably occurred on such occasions, the

* A mule journey in Algeria is generally a very cheap mode of travelling. When mules are hired through the agency of the Bureau Arabe, five or six francs a day for man and mule is the ordinary tariff. When hired through a caïd, or directly from a native, the charge is generally somewhat higher.

mules were an hour or more late in making their appearance, and when they arrived, a still further delay occurred from my strongly demurring to the absence of a bridle. To satisfy my prejudices on the subject, a highly original sample of the article desired was, after a little time, supplied. But no sooner had the bridle question been satisfactorily settled, than another difficulty of a far more serious character arose, for the proprietor of the mules, having found from experience that French Christians could cheat, had sufficient doubts of the honesty of English Christians as to make him demand that we should pay down at once the sum for which we had agreed. As suspicious of his probity, as he was of ours, we stoutly resisted his claim, which happily was soon withdrawn, on his receiving the assurance of a policeman who stood by, that no Anglais or Anglaise was ever known to cheat, or to tell a falsehood. May that highly estimable official speedily become Monsieur le Commissaire!

With the grateful sight overhead of a clouded sky, we at length started forward on our journey. Passing through the narrow belt of verdure that encircled Jemmapes, cultivation ceased until we had reached in half an hour the immediate vicinity of a small French village, which bore the aspect of being yet under the influences of the malaria scourge. Advancing onward through a beautiful copse, principally composed of myrtle, lentisk, and heath, intermingled here and there with a cork-tree, we crossed from time to time a shallow stream or dried-up bed of a watercourse, bordered with the gorgeous blossoms of clustering masses of the oleander.* Save a deserted settler's house, in front of which an Arab had built his gourbi, not another sign of civilised life presented itself to view amidst the rich wilderness of copse and pastures through which we journeyed. Gaining at length an olive wood that covered the summit of a hill, we were well pleased to find ourselves in the immediate vicinity of a French village, where a small house which united the double functions of a café and grocery afforded us a very grateful cup of coffee.

Beautifully situated on the brow of the olive-crowned height that rose immediately above a richly-wooded valley, the village was yet anything but a desirable place of residence; for, elevated and picturesque as was its site, the curse of malaria still weighed heavily on its existence. Not a face I saw but bore the stamp of suffering and sickness. The proprietor of the café was in the hospital at Guelma; and his pale wife, who kept the house, looked as if she were a fit inmate of a similar establishment.

After a short halt, we re-mounted our mules, and, winding downward through the olive-grove, we

* The sap of the oleander has poisonous properties; and it is said that the French, ignorant of this fact, lost many men by drinking the water of the streams into which the cut-down branches of the oleander, along their beds, had been thrown.

entered a richly-wooded valley, watered by a stream fringed by the magnificent clustering blossoms of the oleander, and backed on either hand by pillar-like grey crags, rising amidst a thicket of myrtle in full bloom. Save the white walls of a newly-erected caravanseraï which we passed, no trace of man was visible for miles in the woodland paradise we had entered. Beautifully marked blue pigeons were so little scared by our approach, that they scarcely gave themselves the trouble of moving out of our way. The luxuriant beauty and richness of vegetation amidst which we advanced, was beyond aught that I had yet seen in Algeria; and as, time after time, we crossed the stream, the sight of the gorgeous mass of blossoming oleanders, with which its banks were fringed, made me feel as Linnæus did when, kneeling down upon a gorse-covered hill, he thanked God for having permitted him to live to see a sight so exquisitely beautiful.

The brilliant sunshine which had succeeded to the clouded morning sky, rendering our progress somewhat fatiguing, it was pleasant news to hear, towards noon, that we would soon arrive at a settler's house, where we might halt until the great heat of the day was past; and the large two-storied building, of which we speedily came in sight, was calculated to confirm the agreeable anticipations of rest and refreshment, that naturally resulted from a long ride and a scanty breakfast. Dismounting at the entrance-gate of a large court, half filled with cattle, we crossed the littered ground to the dwelling house, the door of which seemed to stand invitingly open. Not seeing or hearing any sign of inhabitants, I made an impromptu knocker of my parasol as a means of invocation, and that failing in the desired result, we uplifted our voices in a call to the invisible inmates. The smothered tones of the human voice that answered this last appeal were speedily followed by the sound of steps, of an opened door, and in another instant we were confronted by a young woman with a child in her arms.

Slatterns are no very rare productions in any lands, but in all my life I had never seen such a finished specimen of this species, as that presented by the figure who appeared. A sallow dirty face, set in a frame of dishevelled black hair, a large back comb half dropping out, a torn and greasy dark calico dress, hands and nails begrimed with dirt, and bare feet thrust into worn-out slippers, completed a picture which in its way was perfect, and harmonised admirably with the room into which we were shown, after the exchange of a few words, that proved we had the honour of being in the presence of the mistress of the house.

Sitting down on a crazy chair that seemed reluctant to support my far from oppressive weight, the scrutinising glance with which I swept the room acted on my mind as did the unlucky kick that suddenly terminated the glowing visions of Alnaschar; for though two moderator lamps and a machine for making soda water, standing on a shelf well heaped with books, showed me that we were in the house of one considerably above the peasant class, yet when, from a glance at a cobwebbed ceiling, in a corner of which a swallow had built its nest, I turned my eyes upon a dirt-encrusted floor, where a hen and her youthful family ran about underneath a table heaped with chairs, and flanked by three children's beds, in all the disarray that testified to a recent bolster warfare, I felt at once my hopes of a good *déjeûner* collapse into nothingness. Recalling, however, even in the first moments of my dismay, the cows I had seen in the court-yard, I craved a glass of milk.

'I am sorry that we have none to spare,' was the answer; and, having refused the familiar red vinegar which, under the name of wine, was offered us instead, I asked for a glass of water. This request being granted, my enjoyment of the refreshing draught was much enhanced by the conversation of our hostess.

She was sorry we should have found her house in such disorder, but she had not been able to get a servant in place of the one who had lately left. To live so far away from society and amusements was a dreadful fate; if she were not able from time to time to go and spend some days at Guelma with

Madame, the wife of M. le Commissaire, her existence would be intolerable. She hoped in a year or two that there would be a good road to Guelma, which would save the fatigue of a long ride; but she made us understand that she had never demeaned herself by mounting an Arab mule in Arab fashion. No, certainly not; even if she had not had her own horse and side saddle, she would not have journeyed thus. Her boys were unfortunately now running about quite wild, but she hoped that an arrangement would speedily be made with a *professeur* to come and live with them. She really could not inform me how many *hectares* her husband had, she did not concern herself about such things.

With my glance constantly reverting from the swallow's nest above my head, to the hen and chickens at my feet, I had some difficulty in preserving a politely serious expression of countenance whilst Madame spoke; and more especially was this the case, when the contemplated arrangement with the *professeur* was mentioned. Undoubtedly, it may be very interesting to contemplate a swallow's architectural operations, and to watch the proceedings of a hen and chickens, but the coming Monsieur le Professeur would need, I thought, a very enthusiastic love for natural history to approve of the hen and swallow as members of the family circle.

Speedily bidding Madame *bon jour*, we left her presence to seek rest and shade underneath the trees which grew along the banks of a stream close by, and the gorgeous mass of oleander blossoms which there met my view was a welcome sight after that from which we came.

On remounting our mules, in two hours' time, we proceeded onward through a richly wooded valley, that showed for many a mile no traces of inhabitants; and ever advancing amidst vegetation as varied as that through which we had passed that morning, we reached towards evening the foot of a range of bare hills which formed the southern boundary of the rich vale. A somewhat tedious, but easy ascent, having brought us to the summit of the heights, we saw with joy, in the wide valley which suddenly burst upon our sight, a cluster of white walls at no great distance, and our first view of Guelma—striking under any circumstances, from the amphitheatre of hills by which it was encircled—had its attractions immeasurably enhanced, by the assurance it afforded of speedily obtaining rest and refreshment after a long day's ride.

Descending to a cultivated and populous valley, that glowed with the rich golden hue of nearly ripened grain, and fording the wide but shallow bed of the river Seybouse, a short ride brought us to the gates of the French town of Guelma.

CHAPTER XXXIII.

GUELMA—ORPHAN ASYLUM — HAMMAM MESKOUTINE—CURIOUS SCENE—ABANDONED FOUNTAINS—BATHS—ARAB AND KABYLE LEGENDS—BONA—PROSPECTS OF BONA — ROMAN CISTERNS— MONUMENT TO SAINT AUGUSTINE — MOUNT EDOUG — NATIVE HOSPITALITY — EMBARK FOR TUNIS.

AN almost continuous circuit of the ruined ramparts of Roman Calama were standing when the French selected the spot as the site for a French town; and the almost formless piles of stones that then littered the ground have grown under the mason's hand into the bright whitewashed, or stuccoed walls of Guelma. A ruinous amphitheatre, and the still massive but crumbling walls of a temple and baths, yet remain, however, as monuments of the old Roman city.

As, except for its antiquities, Guelma possesses no distinctive feature, it may be dismissed with the remark, that it is a worthy member of the numerous family of French Algerian towns. Built on the lowest slopes of the Mount Maouna, the town overlooks a basin-shaped valley, whose cultivated fields, dotted with villages and farmhouses, give quite a European appearance to the landscape. The district around Guelma looked one of the most flourishing I had seen in Algeria.

The immediate neighbourhood offers few sights of interest to the stranger. A negro village just outside the walls, a ravine lined with luxuriant gardens, and a Government *pepiniere** that will furnish in a few years an agreeable shady promenade, are the only things worth seeing in the vicinity, with the exception of a few surviving antiquities too ruinous to excite much interest in any but antiquarians.

But though Guelma has not much attraction in itself, it possesses, in the baths of Hammam Meskoutine, some ten miles distant, a sight to arrest the tourist for at least a day. 'Be sure you do not fail to see the baths of Hammam Meskoutine when you go to Guelma,' was an injunction we had so often heard that, acting upon this counsel, we lost no time in hiring a cabriolet to convey us there.

Following the course of the Seybouse for some eight miles, our road lay through an evidently fertile, but only half cultivated valley, with wooded hills rising on either side. No native dwelling was visible, although the land, while owned by French proprietors, was mostly cultivated by Arabs, who held *au cinquieme* — a phrase implying that the tenant pays four-fifths of the produce to his landlord.†

---

* A kind of botanical garden.

† A caïd exacts the same proportion of the produce on lands belonging to his tribe; and as these undergo a fresh partition every year, the Arab, it is said, prefers a European landlord.

A large French building situated near the junction of the Seybouse with the small river Bou Hamdan, evidenced, in its empty deserted state, how the curse of malaria prevails in the rich valley where it stands. Built originally in 1851 for an orphan asylum, its doors have been closed for many years, as it was found that it afforded to the children beneath its roof a very expeditious mode of rejoining their parents.

Leaving the valley of the Seybouse for that of the Bou Hamdan, a short drive brought us to a point from which we could discern a tract of ground dotted with conical rocks, immediately in front of a dense white surging steam. Arriving shortly afterwards at a gully crowned on one side by a large French building, and on the other by a thick canopy of vapour gushing upwards with a hissing noise from a snow-white rock, we needed not our driver's intimation that we saw before us the military hospital and the boiling fountain of Hammam Meskoutine.

Gaining the summit of the snowy rock, and standing at the windward side of the dense sulphurous steam which surged aloft in the transparent air, we approached the verge of a number of small shallow and brilliantly white basins, bordered by the sparkling lime-encrusted forms of twigs and leaves, and filled with bubbling water, which in its overflow coursed down the steep side of the marble-like rock in innumerable miniature cascades. The richly-wooded glen into which the gully merged — the canopy of vapour swaying to and fro with every gust of wind —the sparkling rocks and steaming streamlets, all combined to give a high amount of beauty to the curious scene.

Possessing something of the practical character attributed to the English nation, and lacking a thermometer to test the temperature of the steaming water, I dipped my finger into one of the bubbling basins, but withdrew it instantly with a sensation such as any one of an experimental turn of mind can exactly realise through the medium of a kettle of water on the eve of boiling.*

A French soldier, standing on the summit of the rock inhaling the sulphurous vapour, spoke enthusiastically of the curative virtue of the waters. A cripple from rheumatism at the period of his arrival two months ago, he had now thrown aside his crutches. Diverging from the subject of his malady to his private history, he told us that on receiving his *retraite,* which would give him a yearly income of 1,000 francs, he intended to marry an Arab girl, and return to France, to spend the remainder of his days in domestic pleasures. On my suggestion that a French wife might in all probability prove a more agreeable companion, he said that a caïd's daughter, who married an officer in his regiment, spoke French

---

* The temperature of 203 degrees assigned to the waters of Hammam Meskoutine is above that, it is said, of any hot spring in the continent of Europe.

so *divinement bien*, that he would feel himself a fortunate man to find a wife like her.

Under the guidance of another soldier patient, I visited some Roman ruins lying at a distance of a quarter of a mile from the present fountain. The numerous conical rocks which studded the ground over which we passed, had each, in bygone days, been built up by the lime-charged waters. One of the largest of these cones is stated to measure thirty-six feet in height, and nearly forty feet in circumference, but the majority are not probably much more than half that size. With their progress up the valley, the boiling springs seemed to have lost their architectural power, for I could not see a single cone in the act of formation.

The Roman ruins show very forcibly the change that time has wrought upon the level of the soil, for they are now only visible through apertures in the ground. Here, I looked down upon the summit of a broken arch, there, upon the interior of a supposed temple. Antiquarian research has identified these, and some other relics of Roman times in their vicinity, as belonging to the Aquæ Tibilitanæ — the favourite lounge of the gay idle world of ancient Tiblis, whose ruins rise upon the summit of a neighbouring hill.

On returning towards the hospital, we passed a large shallow pool of hot water tenanted by a number of green frogs; but however inured as are their constitutions to a high temperature, it not unfrequently happens that an erratic member of the community terminates his life by an unwary jump into the brook fed by the boiling spring, which in a few minutes converts him into a dainty morsel for the French epicure's table.

The present baths are of the most simple construction, consisting of wooden sheds erected above excavated pits, to which the encrusting water has given the semblance of a lining of the purest Carrara marble. Twelve hours are required to cool the water down to a temperature fit for bathing.

My soldier guide had qualified himself for acting as cicerone, by learning the legends connected with the spot; and, during our progress, he informed me how it came to pass that these boiling springs bore such an ill-omened name as Hammam Meskoutine—words signifying, Baths of the Accursed.

In long bygone days a tribe of Arabs inhabiting this spot had a caïd whose son, named Ali, was the most beautiful youth that ever lived; and Ali, vain of his great beauty, vowed that he would have the most beautiful girl in the whole country for his wife: but let him seek as he might, no girl so beautiful as his sister Aziza could be seen, or heard of anywhere. On this, Ali declaring that Aziza must be his wife, persisted, in spite of every remonstrance, in carrying out his resolve; and, won by his importunities, the caïd at length gave his sanction to the impious marriage, which was to be celebrated with the utmost splendour. But on the appointed day, when the wedding guests had all arrived, and when the ground was dotted with fires employed in roasting sheep and making couscousou for the marriage feast, the earth split open, and whilst the fires and boiling couscousou were swallowed up by the abyss, the assembled party were turned to stone. From that day to this the fires have gone on burning underground, and, to the eye of faith, the conical rocks yield the outline of human features. Certainly, however, though I might hear the simmering couscousou on applying my ear to any of the numerous apertures in the ground, I could not trace, in the pillars bearing Ali's and Aziza's names, the faintest trace of their resplendent beauty.

This, the Arab legend of the origin of the boiling springs, differs widely from the one that prevails amongst the Kabyles, who say that King Solomon had constructed here an immense subterranean palace, in which 200 deaf and dumb demon slaves were perpetually kept at work, to feed the fires to boil water for their master's baths.* And thus still they are employed, for, as King Solomon died in another place, their deafness has prevented them from hearing

* Mohammedans reverence King Solomon as a great magician, who ruled the winds and made genii and demons obey his commands. He understood the language of birds, beasts, and fishes, and read the future by the means of a talismanic ring.

of his death; and, fearful of his wrath if he should find them slackening in their duties, they continue indefatigably feeding fires and boiling water, in expectation of his return.

On the day succeeding our visit to the baths, we left Guelma for Bona, in a public conveyance plying between the towns. The distance, about forty miles, was easily accomplished, owing to the very unusually good road over which we travelled. On leaving the well-cultivated, basin-shaped valley of the Seybouse, we wound through a hilly tract, which, except in the vicinity of three villages we passed, exhibited a thicket of brushwood, chiefly composed of lentisk and myrtle, out of which we emerged at length, to enter upon the plain of Bona, at whose further side the white walls of the town, at the foot of a high hill, gleamed in the bright sunshine. Crossing a perfectly flat and almost treeless plain, extending to the sea, and very sparsely dotted with settlers' houses, we were close to Bona before the prospect changed; and the olive-groves and cultivated fields which lay immediately outside its walls, looked all the more attractive from the monotonous features of the bare plain through which we had come.

Bona bears the character of being '*la plus jolie ville*' in Algeria; but, except for its fine promenade, shaded by long avenues of trees, I could not see that it was entitled to boast of any particular superiority to the many clean, pleasant, and well-built Algerian towns with which I had made acquaintance: and it has this demerit in a tourist's eyes, that, although a seaport, not one glimpse of the fine curving bay of Bona can be obtained from the aristocratic quarter of the town in which the hotels are situated. With a little toil, however, a magnificent view of the coast may be obtained from the summit of the steep citadel-capped promontory at the foot of whose inland side the town is built. Standing on this height, and following the fine curving outline of the Bay of Bona, from its near westward boundary of the bold Cap de Garde, to its distant limit of Cap Rose, the glance takes in a glorious expanse of bright blue sea, edged here, by bristling rocks and fort-crowned cliffs, and there, by a sloping beach fringed with white glistening sands.

No town in all Algeria was so severely scourged as Bona by malaria fever; but the evil has now been almost conquered by the construction of a chain of canals, to receive the overflow of the several sluggish rivers that fall into the sea in the vicinity of the town. With the disappearance of the stagnating marsh-creating inundations of the El Farcha, Boudjema, and Ruisseau d'Or, the deadly Bona fever has vanished. This curse removed, Bona enjoys advantages of position that will probably render it one of the most flourishing towns of Algeria. The forests of cork, the rich mines of iron and copper, and the marble quarries existing in its vicinity, combine, with the fertile plains of which it is the natural outlet, to give it prospects of attaining, with the developement of the resources of the country, to a high degree of commercial prosperity. Even at this present day, Bona, it is said, '*peut marcher seul*,' a phrase implying that, unlike other Algerian towns, it does not solely depend on garrison expenditure for its continued existence. A good safe port is, however, much required, to stimulate its progress.

Some remains of Roman Hippo are visible on a wooded hill lying a little more than a mile to the south-west of Bona; but all are in a fragmentary state, save some vast cisterns, whose still nearly perfect walls are yet partly covered by a massive vaulted roof, which will probably take some centuries to destroy completely. The luxuriant trees which rose above these shattered, but still imposing relics of bygone days, strikingly contrasted in their fresh and vigorous beauty with the mouldering ruins they overshadowed.

Immediately above the cisterns, the French have raised a monument to St. Augustine, who was Bishop of Hippo, at which place he died in 429. The monument consists of a bronze statue of the saint, surmounting a small white altar, containing one of his supposed arm bones, which was deposited here with solemn pomp by seven French bishops in 1842. Since this time, the clergy, followed by the Christian population of the town, annually repair in procession to the spot, to celebrate a commemorative mass over the venerated bone.

Another annual commemorative rite, but of a widely different character, takes place in the same locality, in honour of a female maraboo, termed in Arabic, Lella Bona, Bent-el-Hamra (daughter of the Red), whose sacred remains lie buried within the precincts of the cisterns; and the negro population of the town, who assemble here on a certain day of every year to do her homage, show their devotion by a prodigious slaughter of red cocks, followed by frantic dances, which do not end till the dawn of the succeeding morning. A number of black dots and crosses on the wall of a recess mark the shrine of Lady Bona; and, at the period of our visit to the place, some female devotees were busily engaged in adding to the amount of these fresco decorations through the means of a burnt stick, whilst uttering from time to time a shrill piercing cry.

The beautiful views commanded by the summit of Mount Edoug, a high hill immediately to the west of Bona, well repays the inconsiderable toil of the ascent. Fine as is the character of Algerian seacoast scenery, I had seen nothing grander along the African shores than the view from the top of Edoug, of noble wooded headlands, extending westward from the town of Bona to the grand promontory of the Cap de Fer; and turning from the sea, the large Lake Fezzara, which glittered at the foot of the richly-wooded sides of Edoug, gave to the inland scene a high degree of beauty. In this direction rise the remains of a fine aqueduct, by which, in former times, the vast cisterns of Hippo Regius were supplied with water from the Mount.

Nowhere were we more hospitably treated and welcomed by the natives than at Bona. Happy were the owners of country gardens to offer us the best that they contained, and even the café-keeper munificently refused all payment for the cup he furnished. Indeed, from our first landing to our departure from the shores of Algeria, the natives with whom we came in contact seemed ever actuated by a spirit of the kindliest feeling towards us; and most abundantly we proved how utterly false was the assertion that I heard, not only uttered by French, but English gentlemen, that no Arab would yield obedience, save through the means of blows. Proud of the trust we reposed in them, they showed themselves on all occasions worthy of our confidence. Pilferers and robbers, a mere *canaille*, as they are termed by their Christian masters, we never lost amongst them one single article of our property; and the unfailing respect and prompt obedience ever rendered us, could not have been greater, had we gone amongst them surrounded by a guard of soldiers.

It was nearly the middle of June when, after a few days stay at Bona, the French steamer which was to convey us to Tunis made its appearance in the bay; and for one day, at least, I could have well excused the absence of the daily morning high sea breeze which had hitherto at Bona pleasantly tempered the burning heat of a June sun, for the waves it raised were fraught with prospects of no pleasant nature. Thanks to the Director of the Port, who wound up by a friendly service the many acts of courteous kindness shown to us by French officials, we were rapidly conveyed through the troubled sea in his trim and well manned yawl, to the side of the somewhat distant steamer. Arrived on board, we found ourselves invested with the dignity of being the sole first-class passengers; and that, together with the sight of only some half-dozen second-class passengers, impressed me with the conviction that the steamer did not yield a large dividend to its proprietors.

Watching the shore as, seemingly receding from view, it grew dimmer and dimmer in the distance, I saw Algeria fade ere long into a faint outline, just visible through a silver haze. Before daylight ended, we were off the dominions of the Bey of Tunis.

CHAPTER XXXIV.

ALGERIAN COLONISATION—ITS STATE AND PROSPECTS.

AFTER a visit to nearly all the chief centres of colonisation in Algeria, a few words on its present state and prospects may not unfittingly wind up this work.

What Algeria was in bygone days our libraries can tell. Where the Arab's mud gourbi or ragged tent alone breaks here and there the desolation of its brushwood or weed-covered plains, great populations lived in plenty, and exported food to less favoured lands. The soil in which the dwarf palm now strikes deep its root, once fed the millions of Imperial Rome. Mouldering fragments of ruined cities peer forth amidst the glossy foliage of the luxuriant lentisk, or rise up in solitudes whose silence is unbroken by the voice of man. From Morocco to Tunis, the seaboard of Algeria teems with monuments of the bygone glories of Roman Numidia and Mauritania.

To revive the past, to repeople a region of renowned fertility, lying within four days of Paris, might well seem to France an achievement to be accomplished without effort or cost, and to the European world it bore the same complexion—more especially so to England, accustomed as she is to see an annual voluntary emigration from her shores, to lands only attainable through the means of a long, perilous sea voyage. With the experience that we have of the hardships and perils that the needy classes of our population will voluntarily undergo for the sake of improving their fortunes, it was only natural to suppose that the same classes in France would joyfully rush across a narrow inland sea, bridged over by steamers, to occupy and populate the favoured land which conquest had placed at their disposal. To regulate the stream of emigration, to establish law and order amongst the new founded settlements, might well seem almost the whole duties devolving on the government to perform.

How the result belies such speculations is a widely known fact. Not only has no self-supporting emigration taken place, but in despite of lavish expenditure, and the most energetic efforts of a powerful government to colonise Algeria, a paltry population of 60,000 rural settlers represented in 1857 the whole amount of colonising success, purchased at a cost of some £90,000,000, during an occupation of nearly thirty years. Nor at this present time do the French compose one half of the European population of Algeria. What progress there is made, entails an annual drain of £3,000,000 on the mother country, and at the rate of increase which has prevailed during the last ten years, very many years must elapse before the colonial population numbers 1,000,000.* A result so incommensurate with the efforts used, and money expended, would apparently argue either a high degree of government incapacity, or an utter inaptitude of the French for colonisation.

Such readers, however, who may have borne me company throughout these pages, will probably see reason to assign another cause for the failure of French colonisation in Algeria. The terribly significant phrase, 'they died off like flies,' which followed me from Tlemcen to Bona, as the spoken epitaph of the first, second, third — aye, even, in some places, fourth and fifth generations of colonists — reveals an enemy against which individual enterprise or government efforts might well lack power to contend. In vain do the rich corn lands of Imperial Rome, re-vigorated by ages of fallow, promise the cultivator an abounding harvest, if at the very outset of his career he be stricken down by fever. What

* The European population of Algeria amounted, in 1857, to 180,000. Of this number, only 92,000 were French. The remaining portion consisted of Spaniards, Italians, Maltese, and Germans. The average annual increase of population during the last ten years has been 7,600. The population of Algeria in 1861, as stated in the French Chambers, was 210,000, of which only 100,000 were French. The rural settlers have, of course, proportionally increased, but at this present day the great bulk of the European-Algerian population are the followers of a large army, which, if withdrawn, would leave the French towns of Algeria with scarcely an inhabitant.

availed to him the government bribe of a house and land, free of cost, and daily rations for three years, when, long before that time expired, he and his family were in the grave? When we vaunt our success in New Zealand, Australia, and America, we should remember, that there the fresh upturned soil does not reek with poisonous miasmatic exhalations. Nor is the emigrating impulse of our working classes checked by accounts received, from friends or relatives, of the unhealthiness of the land to which they have gone to seek their fortunes. 'I and my family are in good health, thank God,' which forms the common burden of an Australian settler's letter, is a far greater incentive to emigration than any bribe to poverty which the French government can offer. In the presence of the still raging malaria scourge, it is idle to wrangle, as French statesmen do, over the cause of the ill success of Algerian colonisation. Many governmental errors, doubtless, have occurred. A military régime is evidently not well adapted to foster private enterprise or stimulate individual effort; but its injurious influence is scarcely appreciable in comparison with that of the autumnal fever scourge. Until the demon guardian of the buried riches of the soil is conquered, Algeria must inevitably remain a heavy burden on the finances of the mother country. Algerian colonisation is an exotic that can only thrive through a costly forcing process. Left to itself, if it did not wither and die away, it would cease to grow, and never reach maturity.

But dismal as has been its past career, the colony at this present day is not without some cheering features. The now healthy climate and flourishing look of the lately death-dealing Boufarik and Philippeville is a good augury for the future. With every fresh settlement made, the malaria fever loses some portion of its dominion, and with each loss assumes a milder type. Every district gained to civilisation remains a gain, and acts as an incentive to exertion. And if Algeria advances, like the car of Juggernaut, over scores of victims, yet in days when human life is freely expended on battle fields for the attainment of paltry ends or profitless dominion, we need not recoil in horror from the thought of sacrifices fraught with ultimate profit to humanity. No Algerian colonist who falls a victim to the poisonous exhalations of the rank soil he labours on, but has done somewhat to abate the evil to which he owed his death. The hardest portion of the war with nature has been waged; that which has yet to come, however severe, will be exempt from the terrible calamities that have signalised the past. Taught by the dear-bought lessons of experience, government now affords the emigrant the protection of a well-built house from the moment his toil begins; and a laborious peasant class, inured to agricultural work, has succeeded the bankrupt tradesmen and worthless hordes of camp followers who formed the first and second generation of Algerian colonists. The mockeries of roads over which we travelled are in course of being converted into good highways; and the several railroads now in progress will undoubtedly exercise a highly beneficial influence. If France perseveres, success, though long delayed and bought at a great cost, can scarcely fail at length to reward her efforts.

And when that time arrives, the Arab population of the Tell will have surely disappeared; for, destitute of the industrial instincts of European races, they must inevitably retreat or die away before the advance of civilisation.* Clinging tenaciously to the customs, habits, and mode of living of their forefathers, they have, with rare exceptions, learned nothing from their conquerors but a love of absinthe— a taste which has thinned the numbers of many of their tribes. And even if their religion, with its degrading social influences, were not an insuperable barrier to their existence in the midst of a civilised Christian community, their hatred of labour would ensure their being swept away by the tide of progress. With an ambition limited to the command of little beyond the commonest necessaries of existence, the civilisation which vainly offers its blessings to their grasp, will requite their scorn, by speedily effecting their destruction. The caïd, for whom the

* The native population of Algeria, reckoned at about 2,370,000, is divided thus: Arabs, 1,500,000; Kabyles, 800,000; Moors, 30,000; Jews, 30,000; Koulouglis and Negroes, 10,000. The Arabs inhabiting the Tell are computed to amount to about 1,000,000.

government builds a good stone house, often abandons it for a rude shelter of sods and scraws. Give an Arab a warm burnous, a horse, a gun, a wife, and a daily dish of couscousou, and he craves no more. Driven from spot to spot by the pressure of an ever increasing Christian population, the Arabs of the Tell can scarcely fail eventually to die off, if they do not join their nomade brethren of the Sahara.

And though one cannot fail to pity a conquered nation withering away from contact with a dominant race, yet, in regard to a people like the Algerian Arabs, it would be mere sentimental folly to lament that such should be the case. Possessing Algeria as they did for centuries, they yet never occupied it. Scattered here and there in insignificant clusters over rich alluvial plains, the small plots of ground they annually scratched for their subsistence were but as dots amidst the surrounding wastes. Left in their possession, Algeria would remain, as it has now done for centuries, a hotbed of malaria—a fate ill befitting a land with such a history as it has. And if the Arab dies off under the rule of the conquering race, it is only fair to the French to say that he will owe that doom, not to oppression, but to his own inherent defects of character; for government act fairly by his race, and perhaps too kindly for his good, since it leaves each tribe to the action of agrarian laws, which only befit a savage people.

Far different from the Arab's menaced fate, is the

future apparently awaiting the remaining portion of the native population of Algeria; for the Kabyle, inhabiting rugged heights that can excite no envy, is as secure in their possession as he was before the French became his master. However the dominant race may increase and flourish throughout the land, the tide of progress which sweeps the Arab's gourbi from the plain, will leave the Kabyle's red-tiled-roof dwelling standing uninjured; and his industry, which needs no spur to quicken, cannot fail to attain to a higher phase of developement from the example of the nation under whose rule he lives. The Beni Abbês and the Flissa will fabricate in their forges implements of peace and warfare, with greater skill. The iron mines of the Beni Sliman will give, through better processes of working, a far richer yield. The wood carver, in his mountain forests, will learn to handle his tool with cunning skill. The Kabyle, who wanders to a French seacoast town to seek his fortune, will bring back to his mountains a taste for the knowledge, arts, and luxuries of civilised life. And, Mohammedan as he nominally is, his social institutions interpose no barrier to his elevation to a grade as high as that enjoyed by any Christian people. His wife, neither slave nor toy, respected as well as loved, free as a Christian woman, will aid his rise, instead of keeping him down, as is the case amongst other Mussulman communities. Not unlikely, either, the faith which he forsook in bygone years will claim him yet again as a disciple. Those efforts, and the money now utterly thrown away in an attempt to convert the Arab population of the north of Africa, might well bear good fruit if expended amongst the lukewarm Mussulmen inhabitants of the Atlas mountains. That cross with which the Kabyle woman marks her face may readily come to be, not the memento of an abandoned creed, but a symbol of its acceptance and dominion. Another hundred years may not improbably see the Kabyle altogether emerged from the slough of barbarism.

And even as I dwell with pleasure on the thought of the coming time when the now untrodden wilds of Australia shall abound with human life, and minister to the weal and happiness of my race; so in a similar spirit do I think of a future day, when the now desolate plains of Algeria shall teem with the rich and varied products of its fertile soil, and when, perhaps, its aspect of nearly two thousand years ago will be renewed in all its exterior splendour, but purified from the taint of a deeply-corrupted civilisation.

www.ingramcontent.com/pod-product-compliance
Lightning Source LLC
Chambersburg PA
CBHW021815300426
44114CB00009BA/195